Inter-Organizational Collaboration by Design

Although difficult, complicated, and sometimes discouraging, collaboration is recognized as a viable approach for addressing uncertain, complex, and wicked problems. Collaborations can attract resources, increase efficiency, and facilitate visions of mutual benefit that can ignite the common desires of partners to work across and within sectors. An important question remains: How does one enable successful collaboration?

Inter-Organizational Collaboration by Design examines how collaborations can overcome barriers to innovating and rejuvenating communities, outlining the factors and antecedents that influence successful collaboration. This book proposes a theoretical perspective for collaborators to adopt design science (a solution-finding approach utilizing end-user-centered research, prototyping, and collective creativity to strengthen individuals, teams, and organizations), the language of designers, and a design attitude as an empirically informed pathway for better managing the complexities inherent in collaboration.

Through an integrated framework, evidence-based tools and strategies for building successful collaboration are articulated where successful collaboration performance facilitates innovation and rejuvenation. This volume will be essential reading for academics, researchers, leaders, and managers in nonprofit, private, and government sectors interested in building better collaborations.

Jennifer R. Madden is Assistant Professor of Management and Marketing, Carthage College, USA. She is also Director of the Master of Business Design and Innovation Program.

Routledge Critical Studies in Public Management

Edited by Stephen Osborne

For a full list of titles in this series, please visit www.routledge.com

The study and practice of public management has undergone profound changes across the world. Over the last quarter century, we have seen

- increasing criticism of public administration as the over-arching framework for the provision of public services,
- the rise (and critical appraisal) of the "New Public Management" as an emergent paradigm for the provision of public services,
- the transformation of the "public sector" into the cross-sectoral provision of public services, and
- the growth of the governance of inter-organizational relationships as an essential element in the provision of public services.

In reality, these trends have not so much replaced each other as elided or co-existed together—the public policy process has not gone away as a legitimate topic of study, intra-organizational management continues to be essential to the efficient provision of public services, whist the governance of inter-organizational and inter-sectoral relationships is now essential to the effective provision of these services.

Further, whilst the study of public management has been enriched by the contribution of a range of insights from the "mainstream" management literature, it has also contributed to this literature in such areas as networks and inter-organizational collaboration, innovation, and stakeholder theory.

This series is dedicated to presenting and critiquing this important body of theory and empirical study. It will publish books that both explore and evaluate the emergent and developing nature of public administration, management, and governance (in theory and practice) and examine the relationship with and contribution to the over-arching disciplines of management and organizational sociology.

Books in the series will be of interest to academics and researchers in this field, students undertaking advanced studies of it as part of their undergraduate or post-graduate degree, and reflective policy makers and practitioners.

Local Participatory Governance and Representative Democracy
Institutional Dilemmas in European Cities
Edited by Nils Hertting and Clarissa Kugelberg

Inter-Organizational Collaboration by Design
Jennifer R. Madden

Inter-Organizational Collaboration by Design

Jennifer R. Madden

Routledge
Taylor & Francis Group

LONDON AND NEW YORK

First published 2018
by Routledge

2 Park Square, Milton Park, Abingdon, Oxfordshire OX14 4RN
52 Vanderbilt Avenue, New York, NY 10017

Routledge is an imprint of the Taylor & Francis Group, an Informa business

First issued in paperback 2019

Library of Congress Cataloging-in-Publication Data
A catalog record for this book has been requested

ISBN: 978-1-138-20481-2 (hbk)
ISBN: 978-0-367-88997-5 (pbk)

Typeset in Sabon
by Apex CoVantage, LLC

Contents

Figures and Tables

Figures

Tables

Foreword

Over the past two decades, management theory and application have merged in various ways to establish fields of engaged management (Van De Ven, 2007) and practitioner scholarship (Salipante & Aram, 2003). This idea of practitioner scholarship is not intended to be the be-all and end-all of problem solving; rather, it provides opportunities for contributing empirical evidence toward addressing real world problems that managers encounter in their lived experiences. Practitioner scholars like to attempt to tackle what they call "wicked" problems or those that we all know are important but still fall short of consensus approaches to navigating the challenges incurred in managing the problem.

Building from insight on the wicked problem of affordable housing, this novel and informative book is intended to contribute to the importance of developing inter-organizational collaborations to ensure continued progress for the benefit of individuals, communities, and society as a whole. This important contribution comes from the doctoral and professional practice work of a rising practitioner-scholar, Jennifer Madden, PhD. Dr. Madden is an enormously successful practitioner in bringing inter-organizational collaborative projects to fruition for community benefit and social and societal improvements in urban neighborhoods. This work represents early scholarly attempts to apply her empirical findings toward bold contributions to the problem under investigation. It's this mix of practical successful experiences ranging over a 15-year period, combined with rigorous scholarship, that makes this book a must read for anyone concerned with designing inter-organizational collaborations, affordable housing, and urban development.

Jennifer and I met as doctoral students in the Weatherhead School of Management at Case Western Reserve University. We come from different backgrounds and influences on our journeys toward practitioner scholarship, but we shared passions for finding venues for success throughout Northeast Ohio, for rigorous research applied to practical problems, and the strong desire to make contributions to our communities that can be generalized more broadly to help others apply improved management approaches in the future. Jennifer is bright, bold, and passionate while maintaining a tremendous sense of humor. Her laugh is contagious and usually could be heard throughout the classrooms of the Peter B. Lewis Building during those doctoral study years. However, her professional desire to understand the antecedents and outcomes of inter-organizational collaboration emerged methodically throughout our program. I heard her speak and discuss these research and practice endeavors over a four-year period, and it is very exciting to see these ideas come to life in this well-written and easy to comprehend practitioner-scholar book.

This book represents a strong introduction to and theoretical framing of a wicked problem of practice, and then it embarks on a series of three empirical works with separate and relevant research questions contributing to our understanding of potential approaches toward solutions for this and related problems. In Chapter 1, Dr. Madden outlines a simple yet profound model for inter-organizational collaboration using affordable housing as a framework. In the model we must work to understand pre-conditions, then the process, and review outcomes. This is where previous scholars stopped; however, Dr. Madden propels us forward to also look for "impact" that extends current theory and compels managers to ascribe more meaning to outcomes over time. Chapter 2 covers her initial inductive qualitative research paper, which was published by the Academy of Management (AOM) in the 2011 best paper proceedings for its contributions toward improved inter-organizational collaborations in the area of affordable housing. The detailed background of previous efforts to address the affordable housing problem in the United States are well covered in the literature review of Chapter 2 and should be read by anyone interested in understanding the mistakes and successes of the past that lead us to contemporary management of these issues. Chapter 3 extends the initial work through the presentation of a deductive quantitative paper and introduction of design. This work, also presented at AOM, and subsequent works covered here have been annual favorites for paper presentations at the Association for Research on Nonprofit Organizations and Voluntary Action (ARNOVA) conferences. Chapter 4 integrates the first two studies via sequential mixed methods, which allows us to understand the problem more deeply and arrive at conclusions beyond either of the initial two studies alone. In these studies she provides evidence of factors that influence inter-organizational collaboration that help us overcome barriers to innovation while rejuvenating communities.

Chapter 5 then provides an evidence-based design plan, or a practical and useful blueprint, for successful inter-organizational collaboration with suggestions for tools and training for the serious practitioner while further clarifying how to arrive at success factors. Finally, Chapter 6 is a dynamic summary of tremendously successful outcomes that emanated from Dr. Madden's contributions to collaborative efforts in improving urban communities through similar approaches, studied in the context and framework of the empirical studies contained herein. The research is rigorous, but the application to practice is so compelling that the final chapter leaves the reader wanting to immediately attempt to apply the lessons learned to real world situations. Most importantly, it compels the reader to take action toward improved collaboration and support of noteworthy causes that help level the playing field in communities in need of support and opportunity.

This book inspires me, even after a distinguished 25-year plus career in the management of research at a major academic medical center (Case Western Reserve University and its affiliate University Hospitals Cleveland Medical Center) to continue to make broad and bold contributions to the field of management scholarship and practice. I have had terrific opportunities to support urban communities as a founding Board of Trustee member of the Cleveland School of Science and Medicine, which helped elevate this urban high school to the top performing high school in the Cleveland Metropolitan School District as well as one of the best public high schools in the state of Ohio. Even with the perspective of these successes in my own career, Dr. Madden's style and approach in her work will inevitably invigorate all readers and help individuals realize how to make important contributions to management practice and research. Collaboration is not easy, but we learn in this book that it is often necessary and desirable. We will now know better approaches to ensuring and sustaining collaborative efforts.

I cannot think of a more exciting approach to living out one's passion as Dr. Madden has done here while bringing new insights to urban redevelopment by combining her real world experiences with solid research and integrating results to improve our understanding. I picture this book in the future (even in the new digital age) as a well-worn hard copy tool that managers use and reference in generalizable ways across any and all management practices that require insights into collaboration for the betterment of society. Please enjoy this contribution, and I am sure you will find the practical applicability that is in abundance here will apply to your own personal passions and interests.

Philip A. Cola, PhD
Associate Professor of Design & Innovation
Weatherhead School of Management
Case Western Reserve University
Cleveland, Ohio
March 12, 2017

References

Salipante, P., & Aram, J. D. (2003). Managers as knowledge generators: The nature of practitioner-scholar research in the nonprofit sector. *Nonprofit Management and Leadership*, 14(2), 129–150.

Van de Ven, A. H. (2007). *Engaged scholarship: A guide for organizational and social research*. Oxford: Oxford University Press on Demand.

Acknowledgments

Many thanks to my wonderful friends and colleagues who provided such tremendous support in reviewing this book to ensure my quantitative and qualitative research was exceptional—Dr. Philip Cola, Dr. Yunmei Wang, Dr. Michele Hancock, and Dr. Joseph Wall.

A special thank you to my mother, Lynda Jeanne Bivins, my biggest cheerleader, and my dad, Tyrone Madden, Sr., for endless support. Lastly, a special thanks to my husband, Kahlil, for his never-ending encouragement; without him my work would not be possible.

1 Introduction

Although difficult, complicated, and sometimes discouraging, collaboration is recognized as a viable approach for addressing uncertain and complex problems. Inter-organizational collaborations can attract resources and increase efficiency, facilitate visions of mutual benefit that can ignite common desires of partners to work across and within sectors, and create shared feelings of responsibility. Collaboration can also promote conceptualized synergy, the sense that something will "be achieved that could not have been attained by any of the organizations acting alone" (Huxham, 2003). However, previous inquiries into the problems encountered in collaborations have not solved an important question: How can successful inter-organizational collaboration be enabled? Through exploratory sequential mixed-methods research conducted in three empirical studies, I discover how inter-organizational collaborations can overcome barriers to innovate and rejuvenate communities and understand the factors and antecedents that influence successful collaboration.

In the first study (Chapter 2), I use a grounded theory approach to identify the emergent factors involved in successful collaboration. My interviews with leaders in affordable housing as an example of inter-organizational collaborations revealed most collaborations for affordable housing encounter a common set of obstacles: funding, partnering, community, and/or government. Key findings suggest leaders of successful collaborations exhibit heightened emotional and social competencies, take actions intended to create a better future, remain mission-focused, and continuously redesign to meet ongoing challenges. Further, successful inter-organizational collaborations were innovative—creating solutions that rejuvenated their communities.

To confirm and validate the findings in the first study, I proposed a theoretical model emerging from the qualitative research, designed and empirically tested through a survey of 452 leaders and managers participating in ongoing or recently completed inter-organizational collaborations. In this second study (Chapter 3), after establishing proper reliability and validity of the constructs examined, I found design attitude ($\beta = 0.45$, $p < 0.001$), shared vision ($\beta = 0.32$, $p < 0.001$), and autonomy ($\beta = 0.16$, $p < 0.01$) all positively affect successful collaboration performance. The study proposed a theoretical perspective for collaborators to adopt design science (i.e., a solution-finding approach utilizing end-user-centered research, prototyping, and collective creativity) to strengthen individuals, teams, and organizations; (Madden, 2015), the language of designers, and a design attitude as an empirically informed pathway for better managing the complexities inherent in inter-organizational collaboration. This research is also the first to quantitatively validate a design attitude scale for building better collaborations.

In my third study (Chapter 4), I examine mutuality as a critical antecedent of successful inter-organizational collaboration performance and the importance of active listening in team interaction. This study uncovers the positive and significant links between mutually beneficial exploration and boundary spanning ($\beta = 0.73$, $p < 0.001$), design attitude ($\beta = 0.65$, $p < 0.001$), shared vision ($\beta = 0.35$, $p < 0.001$), and autonomy ($\beta = 0.34$, $p < 0.001$). The constructs are validated in my second quantitative study. Again, these data are revealed following the proper statistical techniques that show reliability and validity of the constructs utilized in the hypothesized model. Finally, I propose how successful collaboration performance research can contribute to the development of evidence-based strategies for creating practitioner tools (Chapter 5). I provide examples and resulting implications both as evidence and to guide practitioners (Chapter 6).

This book makes theoretical and empirical contributions to the literature on inter-organizational collaboration, extending the traditional theoretical framework to include nontraditional literature streams and theories and connecting theory to practice. Through an integrated framework, evidence-based tools and strategies for building successful collaboration is examined and articulated in real world situations where successful collaboration performance and innovation facilitates rejuvenative collaboration. This book is useful for leaders and managers in nonprofit, private, and government sectors interested in building better and more meaningful collaborations.

1.1. The Collaboration Conundrum

A change in the nature of problems has caused a pivotal shift. Contemporary problems are now indivisible (Aldrich, 1976), wicked (Rittel & Webber, 1973; Kimbell, 2011), open-ended and unstable messes (Schon, 1971; Ackoff, 1974) or meta-problems (Trist, 1983; Shapiro, 2014), suggesting that the increased difficulty of problem solving (or solution finding) now exceeds the ability of single organizations (Gray, 1985). The growing need for collaborative problem solving cannot be overstated. Yet although a viable strategy, scholars note "collaboration may be necessary and desirable, but the research evidence indicates that it is hardly easy" (Bryson, Crosby, & Stone, 2006, p. 44).

Collaboration is "a process in which autonomous or semi-autonomous actors interact through formal and informal negotiation, jointly creating rules and structures governing their relationships and ways to act or decide on the issues that brought them together" (Thomson, Perry, & Miller, 2009, p. 25). There is a variety of extant research on collaboration, with topics ranging from accountability (Andersson & Wikström, 2014; Romzek, LeRoux, Johnston, Kempf, & Piatak, 2014; Forrer, Kee, Newcomer, & Boyer, 2010; Tschirhart, Christensen, & Perry, 2005; Page, 2004; Sullivan, Barnes, & Matka, 2002; Foster-Fishman, Salem, Allen, & Fahrback, 2001; Wolff, 2001; Mitchell & Shortell, 2000; Bardach, 1998; Huxham, 1996; Wood & Gray, 1991; Van de Ven, Emmett, & Koenig, 1975) to sustainability (Bryson, 2011; Kumar & van Dissel, 1996; Huxham, 1996; Oliver, 1990). Examples of select collaboration research topics are presented in Table 1.1 as a summary of relevant literature streams in this area.

Table 1.1 Selected Collaboration Research Topics

Collaboration Research Topic	Source
Collaboration Accountability	Andersson and Wikström (2014) Romzek et al. (2014) Forrer et al. (2010) Tschirhart et al. (2005) Page (2004) Sullivan et al. (2002) Foster-Fishman et al. (2001) Wolff (2001) Mitchell and Shortell (2000) Bardach (1998) Huxham (1996) Wood and Gray (1991) Van de Ven, Emmett, & Koenig, (1975)
Collaboration Advantages	Huxham (2003) Kanter (1994)
Collaboration Alliances	Anslinger and Jenk (2004) Austin (2000) Gulati (1998) Eisenhardt and Schoonhoven (1996) Mitchell and Singh (1996) Hagedoorn and Schakenraad (1994) Gray and Wood (1991)
Collaboration Alignment of Expectations	Foster-Fishman et al. (2001) Wolff (2001) Lister (2000) Mitchell and Shortell (2000)
Collaboration Antecedents	Concha (2014) Radin et al. (1996) Alter and Hage (1993) Pasquero (1991) Powell (1990) Axelrod (1984) Levine and White (1961) Nathan and Mitroff (1991)

(Continued)

Table 1.1 (Continued)

Collaboration Research Topic	Source
Collaboration Design	Bryson et al. (2006)
Collaboration Governance	Ansell and Gash (2007) Crosby and Bryson (2005) Thomson (2001) McCaffrey, Faerman, and Hart (1995) Chrislip and Larson (1994) Gray (1989) Van de Ven and Ferry (1980)
Collaborative Leadership	Crosby and Bryson (2010) Vangen and Huxham (2003a) Chrislip and Larson (1994)
Collaborative Networks	Rethemeyer and Hatmaker (2007) Agranoff (2006) Agranoff and McGuire (1999) Agranoff and McGuire (1998) O'Toole (1997) Walker, Kogut, and Shan (1997) Klijn, Koppenjan, and Termeer (1995) Nohria (1992) Logsdon (1991)
Collaboration Processes	Thomson and Perry (2006)
Collaboration for Public Services Delivery	Sowa (2008, 2009) Graddy and Chen (2006) Guo and Acar (2005) Hill and Lynn (2003) Page (2003)
Collaboration Opposition/ Disadvantages/Difficulties	Gazely (2010) Cheek (2008) Morse (2008) Bryson et al. (2006) Hodge and Greve (2005) Gray (2004) Huxham and Vangen (2000b) Wondolleck & Yaffee (2000) Huxham (1996)
Collaboration Synergy/ Failure of Synergy	Austin and Seitanidi, M. M. (2012) Lindgreen and Swaen (2010) Lin, Yang, and Arya (2009) Huxham and Vangen (2005) Foster-Fishman et al. (2001) Lasker, Weiss, and Miller (2001) Simonin (1997) Mohr and Spekman (1994)
Collaboration Research	Bardach (1998) Ring and Van de Ven (1994) Mattessich, Murray-Close, and Monsey (2001)

Collaboration Research Topic	Source
Collaboration to Attract/ Sustain Funding	Berman (2008) Morse (2008) Ostrower (2005) Brinkerhoff (2002) Smith (2001) Barringer and Harrison (2000)
Collaboration Strategy to Address Social Issues	Gardner (2005) Vangen and Huxham (2003b) Keast, Mandell, Brown, and Woolcock (2004) Foster-Fishman et al. (2001) Huxham and Vangen (2000a)
Collaboration Trust, Control and Risk	Diallo and Thuillier (2005) Paul and McDaniel (2004) Das and Teng (1996, 1998, 2000, 2001) Shortell et al. (2002) Lewicki, McAllister, and Bies (1998) Zaheer, McEvily, and Perrone (1998) Mohr and Spekman (1994)
Improving Success	Das & Teng (1998) Dacin, Hitt, and Levitas (1997) Gray (1985)
Measurement and Evaluation of Efforts	Thomson et al. (2009) Foster-Fishman et al. (2001) Thomson (2001) Mitchell and Shortell (2000)
Member Selection/Partner Process	Austin and Seitanidi (2012) Austin (2000) Keast et al. (2004) Shortell et al. (2002) Wolff (2001) Mitchell and Shortell (2000)
Optimizing Scarce Resources	Lister (2000) Mitchell and Shortell (2000)
Successful Collaboration Arrangements	Brinkerhoff and Brinkerhoff (2004)
Sustaining Collaborations	Bryson (2011) Kumar and van Dissel (1996) Huxham (1996) Oliver, (1990)

On reviewing existing research on collaboration, inconsistencies and the absence of a single theoretical perspective for a comprehensive model of collaboration presents a major challenge. In other words, with no single theory serving as a general foundation for a theory of collaboration, different theoretical perspectives provide different understandings of collaboration

(Gray & Wood, 1991). Moreover, the various theoretical perspectives often fail to address all three components of the "traditional" collaboration framework defined as "preconditions," "processes," and "outcomes." Thus, even though collaboration can be a critical factor for success (in theory and practice), an inter-organizational collaboration design plan and strategy for implementation is needed.

1.2 Theoretical Pluralism and Case Study Research

The collaboration literature is characterized by theoretical pluralism and case study research. Examples of multiple theories include: exchange theory, resource dependency theory, network theory, stakeholder theory, corporate social performance theory, and transaction cost theory. Inter-organizational relationships have typically followed exchange theory (Levine & White, 1961) or resource dependency theory (Pfeffer & Salancik, 1978) and their related research streams. The exchange perspective evokes expectations of mutual benefit or gain, motivating interaction where the nature of the relationship involves a high level of problem solving and cooperation (Schmidt & Kochan, 1977). Conversely, the resource dependency perspective is asymmetrical, where external pressure, lack of power or lack of resources motivates the interaction, and the nature of the relationship involves conflict and bargaining (March & Simon, 1958) to reduce the significance of the gap. Schmidt and Kochan (1977) complicate the idealities of exchange theory and resource dependency theory by outlining organizations that have mixed motives and inter-organizational relationships with both exchange and power-dependency tendencies.

In addition to theoretical pluralism, there is a great deal of formative collaboration case study research that collaboration topics build upon, including: steps for creating alliances (Gricar & Brown, 1981; McCann, 1983; Susskind & Madigan, 1984); the need for public–private partnerships (Brooks, Liebman, & Schelling, 1984; Levitt & Kirlin, 1985); conditions facilitating inter-organizational relationships (Gray, 1985; Gray & Hay, 1986); the ability of collaborations to address negative consequences (Gricar & Baratta, 1983; Taber, Walsh, & Cooke, 1979); design and innovation (Dimancescu & Botkin, 1986; Hallisey & Sanabria, 1987; Ahuja, 2000; Verganti, 2006); and conflict resolution (Bingham, 1986; Carpenter & Kennedy, 1988). The case studies demonstrate promise for collaboration in problem solving. For example, in an effort to build a framework for understanding social problem solving, McCann (1983, p. 180) outlined the development phases of collaborations: problem setting (including identification of the problem, stakeholder interaction for achieving a consensus regarding the existence the problem, and mutual impact and interdependence), direction setting (including the identification of values and a shared mission, and building consensus on desired action), and structuring ("functional

viability"). Gray (1985, p. 916), building upon McCann's research, analyzed case studies to articulate problem setting, direction setting, and structuring as stages necessary for collaboration. This process model improved
our understanding of collaboration theory, specifically how collaboration
can be achieved and sustained. However, a key weakness is that the process
model proposed by McCann (1983), cannot be readily followed in practice,
and the fidelity of this model is in the sequence. A critical review of this
research reveals that the social problem-solving model was not followed
by the organization described in the case study. The reviewer argues that
"[o]nce a problem is well defined, direction setting and structuring follows
as night the day" (Chiles, 1983, p. 191). This commentary illustrates a dis-
connection between theory and practice, which is a significant gap in this
theory building.

Gray (1989), using case study research, presents innovative approaches
for resolving conflicts, solving problems, and facilitating successful collaborations. The need for understanding collaboration and creating a
theory of collaboration compelled Wood and Gray (1991) to map a
research agenda for collaboration scholars to move collaboration from
practice to theory given the lag of theory behind practice. The Journal of
Applied Behavioral Science dedicated two special issues (1991, Volume
27, Issue 1 and Issue 2) to examine theories of collaboration. As a result
of this seminal work, scholars built upon "both case research and theoretical analysis . . .to move beyond pragmatic descriptions to a deeper,
more systematic understanding of the theoretical issues involved in forming and maintaining collaborative alliances" (Gray & Wood, 1991, p. 4).
The outcome of this work was new insight into inter-organizational
collaboration where six major existing theoretical perspectives emerged
from nine case studies on collaboration. The theories were: a) resource
dependency theory, b) corporate social performance theory/institutional
economic theory, c) strategic management theory/social ecology theory,
d) microeconomics theory, e) institutional theory/negotiated order theory, and f) political theory.

Case study research is useful for theorizing (Creswell, 2013). The nine
studies published in the Journal of Applied Behavioral Science advanced
collaboration research and scholarship but did not produce a singular theoretical framework to follow. This body of research brought us closer to
constructing a theory of collaboration. There are, however, gaps in our
knowledge. There are challenges with the theoretical pluralism and ability to address the traditional collaboration framework (i.e., preconditions,
process, and outcomes). For example, all nine studies address preconditions
for collaboration, but not the same preconditions; some studies addressed
process, whereas other studies ignored it. Eight of the studies addressed preconditions as an issue across all six theoretical perspectives; four studies
addressed process as an issue across three theoretical perspectives. All nine

studies addressed outcomes across all six theoretical perspectives. However, none of theoretical perspectives address all three broad issues of collaboration (Logsdon, 1991; Pasquero, 1991; Westley & Vredenburg, 1991; Selsky, 1991; Fleisher, 1991; Nathan & Mitroff, 1991; Sharfman, Gray & Yan, 1991; Roberts & Bradley, 1991; Golich, 1991).

Following the publication of the case studies in the Journal of Applied Behavioral Science, collaboration emerged as a focus of research and scholarship (Thomson et al., 2009). Building upon Thomson's (2001) dissertation, Thomson et al. (2009) developed an empirically validated theory of collaboration. The first step in this research was the development of a structural equation model (SEM) to better understand causal relationships among five dimensions (i.e., governance, administration, autonomy, mutuality, and norms) and a conceptualization of a collaboration construct. The strength of the study is the empirically validated theory of collaboration, which is rooted in a wide cross-disciplinary body of research. This theory provides insight into the meaning and measurement of collaboration. However, weaknesses include a lack of statistical support in the measurement model for reciprocity, which is an especially critical failing given the strong support found elsewhere in the literature for reciprocity in collaboration (Axelrod, 1984; Vangen & Huxham, 2003b; Ostrom, 1990). Further, even though autonomy is an important dimension of collaboration, the researchers still found it difficult to operationalize (Thomson et al., 2009). Finally, while the research design was cross-sectional, it lacked variation in the samples (e.g., including examples of less successful or failed collaborations). Although there has been significant scholarship contributing to research, practice, and the creation of an integrative framework and model of collaboration, it is clear that gaps remain.

1.3 Proposition: Integrated Theoretical Framework for Rejuvenative Collaboration

To address the gaps in the collaboration literature and contribute to successful inter-organizational collaboration, this book makes three critical suggestions. First, integrate nontraditional literature and research (e.g., teleology, experiential learning theory, team interaction, and design). Second, expand the traditional collaboration framework to include "impact" (see Figure 1.1). Third, connect theory to practice. This integrated theoretical framework can contribute to the design and building of successful inter-organizational collaboration facilitating innovation and rejuvenation (i.e., rejuvenative collaboration). These suggestions are based upon the results from three empirical studies, validated through inter-organizational collaborations that have secured significant funding to implement transformational projects described in detail in this book (see Figure 1.2).

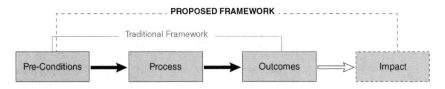

Figure 1.1 Commonly Used and Proposed Collaboration Framework

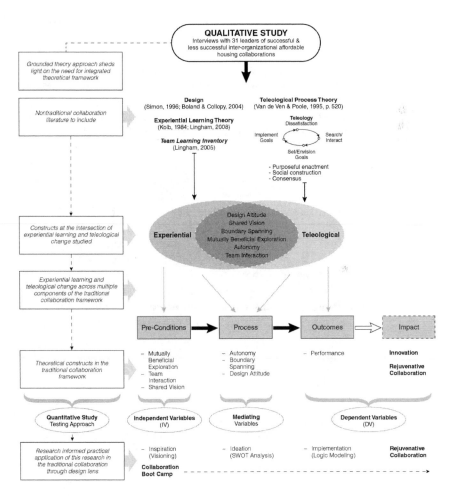

Figure 1.2 Proposed Integrated Theoretical Framework

1.3.1 Using Nontraditional Literature

The proposed nontraditional literature includes: teleology, experiential learning, team interaction, and design. Integrating teleological theory (a theoretical perspective) and experiential learning theory (a practical perspective) creates a potentially interesting theoretical contribution. Collaboration theories are motivated by external pressure or lack of power (i.e., resource dependency theory), potential benefit or gain (i.e., exchange theory), and efficiency through governance or contracts (i.e., transaction cost theory). However, teleology is a socially constructed recursive process theory of development in which participants work towards a goal (Van de Ven & Pool, 1995). According to Van de Ven and Poole (1995, pp. 515–516), teleological theory is:

> the philosophical doctrine that purpose or goal is the final cause for guiding movement of an entity. This approach underlies many organizational theories of change, including functionalism (Merton, 1968), decision making (March & Simon, 1958), epigenesis (Etzioni, 1963), voluntarism (Parsons, 1951), social construction (Berger & Luckmann, 1966), adaptive learning (March & Olsen, 1976), and most models of strategic planning and goal setting (Chakravarthy & Lorange, 1991). According to teleology, development of an organizational entity proceeds toward a goal or an end state. It is assumed that the entity is purposeful and adaptive; by itself or in interaction with others, the entity constructs an envisioned end state, takes action to reach it, and monitors the progress. Thus, proponents of this theory view development as a repetitive sequence of goal formulation, implementation, evaluation, and modification of goals based on what was learned or intended by the entity. The theory can operate for an individual or for a group of individuals or organizations who are sufficiently like-minded to act as a single collective entity. Teleology inherently affords creativity because the entity, consisting of an individual or group, has the freedom to enact whatever goals it likes.

From a practical perspective, collaboration is a recursive process in which individuals, teams, and organizations learn, develop relationships, share knowledge, build consensus, and implement goals (Dietrich, Eskerod, Dalcher, & Sandhawalia, 2010). Because collaboration is experiential in nature, in addition to teleological theory, experiential learning theory also has the potential to be useful for collaboration research. Experiential learning theory, developed by David Kolb (1984), combines the grasping and transformation of knowledge through experience as well as facilitating team learning. In addition, team learning builds upon experiential learning theory and provides critical insight given the complexities of team interaction (Lingham, 2009). See again Figure 1.2 above.

The intersection of teleological process theory and experiential learning theory are where the constructs studied in my research—autonomy, boundary spanning, design attitude, mutually beneficial exploration, shared vision, and the active listening attribute of team interaction—may be found. Understanding teleological process and experiential learning theories illuminates the performance of successful collaborations and contributes to theory and practice. Experiential learning theory and teleological process theory apply to multiple components of the traditional collaboration framework of preconditions, process, and outcomes. It is through the intersection of these well-established theories that impact is proposed for inclusion into the traditional collaboration framework.

1.3.2 Expanding the Traditional Collaboration Framework

An expansion of the traditional collaboration framework that includes an "impact" component results in the creation of a "preconditions," "processes," "outcomes," and "impact" frame for collaboration. Adding impact to the framework proposes a shift in focus from outcome to impact. Shifting the focus of the inter-organizational collaboration from outcomes to impact embeds a resiliency into the work and reinforces the critical idea of shared or common vision necessary for overcoming barriers and actualizing rejuvenative collaboration. See again Figure 1.1 above.

1.3.3 Connecting Theory to Practice

Directly connecting quantitatively validated grounded theory back to practice (through a design lens) facilitates the development of evidence-based and research-informed practical application. It also provides tools useful for inter-organizational collaborations to actualize funding to implement transformational programs. The connection of theory to practice as demonstrated in this book documents the power of, and replicable pathway for, engaged scholarship, as well as a clear design plan (or blueprint) for viable inter-organizational collaboration. This answers the question of how to enable successful collaboration.

These results emerge from a mixed methods research design. The mixed method approach allows for a deeper analysis than qualitative or quantitative methods alone would achieve (Johnson & Onwuegbuzie, 2004). A brief description of the research design is provided followed by abridgements of the three studies (i.e., Study I, Study II, and Study III) detailed in this book.

1.4 Research Design

This book is the result of an exploratory sequential mixed methods research design (Creswell & Plano Clark, 2011) in which qualitative (QUAL) research precedes a quantitative (QUANT) study (QUAL → QUANT). The use of a mixed methods research design is robust. The qualitative data collection and analysis in Study I (Chapter 2) build to quantitative data collection and analysis in Study II (Chapter 3). This building results in meta-inferences that are quantitatively analyzed in Study III (Chapter 4), leading to data-driven results and interpretation.

The use of mixed methods provides triangulation, complementarity, and expansion of the data (Greene, Caracelli, & Graham, 1989). Triangulation is achieved through literature review and qualitative research (Tashakkori & Teddlie, 2003). Complementarity is achieved by the qualitative research enhancing and clarifying results from the quantitative studies. Expansion is achieved by building a conceptual model for practice, which in turn is used to develop innovative evidence-based practitioner tools and a strategy for building successful inter-organizational collaborations.

In this research design, the qualitative analysis is used to develop and inform the quantitative study, allowing for the expansion of the scope of the research. The quantitative studies build upon the results and interpretation of the qualitative research to inform the development of a survey with adapted and developed scales. The resulting quantitative data analysis tests hypotheses and research models using structural equation modeling (SEM) and provides additional insight through descriptive statistics on inter-organizational collaborations in general.

A map of the research approach is included to illustrate the studies, procedures, and resulting product (see Figure 1.3). The results and interpretations from the qualitative study inform the survey development in the two subsequent quantitative studies that are analyzed sequentially.

1.4.1 Study I

Qualitative research is conducted to gain insight into a series of questions: Why are some inter-organizational, affordable-housing collaborations successful and others less successful? How do successful inter-organizational collaborations handle challenges differently from less successful collaborations?

Using a grounded theory approach, the first study examines inter-organizational collaborations building affordable housing to shed light on why some collaborations are successful whereas others are less successful. The 31 semi-structured interviews facilitating 15 case studies of affordable-housing collaborations in the United States provide insights that are built upon in two subsequent quantitative studies. Interpreting the qualitative study provides emergent factors and behaviors of successful collaborations that are further examined through quantitative analyses in Study II and Study III.

1.4.2 Study II

Quantitative research is conducted to empirically validate a series of constructs that emerged in the qualitative study. These constructs are at the

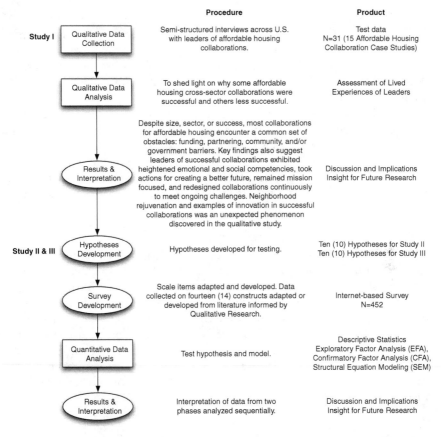

		Procedure	Product
Study I	Qualitative Data Collection	Semi-structured interviews across U.S. with leaders of affordable housing collaborations.	Test data N=31 (15 Affordable Housing Collaboration Case Studies)
	Qualitative Data Analysis	To shed light on why some affordable housing cross-sector collaborations were successful and others less successful.	Assessment of Lived Experiences of Leaders
	Results & Interpretation	Despite size, sector, or success, most collaborations for affordable housing encounter a common set of obstacles: funding, partnering, community, and/or government barriers. Key findings also suggest leaders of successful collaborations exhibited heightened emotional and social competencies, took actions for creating a better future, remained mission focused, and redesigned collaborations continuously to meet ongoing challenges. Neighborhood rejuvenation and examples of innovation in successful collaborations was an unexpected phenomenon discovered in the qualitative study.	Discussion and Implications Insight for Future Research
Study II & III	Hypotheses Development	Hypotheses developed for testing.	Ten (10) Hypotheses for Study II Ten (10) Hypotheses for Study III
	Survey Development	Scale items adapted and developed. Data collected on fourteen (14) constructs adapted or developed from literature informed by Qualitative Research.	Internet-based Survey N=452
	Quantitative Data Analysis	Test hypothesis and model.	Descriptive Statistics Exploratory Factor Analysis (EFA), Confirmatory Factor Analysis (CFA), Structural Equation Modeling (SEM)
	Results & Interpretation	Interpretation of data from two phases analyzed sequentially.	Discussion and Implications Insight for Future Research

Figure 1.3 Research Approach

intersection of experiential learning theory and teleological process theory: design attitude, shared vision, boundary spanning, mutually beneficial exploration, autonomy, and team interaction. The second study specifically examines the effect of autonomy, shared vision, and boundary spanning on inter-organizational collaboration performance; the effect of design attitude on the success or failure in inter-organizational collaboration; and the mediating role of design attitude on inter-organizational collaboration.

Study II empirically supports the positive impact of autonomy, boundary spanning, and common (or shared) vision as well as the mediating role of a design attitude as key to successful inter-organizational collaboration performance. Study II also proposes that increasing successful collaboration performance research will contribute to the development of evidence-based and research informed strategies for creating practitioner tools for building better collaborations.

1.4.3 Study III

Additional quantitative research is conducted to determine other key anteced-ents. To what extent does mutually beneficial exploration assist in building successful inter-organizational collaborations? Which components of team interaction are most critical and to what extent? This study tests a measure developed for mutually beneficial exploration and builds upon the first and second studies.

Study III examines mutually beneficial exploration (a construct that emerged from Study I) to confirm that mutually beneficial exploration is a key antecedent to the previously validated constructs in Study II (i.e., auton-omy, boundary spanning, shared vision, and design attitude)—the factors that have a positive impact on successful collaboration. Study III also deter-mines the active listening attribute in team interactions as a key antecedent for shared vision and autonomy.

1.5 Significance of the Research

Inter-organizational collaboration is recognized as a feasible tactic for addressing complex social problems. Theoretical and practical insights on collaboration are critical for both scholars and practitioners. Building from qualitative inquiry, the present research shows how to enable successful inter-organizational collaboration, realize innovation, and rejuvenate com-munities. This research also sheds light on factors that influence success-ful inter-organizational collaboration as well as the key antecedents that can serve as starting points for success. Finally, this research bridges the theory-practice gap.

1.6 Overview of the Book

Following this introduction, Chapter 2 (Learning from Inter-Organizational Col-laboration in Action: Overcoming Barriers in Affordable Housing Cross-Sector Collaborations) presents the qualitative research (Study I). The chapter inter-rogates the success or failure of affordable-housing, inter-organizational col-laborations, uncovering emergent factors of successful collaboration using the lived experiences of leaders. This critical initial study informs the work of subsequent chapters in this book and is discussed in great detail to provide background information on affordable-housing policy and actors, to begin the introduction of nontraditional literature (i.e., design, redesign), to demon-strate the rigorous methodological approach, and to discuss the implications of the findings.

Chapter 3 (The ABCDs of Successful Collaboration) presents the first quantitative analysis (Study II). The chapter examines the impact of emer-gent factors from Study I (autonomy, boundary spanning, shared vision, and design attitude) on successful collaboration performance.

Chapter 4 (Mutually Beneficial Exploration as a Key Antecedent for Successful Collaboration) presents the second quantitative analysis (Study III). The chapter measures mutually beneficial exploration as a key antecedent to the emergent factors in Study II and the impact of active listening in team interactions on shared vision and autonomy.

Chapter 5 (Creating the Collaboration Blueprint: Connecting the Practical & Theoretical Perspectives) presents an overview of the integrated findings and a discussion of the three studies. The chapter diagrams the connection of lived experiences of practitioners in the qualitative research to theory tested in the quantitative study for the creation of an evidence-based design plan (or blueprint) for successful inter-organizational collaboration. The chapter also proposes additional useful tools (i.e., facilitated inter-organizational collaboration and skill building in design thinking, team learning, and emotional intelligence).

Finally, Chapter 6 (Leverage Point Development: Examples of Inter-Organizational Collaborations Utilizing the Collaboration Blueprint) connects theory to practice through a design lens. The resulting evidence-based practitioner strategies presented in the blueprint can be facilitated via a boot camp style. This chapter also includes real-world examples of projects I have worked on using the design plan (or blueprint) detailed in this book to actualize successful inter-organizational collaborations by design.

References

Ackoff, R. R. (1974). *Redesigning the future*. New York, NY: Wiley.

Agranoff, R. (2006). Inside collaborative networks: Ten lessons for public managers. *Public Administration Review, 66*(Special Issue), 56–65.

Agranoff, R., & McGuire, M. (1998). Multinetwork management: Collaboration and the hollow state in local economic policy. *Journal of Public Administration Research & Theory, 8*(1), 67–91.

Agranoff, R., & McGuire, M. (1999). Managing in network settings. *Policy Studies Review, 16*(1), 18–41.

Ahuja, G. (2000). Collaboration networks, structural holes, and innovation: A longitudinal study. *Administrative Science Quarterly, 45*(3), 425–455.

Aldrich, H. (1976). Resource dependence and interorganizational relations: Local employment service offices and social services sector organizations. *Administration & Society, 7*(4), 419–454.

Alter, C., & Hage, J. (1993). *Organizations working together*. Newbury Park, CA: Sage.

Andersson, J., & Wikström, E. (2014). Constructing accountability in inter-organisational collaboration: The implications of a narrow performance-based focus. *Journal of Health Organization and Management, 28*(5), 619–634.

Ansell, C., & Gash, A. (2007). Collaborative governance in theory and practice. *Journal of Public Administration Research & Theory, 18*(4), 543–571.

Anslinger, P., & Jenk, J. (2004). Creating successful alliances. *Journal of Business Strategy, 25*(2), 18–22.

Austin, J. (2000). Strategic collaboration between nonprofits and businesses. *Nonprofit & Voluntary Sector Quarterly, 29*, 69–97.

Austin, J. E., & Seitanidi, M. M. (2012). Collaborative value creation: A review of partnering between nonprofits and businesses. Part 2: Partnering processes and outcomes. *Nonprofit & Voluntary Sector Quarterly, 41*(6), 929–968.

Axelrod, R. (1984). *The evolution of cooperation.* Princeton, NJ: Princeton University Press.

Bardach, E. (1998). *Getting agencies to work together: The practice and theory of managerial craftsmanship.* Washington, DC: Brookings Institution Press.

Barringer, B. R., & Harrison, J. S. (2000). Walking a tightrope: Creating value through interorganizational relationships. *Journal of Management, 26*(3), 367–403.

Berger, P., & Luckmann, T. (1966). *The social construction of knowledge: A treatise in the sociology of knowledge.* Open Road Media: Soho, NY, USA.

Berman, J. (2008). Connecting with industry: Bridging the divide. *Journal of Higher Education Policy & Management, 30*(2), 165–174.

Bingham, G. (1986). *Resolving environmental disputes: A decade of experience.* Washington, DC: Conservation Foundation.

Brinkerhoff, D. W., & Brinkerhoff, J. (2004). Partnerships between international donors and non-governmental development organizations: Opportunities and constraints. *International Review of Administrative Sciences, 70*(2), 253–270.

Brinkerhoff, J. M. (2002). Assessing and improving partnership relationships and outcomes: A proposed framework. *Evaluation & Program Planning, 25*(3), 215–231.

Brooks, H., Liebman, L., & Schelling, C. (1984). *Public private partnership: New opportunities for meeting social needs.* Cambridge, MA: Ballinger Publishing Company.

Bryson, J. (2011). *Strategic planning for public and nonprofit organizations: A guide to strengthening and sustaining organizational achievement.* New York, NY: Wiley.

Bryson, J., Crosby, B., & Stone, M. (2006). The design and implementation of cross-sector collaborations: Propositions from the literature. *Public Administration Review, 66*(Special Issue), 44–55.

Carpenter, S. L., & Kennedy, W. (1988). *Managing public disputes: A practical guide to handling conflict and reaching agreements.* San Francisco, CA: Jossey-Bass.

Chakravarthy, B. S., & Lorange, P. (1991). *Managing the strategy process: a framework for a multibusiness firm.* Prentice Hall.

Cheek, J. (2008). Researching collaboratively: Implications for qualitative research and researchers. *Qualitative Health Research, 18*(11), 1599–1603.

Chiles, C. L. (1983). Comments on "Design guidelines for social problem-solving interventions." *Journal of Applied Behavioral Science, 19*(2), 189–191.

Chrislip, D. D., & Larson, C. E. (1994). *Collaborative leadership.* San Francisco, CA: Jossey-Bass.

Concha, M. (2014). Exploring collaboration, its antecedents, and perceived outcomes in service partnerships of community-based organizations in South Florida. *International Journal of Public Administration, 37*(1), 44–52.

Creswell, J. W. (2013). *Research design: Qualitative, quantitative, and mixed methods approaches.* Thousand Oaks, CA: Sage.

Creswell, J. W., & Plano Clark, V. (2011). *Designing and conducting mixed methods research.* Thousand Oaks, CA: Sage.

Crosby, B. C., & Bryson, J. M. (2005). *Leadership for the common good: Tackling public problems in a shared-power world.* San Francisco, CA: Jossey-Bass.

Crosby, B. C., & Bryson, J. M. (2010). Integrative leadership and the creation and maintenance of cross-sector collaborations. *Leadership Quarterly, 21*(2), 211–230.

Dacin, M. T., Hitt, M. A., & Levitas, E. (1997). Selecting partners for successful international alliances: Examination of US and Korean firms. *Journal of World Business, 32*(1), 3–16.

Das, T. K., & Teng, B. S. (1996). Risk type and inter-firm alliance structures. *Journal of Management Studies, 33*(6), 827–843.

Das, T. K., & Teng, B. S. (1998). Between trust and control: Developing confidence in partner cooperation in alliances. *Academy of Management Review, 23*(3), 491–512.

Das, T. K., & Teng, B. S. (2000). A resource-based theory of strategic alliances. *Journal of Management, 26*(1), 31–61.

Das, T. K., & Teng, B. S. (2001). Trust, control, and risk in strategic alliances: An integrated framework. *Organization Studies, 22*(2), 251–283.

Diallo, A., & Thuillier, D. (2005). The success of international development projects, trust and communication: An African perspective. *International Journal of Project Management, 23*, 237–252.

Dietrich, P., Eskerod, P., Dalcher, D., & Sandhawalia, B. (2010). The dynamics of collaboration in multipartner projects. *Project Management Journal, 41*(4), 59–78.

Dimancescu, D., & Botkin, J. (1986). *The new alliance: America's R & D consortia.* Cambridge, MA: Ballinger.

Eisenhardt, K. M., & Schoonhoven, C. B. (1996). Resource-based view of strategic alliance formation: Strategic and social effects in entrepreneurial firms. *Organization Science, 7*(2), 136–150.

Etzioni, A. (1963). The epigenesis of political communities at the international level. *American Journal of Sociology, 68*(4), 407–421.

Fleisher, C. S. (1991). Using an agency-based approach to analyze collaborative federated interorganizational relationships. *Journal of Applied Behavioral Science, 27*(1), 116–130.

Forrer, J., Kee, J. E., Newcomer, K. E., & Boyer, E. (2010). Public–private partnerships and the public accountability question; *Public Administration Review, 70*(3), 475–484.

Foster-Fishman, P. G., Salem, D. A., Allen, N. A., & Fahrback, K. (2001). Facilitating interorganizational collaboration: The contributions of interorganizational alliances. *American Journal of Community Psychology, 29*(6), 875–905.

Gardner, D. B. (2005). 10 lessons in collaboration. *Online Journal of Issues in Nursing, 10*(1). Retrieved from http://gm6.nursingworld.org/MainMenuCategories/ANAMarketplace/ANAPeriodicals/OJIN/TableofContents/Volume102005/No1Jan05/tpc26_116008.aspx

Gazely, B. (2010). Why not partner with local government? Nonprofit managerial perceptions of collaborative disadvantage. *Nonprofit & Voluntary Sector Quarterly, 39*, 51–76.

Golich, V. L. (1991). A multilateral negotiations challenge: International management of the communications commons. *Journal of Applied Behavioral Science, 27*(2), 228–250.

Graddy, E. A., & Chen, B. (2006). Influences on the size and scope of networks for social service delivery. *Journal of Public Administration Research & Theory, 16*(4), 533–552.

Gray, B. (1985). Conditions facilitating interorganizational collaboration. *Human Relations, 38*(10), 911–936.

Gray, B. (1989). *Collaborating: Finding common ground for multiparty problems.* San Francisco, CA: Jossey-Bass.

Gray, B. (2004). Strong opposition: Frame-based resistance to collaboration. *Journal of Community & Applied Social Psychology, 14,* 166–176.

Gray, B., & Hay, T. M. (1986). Political limits to interorganizational consensus and change. *Journal of Applied Behavioral Science, 22*(2), 95–112.

Gray, B., & Wood, D. J. (1991). Collaborative alliances: Moving from practice to theory. *Journal of Applied Behavioral Science, 27*(1), 3–22.

Greene, J. C., Caracelli, V. J., & Graham, W. F. (1989). Toward a conceptual framework for mixed-method evaluation designs. *Educational Evaluation and Policy Analysis, 11*(3), 255–274.

Gricar, B. G., & Baratta, A. J. (1983). Bridging the information gap at Three Mile Island: Radiation monitoring by citizens. *Journal of Applied Behavioral Science, 19*(1), 35–49.

Gricar, B. G., & Brown, L. D. (1981). Conflict, power, and organization in a changing community. *Human Relations, 34*(10), 877–893.

Gulati, R. (1998). Alliances and networks. *Strategic Management Journal, 19*(4), 293–317.

Guo, C., & Acar, M. (2005). Understanding collaboration among nonprofit organizations: Combining resource dependency, institutional, and network perspectives. *Nonprofit & Voluntary Sector Quarterly, 34*(3), 340–361.

Hagedoorn, J., & Schakenraad, J. (1994). The effect of strategic technology alliances on company performance. *Strategic Management Journal, 15*(4), 291–309.

Hallisey, B., & Sanabria, S. (1987). *TC2 and the apparel industry.* Boston, MA: Harvard Business School Press.

Hill, C. J., & Lynn, L. E., Jr. (2003). Producing human services: Why do agencies collaborate? *Public Management Review, 5,* 63–81.

Hodge, G., & Greve, C. (2005). *The challenge of public-private partnerships: Learning from international experience.* Cheltenham, England: Edward Elgar.

Huxham, C. (1996). *Creating collaborative advantage.* London, England: Sage.

Huxham, C. (2003). Theorizing collaboration practice. *Public Management Review, 5*(3), 401–423.

Huxham, C., & Vangen, S. (2000a). Leadership in the shaping and implementation of collaboration agendas: How things happen in a (not quite) joined-up world. *Academy of Management Journal, 43*(6), 1159–1175.

Huxham, C., & Vangen, S. (2000b). Ambiguity, complexity and dynamics in the membership of collaboration. *Human Relations, 53*(6), 771–806.

Huxham, C., & Vangen, S. (2005). *Managing to collaborate: The theory and practice of collaborative advantage.* New York, NY: Routledge.

Johnson, R. B., & Onwuegbuzie, A. J. (2004). Mixed methods research: A research paradigm whose time has come. *Educational Researcher, 33*(7), 14–26.

Kanter, R. M. (1994). Collaborative advantage. *Harvard Business Review* (July–August), 72 (4), 96–108.

Keast, R., Mandell, M. P., Brown, K., & Woolcock, G. (2004). Network structures: Working differently and changing expectations. *Public Administration Review, 64*(3), 363–371.

Kimbell, L. (2011). Rethinking design thinking: Part I. *Design and Culture, 3*(3), 285–306.

Klijn, E. H., Koppenjan, J., & Termeer, K. (1995). Managing networks in the public sector: A theoretical study of management strategies in policy networks. *Public Administration, 73*(3), 437–454.

Kolb, D. A. (1984). *Experiential learning: Experience as the source of learning and development.* Englewood Cliffs, NJ: Prentice Hall.

Kumar, K., & van Dissel, H. G. (1996). Sustainable collaboration: Managing conflict and cooperation in interorganizational systems. *MIS Quarterly, 20*(3), 279–300.

Lasker, R., Weiss, E., & Miller, R. (2001). Partnership synergy: A practical framework for studying and strengthening the collaborative advantage. *Milbank Quarterly, 79*(2), 179–205.

Levine, S., & White, P. E. (1961). Exchange as a conceptual framework for the study of interorganizational relationships. *Administrative Science Quarterly, 5*(4), 583–601.

Levitt, R., & Kirlin, J. (1985). *Managing development through public/private negotiations.* Washington, DC: Urban Land Institute.

Lewicki, R. J., McAllister, D. J., & Bies, R. J. (1998). Trust and distrust: New relationships and realities. *Academy of Management Review, 23*(3), 438–458.

Lin, Z. J., Yang, H., & Arya, B. (2009). Alliance partners and firm performance: Resource complementarity and status association. *Strategic Management Journal, 30*(9), 921–940.

Lindgreen, A., & Swaen, V. (2010). Corporate social responsibility. *International Journal of Management, 12*(10), 1–7.

Lingham, T. (2009, July). *An experiential approach to team interaction: Developing a measure to capture its diverse dimensions and aspects.* Paper presented at the Interdisciplinary Group Research Conference, Colorado Springs, CO.

Lister, S. (2000). Power in partnerships? An analysis of an NGO's relationships with its partners. *Journal of International Development, 12*, 227–239.

Logsdon, J. M. (1991). Interests and interdependence in the formation of social problem-solving collaborations. *Journal of Applied Behavioral Science, 27*(1), 23–37.

Madden, J. (2015). Leveraging design: How the design process and a design framework strengthen nonprofit management pedagogy. *Journal of Nonprofit Education & Leadership, 5*(1), 6–11.

March, J. G., & Olsen, J. P. (1976). *Organizational choice under ambiguity. Ambiguity and choice in organizations, 2*, 10–23.

March, J. G., & Simon, H. A. (1958). *Organizations.* Oxford, England: Wiley.

Mattessich, P. W., Murray-Close, M., & Monsey, B. R. (2001). *Collaboration: What makes it work: A review of research literature on factors influencing successful collaboration.* St. Paul, MN: Amherst H. Wilder Foundation.

McCaffrey, D. P., Faerman, S. R., & Hart, D. W. (1995). The appeal and difficulties of participative systems. *Organization Science, 6*(6), 603–627.

McCann, J. E. (1983). Design guidelines for social problem-solving interventions. *Journal of Applied Behavioral Science, 19*(2), 177–189.

Merton, R. K. (1968). *Social theory and social structure.* Simon and Schuster.

Mitchell, S. M., & Shortell, S. M. (2000). The governance and management of effective community health partnerships: A typology for research, policy and practice. *Milbank Quarterly, 78*(2), 241–289.

Mitchell, W., & Singh, K. (1996). Survival of businesses using collaborative relationships to commercialize complex goods. *Strategic Management Journal, 17*(3), 169–196.

Mohr, J., & Spekman, R. (1994). Characteristics of partnership success: Partnership attributes, communication behavior and conflict resolution techniques. *Strategic Management Journal, 15*, 135–152.

Morse, J. (2008). Styles of collaboration in qualitative inquiry. *Qualitative Health Research, 18*, 3–4.

Nathan, M. L., & Mitroff, I. I. (1991). The use of negotiated order theory as a tool for the analysis and development of an interorganizational field. *Journal of Applied Behavioral Science, 27*(2), 163–180.

Nohria, N. (1992). Introduction: Is a network perspective a useful way of studying organizations? In N. Nohria & R. G. Eccles (Eds.), *Networks and organizations: Structure, form, and action* (pp. 1–22). Boston, MA: Harvard Business School Press.

Oliver, C. (1990). Determinants of interorganizational relationships: Integration and future directions. *Academy of Management Review, 15*(2), 241–265.

Ostrom, E. (1990). *Governing the commons: The evolution of institutions for collective action.* Cambridge, England: Cambridge University Press.

Ostrower, F. (2005). The reality underneath the buzz of partnerships: The potentials and pitfalls of partnering. *Stanford Social Innovation Review* (Spring). Retrieved from www.ssireview.org

O'Toole, L. J., Jr. (1997). Treating networks seriously: Practical and research-based agendas in public administration. *Public Administration Review, 57*(1), 45–52.

Page, S. (2003). Entrepreneurial strategies for managing interagency collaboration. *Journal of Public Administration Research & Theory, 13*(3), 311–340.

Parsons, T., & Shils, E. A. (1951). *Values, motives, and systems of action. Toward a general theory of action, 33*, 247–275.

Pasquero, J. (1991). Supraorganizational collaboration: The Canadian environmental experiment. *Journal of Applied Behavioral Science, 27*(1), 38–64.

Paul, D. L., & McDaniel, R. R., Jr. (2004). A field study of the effect of interpersonal trust on virtual collaborative relationship performance. *MIS Quarterly, 28*(2), 183–227.

Pfeffer, J., & Salancik, G. (1978). *The external control of organizations: A resource dependence perspective.* New York, NY: Harper & Row.

Powell, W. W. (1990). Neither market nor hierarchy: Network forms of organization. *Research in Organizational Behavior, 12*, 295–336.

Radin, B. S., Agranoff, R., Bowman, A., Buntz, C. G., Ott, J. S., Romzek, B. S., & Wilson, R. H. (1996). *New governance for rural America: Creating intergovernmental partnerships.* Lawrence, KS: University of Kansas Press.

Rethemeyer, R. K., & Hatmaker, D. M. (2007). Network management reconsidered: An inquiry into management of network structures in public sector service provision. *Journal of Public Administration Research & Theory, 18*, 617–646.

Ring, P. S., & Van de Ven, A. H. (1994). Development processes of cooperative interorganizational relationships. *Academy of Management Review, 19*(1), 90–118.

Rittel, H., & Webber, M. (1973). Dilemmas in a general theory of planning. *Policy Sciences, 4*(2), 155–169.

Roberts, N. C., & Bradley, R. T. (1991). Stakeholder collaboration and innovation: A study of public policy initiation at the state level. *Journal of Applied Behavioral Science, 27*(2), 209–227.

Romzek, B., LeRoux, K., Johnston, J., Kempf, R. J., & Piatak, J. S. (2014). Informal accountability in multisector service delivery collaborations. *Journal of Public Administration Research and Theory, 24*(4), 813–842.

Schmidt, S. M., & Kochan, T. A. (1977). Interorganizational relationships: Patterns and motivations. *Administrative Science Quarterly, 22*(2), 220–234.

Schon, D. A. (1971). *Beyond the stable state.* London, England: Temple Smith.

Selsky, J. W. (1991). Lessons in community development: An activist approach to stimulating interorganizational collaboration. *Journal of Applied Behavioral Science, 27*(1), 91–115.

Shapiro, S. (2014). Poor people, poor planet: The psychology of how we harm and heal humanity and earth. In E. Mustakova-Possardt, M. Lyubansky, M. Basseches, & J. Oxenberg (Eds.), *Toward a socially responsible psychology for a global era* (pp. 231–254). New York, NY: Springer.

Sharfman, M., Gray, B., & Yan, A. (1991). The context of interorganizational collaboration in the garment industry: An institutional perspective. *Journal of Applied Behavioral Science, 27*(2), 181–208.

Shortell, S. M., Zukoski, A. P., Alexander, J. A., Bazzoli, G. J., Conrad, D. A., Hasnain-Wynia, R., & Margolin, F. S. (2002). Evaluating partnerships for community health improvement: Tracking the footprints. *Journal of Health Politics, Policy & Law, 27*(1), 49–92.

Simonin, B. L. (1997). The importance of collaborative know-how: An empirical test of the learning organization. *Academy of Management Journal, 40*(5), 1150–1174.

Smith, D. (2001). Collaborative research: Policy and the management of knowledge creation in UK universities. *Higher Education Quarterly, 55*(2), 131–157.

Sowa, J. E. (2008). Implementing inter-agency collaborations: Exploring variation in collaborative ventures in human service organizations. *Administration & Society, 40*(3), 298–323.

Sowa, J. E. (2009). The collaboration decision in nonprofit organizations: Views from the front line. *Nonprofit & Voluntary Sector Quarterly, 38*(6), 1003–1025.

Sullivan, H., Barnes, M., & Matka, E. (2002). Building collaborative capacity through "theories of change." *Evaluation, 8*(2), 205–226.

Susskind, L., & Madigan, D. (1984). New approaches to resolving disputes in the public sector. *Justice System Journal, 9*(2), 179–203.

Taber, T. D., Walsh, J. T., & Cooke, R. A. (1979). Developing a community-based program for reducing the social impact of a plant closing. *Journal of Applied Behavioral Science, 15*(2), 133–155.

Thomson, A. M., & Perry, J. L. (2006). Collaboration processes: Inside the black box. *Public Administration Review, 66*(s1), 20–32.

Tashakkori, A., & Teddlie, C. (2003). The Past and the future of mixed methods research: From 'Methodological Triangulation' to 'Mixed Methods Designs'. *Handbook of Mixed Methods in Social and Behavioral Research, 671*–701.

Trist, E. (1983). Referent organizations and the development of inter-organizational domains. *Human Relations, 36*(3), 269–284.

Thomson, A. M. (2001). *Collaboration: Meaning and measurement* (Unpublished doctoral dissertation). Indiana University, Bloomington, IN.

Thomson, A. M., Perry, J., & Miller, T. (2009). Conceptualizing and measuring collaboration. *Journal of Public Administration Research & Theory, 19*(1), 23–56.

Trist, E. (1983). Referent organizations and the development of inter-organizational domains. *Human Relations, 36*(3), 269–284.

Tschirhart, M., Christensen, R. K., & Perry, J. L. (2005). The paradox of branding and collaboration. *Public Performance & Management Review, 29*(1), 67–84.

Van de Ven, A. H., Emmett, D. C., & Koenig, R., Jr. (1975). Theoretical and conceptual issues in inter-organizational theory. In A. R. Negandhi (Ed.), *Inter-organizational theory* (pp. 19–38). Kent, OH: Kent State University Press.

Van de Ven, A. H., & Ferry, D. L. (1980). *Measuring and assessing organizations.* New York, NY: Wiley.

Van de Ven, A. H., & Poole, M. S. (1995). Explaining development and change in organizations. *Academy of Management Review, 20*(3), 510–540.

Vangen, S., & Huxham, C. (2003a). Enacting leadership for collaborative advantage. *British Journal of Management, 14*, S61–S76.

Vangen, S., & Huxham, C. (2003b). Nurturing collaborative relations: Building trust in interorganizational collaboration. *Journal of Applied Behavioral Science 39*(1), 5–31.

Verganti, R. (2006). Innovation through design. *Harvard Business Review, 84*(12), 114.

Walker, G., Kogut, B., & Shan, W. (1997). Social capital, structural holes and the formation of an industry network. *Organization Science, 8*(2), 109–125.

Westley, F., & Vredenburg, H. (1991). Strategic bridging: The collaboration between environmentalists and business in the marketing of green products. *Journal of Applied Behavioral Science, 27*(1), 65–90.

Wolff, T. (2001). A practitioner's guide to successful coalitions. *American Journal of Community Psychology, 29*(2), 173–192.

Wondolleck, J. M., & Yaffee, S. L. (2000). *Making collaboration work: Lessons from innovation in natural resource managment.* Island Press.

Wood, D., & Gray, B. (1991). Toward a comprehensive theory of collaboration. *Journal of Applied Behavioral Science, 27*(1), 139–162.

Zaheer, A., McEvily, B., & Perrone, V. (1998). Does trust matter? Exploring the effects of interorganizational and interpersonal trust on performance. *Organization Science, 9*(2), 141–159.

2 Learning From Inter-Organizational Collaboration in Action

Overcoming Barriers in Affordable-Housing Collaborations[1]

My work as a housing and community development practitioner has always been in urban communities where there is tremendous need, yet never enough resources, but the people are resilient and creative. I have seen organizations accomplish tasks beyond their means because the required activities were managed through inter-organizational collaborations. Sometimes the collaborations worked, and sometimes they did not work. It became clear to me, if I could gain insight on how to enable successful collaboration, I could discover knowledge that contributes to sustainable urban economic development and transformation.

Inter-organizational collaborations are defined as "those involving government, business, nonprofits, and/or communities and the public or citizenry as a whole" (Bryson & Crosby, 2008, p. 3). This chapter is an inquiry into why some inter-organizational collaborations for affordable housing are successful whereas others are less successful. The chapter presents background information on affordable-housing policy and describes key actors. The qualitative research and findings are then presented. I return to the literature to formulate a response to the inquiry on successful inter-organizational collaborations focused on design, redesign, and two key factors that affect collaboration outcomes: power and leadership. The chapter concludes with a discussion of the implications of this research and study limitations.

2.1 Affordable-Housing, Inter-Organizational Collaborations

There is a continual shortage of affordable housing in the United States (Davidson, 2009; Graddy & Bostic, 2009; Schwarz, 2008) with approximately 7.72 million households in need (Steffen, B.L., Carter, G.R., Martin, M., Pelletiere, D., Vandenbroucke, D.A., Yao, Y-G. D., 2015). Overall, nonprofit housing organizations have produced more than 1.5 million units (Bratt, 2009) but have still not met the demand. To address this shortage, community development corporations (CDCs) and other nonprofit organizations often collaborate with each other, private developers, and government agencies to build low-income housing (Bratt, 2009; Finkenstaedt, 2009). Inter-organizational collaborations attract resources and increase efficiency (Asian Development Bank [ADB], 2008), making them a viable strategy for addressing complex social problems (Bryson et al., 2006; Roberts, 2000) like the lack of affordable housing.

Some scholars have studied inter-organizational collaborations as ways of addressing social problems, especially affordable housing. For example, in his studies of affordable-housing developers, Myerson (2002) reviewed collaboration strengths and pitfalls; Bratt (2008) focused on resources and capabilities of affordable-housing partners; Kroopnick (2008) demonstrated effective strategies to inform partnership composition and modeling; and Chung (2004) identified key drivers of inter-organizational partnerships and their negotiated terms. The literature is silent, however, on the why, how, and to what extent some collaborations are successful in building affordable housing whereas others have failed.

Despite growing interest by practitioners and scholars in the affordable-housing deficit and some empirical work conducted in search of solutions for it, we lack a comprehensive theory or approach, or the key elements to explain success or failure in inter-organizational collaborations in affordable housing. By determining what makes some collaborations successful and others less successful, we may increase the production of affordable housing. There is also a paucity of knowledge of the characteristics of successful collaborations that can be captured as "best practices" and deployed to improve the performance of less successful collaborations and therefore improve our overall ability to build more affordable housing in the United States.

Semi-structured qualitative interviews with 31 participants, across 15 U.S. affordable-housing collaboration case studies, were conducted to shed light on why some affordable-housing, inter-organizational collaborations were successful and others less successful. The data are grounded in the experiences of leaders from nonprofit agencies, private developers, and local governments participating in affordable-housing developments. I found effective collaboration management is a necessary and viable strategy for developing affordable housing.

The data revealed that most affordable-housing collaborations must overcome a common set of barriers: financing problems, the inability to resolve conflicts in the partnership, and community and/or political opposition. The data uncovered distinct differences between leaders of successful and less successful collaborations in overcoming these challenges. Although the data confirmed previous findings by scholars pointing out that trust (Das & Teng, 1998; Dirks & Ferrin, 2001; Lane & Bachmann, 1998; Nooteboom, Berger, & Noorderhaven, 1997; Snavely & Tracy, 2002) and alignment of mission (Berger, Cunningham, & Drumwright, 2004) are key components for successful collaboration, leaders of successful collaborations in this research demonstrated emotional intelligence, took actions for creating a better future, remained focused on the mission, and continuously redesigned plans and strategies to meet ongoing challenges.

The findings are relevant for scholars and practitioners in search of solutions to obstacles that impede the development of affordable housing. This knowledge may contribute to increasing the number of successful affordable-housing, inter-organizational collaborations.

2.2 Affordable Housing Policy

There is substantial academic and professional literature on the successes and failures of the U.S. affordable-housing program (Katz, Turner, Brown, Cunningham, & Sawyer, 2003). This section presents a brief historical summary of major federal programs for the redevelopment of urban areas. These programs—Urban Renewal, Model Cities, Community Development Block Grant, Low-Income Housing Tax Credit, and Neighborhood Stabilization Program—demonstrate the need for inter-organizational collaborations.

2.2.1 Urban Renewal

Between 1949 and 1974, the Urban Renewal program, created by the Housing Act of 1949, spurred urban development (Ho, 2008). With the initial idea of reversing the decline of the urban areas (or inner cities) and replacing slums with new affordable housing, two key features of the program maximized the role of the private sector and gave local governments the ability to initiate and implement renewal projects. The program authorized the construction of 810,000 units of new decent, safe, and sanitary housing to replace blighted and dilapidated buildings in poor urban neighborhoods. Little affordable housing, however, was actually created (Euchner & McGovern, 2003). Eminent domain was regularly utilized and renewal projects yielded prime land in the city center for business and developers (Euchner & McGovern, 2003). With substantial subsidies, the private sector was responsible for rebuilding communities, but without meaningful community involvement. The collaboration entailed municipal governments acquiring, demolishing, or renovating existing buildings and improving the infrastructure, after which the private sector would redevelop the area (Ho, 2008). The program was terminated in 1974.

2.2.2 Model Cities

Between 1966 and 1974, the Model Cities program, created by the Demonstration Cities and Metropolitan Development Act of 1966, worked to address some of the failures of the Urban Renewal program (Ho, 2008). The U.S. Department of Housing and Urban Development (HUD), established in 1965, would coordinate urban redevelopment efforts, address social and physical development needs, and ensure citizen participation. The private sector maintained its role as developer and continued to work and be receptive mostly to local government because of the absence of power-sharing between local governments and the community (Ho, 2008). The program ended because of administration changes, lack of power-sharing with the local community, and questions regarding the program's legitimacy (Ho, 2008).

2.2.3 Community Development Block Grant

The Community Development Block Grant (CDBG) program was created from the Community Development Act of 1974 for the purpose of shifting federal housing policy oversight and control to local governments because local housing needs did not always match the priorities set by federal programs (Ho, 2008). The program required community participation and provided developer incentives, although funding was more specifically outlined than in earlier programs. CDBG continues to fund a variety of community development programs.

2.2.4 Low-Income Housing Tax Credit

In 1986, the Low-Income Housing Tax Credit (LIHTC) program was created by the Tax Reform Act of 1986, and in 1990 the Home Improvement Partnership Program (HOME) was created under Title II of the National Affordable Housing Act of 1990. These programs marked the devolution of the design and implementation of affordable housing to local government, private sector developers, nonprofit developers, and the community (Katz et al., 2003). Both programs rely on the nonprofit sector for the delivery of services, and CDCs have been working to address the affordable-housing deficit created by the federal government's retrenchment in housing policy (Silverman, 2009) and both LIHTC and HOME remain useful programs today.

2.2.5 Neighborhood Stabilization Program

In 2008, the Neighborhood Stabilization Program (NSP) was created by the Housing and Economic Recovery Act (HERA) of 2008 under Title III ("Emergency Assistance for the Redevelopment of Abandoned and Foreclosed Homes"). The NSP is a component of the Community Development Block Grant (CDBG). The first tranche of funding ($3.92 billion; NSP1) awarded funding to 309 grantees, including 55 states and territories as well as selected local governments, to stabilize communities hardest hit by housing foreclosures and delinquencies. The NSP grantees develop their own programs and funding priorities (U.S. Department of Housing and Urban Development [HUD], 2009). Under an allocation of funds provided under the American Reinvestment and Recovery Act of 2009, a second tranche of funding ($1.93 billion; NSP2) was awarded to eligible applicants, including states, municipal government, nonprofits, and nonprofits

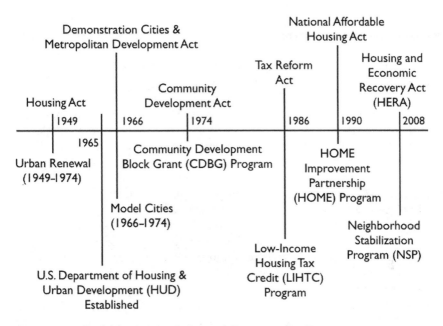

Figure 2.1 Affordable-Housing Policy and Corresponding Programs

collaborating with other nonprofits or for-profit entities (HUD, 2009). In 2010, a final tranche of funding ($1 billion; NSP3) was authorized for additional neighborhood assistance through the "Dodd-Frank Wall Street Reform and Consumer Protection Act" (U.S. Department of Housing and Urban Development [HUD], 2012).

As detailed above, affordable-housing policy has been critical in providing funding for housing development in urban communities. A historical timeline of public policy and major federal programs for the redevelopment of urban areas is provided in Figure 2.1. The figure summarizes the statutes enacted in the top section of the diagram and identifies the public policy connected to the funded program below the timeline.

2.3 Community Development Corporations

Community development corporations (CDCs) leverage affordable-housing policy programs for local economic development. CDCs were established as a model for the revitalization of urban neighborhoods (Frisch & Servon, 2006; Vidal, 1992; Vidal & Keating, 2004). Beginning in 1992, a CDC "industry" (Frisch & Servon, 2006; Walker, Gustafson, & Snow, 2002; Yin, 1998) developed, and CDCs evolved from local community residents working to make their neighborhoods better to a community development "system" with relationships with banks, government, foundations, churches

(Walker, 2002; Yin, 1998), and intermediaries offering training, best practices, and capacity building (Bockmeyer, 2003; Frisch & Servon, 2006; Glickman & Servon, 1999, 2003). Foundations and governments made significant investments in CDCs because they are more flexible than government agencies, and unlike private developers, CDCs involve residents in their governance, planning, and development activities (Galster, Levy, Sawet, Temkin, & Walker, 2005).

Most CDCs develop housing. Successful CDC developments in affordable housing combine the aggressiveness of private-sector developers with the public mission of the government to build and rehabilitate housing units (Kroopnick, 2008). Three key abilities of CDCs as development organizations versus for-profit developers include CDCs' ability to secure support from residents for redevelopment projects and policies, the ability to secure support from public agencies, and the ability to coordinate public investments. Weaknesses include liquidity or cash-flow problems, substantial political involvement because CDCs are an alternative to having local governments managing community development programs, and a lack of capacity to complete projects in a cost-effective and efficient manner (Walker, 2002).

Three financial intermediaries—Enterprise Foundation (now Enterprise Community Partners), Local Initiatives Support Corporation (LISC), and Neighborhood Reinvestment Corporation (d.b.a. NeighborWorks America)—have been critical to building the capacity, growth, development, and success of CDCs in particular (Vidal, 1997) and communities in general. For example, since 1980, Local Initiatives Support Corporation (2016) has invested $16.2 billion in communities (leveraging $48.5 billion in total development); it invested $1.3 billion in 2015 alone (leveraging $4.2 billion in total development). The Enterprise Foundation (2015) has invested $20.8 billion in communities since 1982. NeighborWorks America (2014) provided $5.8 billion in total direct investment for fiscal year 2013.

Intermediaries secure resources from foundations, governments, and corporations and strategically distribute funds to CDCs (Glickman & Servon, 2003). The activities supported by intermediaries positively affect CDC performance (Rohe & Bratt, 2003; Walker, 2002; Walker et al., 2002) resulting in CDCs, especially larger ones, having an impact in the neighborhoods in which they operate (Cowan, Rohe, & Baku, 1999). CDCs are frequently the only hope for the communities that they serve because private developers often ignore high-poverty neighborhoods (Knotts, 2006) leaving CDCs as the main organizational vehicle for development in urban areas (Stoecker, 2003). Despite impressive work completed under difficult conditions and the fact that CDCs are critical in their role as neighborhood change agents (Bratt & Rohe, 2007), CDCs, like many nonprofit organizations, have remained small, underfunded, and staffed by inexperienced personnel (Euchner & McGovern, 2003; Kroopnick, 2008), and their production numbers are limited.

In 1991, there were 2,000 CDCs in the United States producing 320,000 housing units. By 2005, that number had more than doubled to 4,600 and production totaled 1,252,000 units (National Congress for Community Economic Development [NCCED], 2005). Despite these advances, in 2005, only 44% of CDCs had produced more than 100 units of housing over their existence, and only 20% had produced more than 25 units for four consecutive years (NCCED, 2005). Although CDCs that received funding and support from intermediaries were the most productive providers of affordable housing (Glickman & Servon, 2003), even these productive CDCs averaged only 24 units per year (Glickman & Servon, 2003). Moreover, the number of community development organizations decreased significantly, dropping by half between 2002 and 2010 (Von Hoffman, 2013). With an early history of affordable-housing development, CDCs have expanded their community development operations (Reuter, 2014) to include programming around workforce development, community engagement, leadership development, foreclosure prevention, homeownership counseling, asset management, health promotion, healthy eating, and active living.

2.4 Methodological Approach

For this research, a grounded theory approach (Corbin & Strauss, 2008) was adapted, collecting data from semi-structured interviews to inductively develop theory. The grounded theory approach permits a naturalistic study that uses qualitative data in a systematic and rigorous way (Babbie, 2010; Corbin & Strauss, 2008), providing a rich understanding of social phenomena by examining patterns, themes, and common categories discovered in observational data (Babbie, 2010).

Two key features—comparative analysis and theoretical sampling—characterize grounded theory in this study. The goal was to generate theory on how to design a successful collaboration that was grounded on the real experiences of leaders from the nonprofit, private, and government sectors participating in affordable-housing collaborations.

2.4.1 Sample

The sample consisted of 31 participants, engaged in 15 established or recently completed affordable-housing collaborations, in 10 U.S. states. The collaborations were identified with the assistance of two national organizations that secure resources, provide management and technical advice, and serve as industry experts on housing and neighborhood revitalization. These organizations directed me to 10 collaborations described as "successful" and 5 deemed "less successful." The experts defined "successful" collaborations as those that completed high-quality affordable housing, engaged residents, and exhibited a sustainable partnership model that could complete future affordable-housing developments. "Less successful" collaborations were

Table 2.1 Inter-organizational Collaboration Sample

Collaboration Type	Successful	Less Successful	Total
Tri-Sector Collaborations (Government, Nonprofit & For-profit)	4	2	6
Government, Nonprofit & Nonprofit	5	2	7
Government, For-profit & For-profit	0	1	1
Government & For-profit	1	0	1
TOTAL	10	5	15

defined as those that struggled; took longer than expected; were a severe strain on the partners; may have yielded some good results, but whose process lacked follow-through, clarity of roles, or developed an inferior product; or failed completely (i.e., no housing units were built or the collaboration was disbanded). The respondents included 20 nonprofit, 7 for-profit, and 4 government collaboration representatives. Six of the 15 collaborations were tri-sector (nonprofit, for-profit, and government participants) and.9 were either a nonprofit or for-profit organizations in collaboration with government (see Table 2.1).

The nonprofit agencies were tax-exempt organizations that primarily focused on the redevelopment of inner-city neighborhoods. The for-profit organizations were private builders, developers, and/or general contractors. Government respondents were either county or municipal governments. Ten of the collaborations were located in the Midwest; three were in the South and two in the West.

Interview participants held senior positions in their organizations, including executive director (16), housing director (1), president (7), executive vice president (1), managing member (1), manager (4), and planner (1). Twenty-one of the respondents were male and 10 were female. Racial representation included African American (11), Asian (1), and white (17). Participants had been with their organizations from 3 to 30 years. To provide additional insight on the complexities of the collaborations studied, profiles of 5 (of the 15) affordable-housing inter-organizational collaborations case studies are summarized in 2.4.2.

2.4.2 Sample Collaboration Case Study Profiles

Profile 1: Government and Two Nonprofit Organizations

Two nonprofits collaborated to bring order and hope to a city devastated after a natural disaster. The governor sets up a one-stop shop bringing together insurance companies, housing manufacturers, architects, etc. to assist residents. Residents were paralyzed and overwhelmed. They did not have construction backgrounds, didn't know what they needed, and did not understand all the information shared over a short period of time. Residents would leave the one-stop shop with nice brochures but very little progress. Volunteers arrived en masse to assist with the rebuilding efforts. However, volunteers were not organized; volunteer contractors were duplicating efforts or completing construction out of order (e.g., sheetrock installed before electrical), with limited transition because people were volunteering two weeks at a time. Volunteers converged to help, but nobody knew where to start and everything was completely disorganized. The nonprofit director pulled out a map, drew grids (3–4 streets), picked the center, and worked outward. The nonprofit organization coordinated volunteer groups, increased production, and enabled groups to work together as a team. A different attitude is created (from "I can't" to "I can"), and grids are assigned to groups, creating a sense of ownership of the area and an ability to make a difference because the area is a manageable size, and people were empowered.

The nonprofit focused on case management and organizing, so the community design center could focus on working with families to not only replace homes, but also rebuild communities that were suffering before the disaster.

Profile 2: Government and Two Nonprofit Organizations

Because of an outcry from neighborhood residents about building a facility to house chronic inebriates, the nonprofit organization does not move forward with the project, losing $3 million dollars in funding that had been secured for the site. The nonprofit identified a different site, and their nonprofit partner helped them secure $3 million dollars in bond funds to complete the development on this second site. Building on the second site required a special permit. The City denied the permit but did not do it within their legal time frame of 60 days. With the support of a partner, the nonprofit organization sued the city under both violation of fair housing laws (permit denied because of NIMBYism) and violation of the 60-day rule. The nonprofit organization won the lawsuit. There was a strained relationship with the city after winning the lawsuit. The nonprofit apologized to the city's planning department, explained why it had to file suit and why it was important. The organization was able to work with the city to complete the project.

Profile 3: Government, Nonprofit Organization, and
Private-Sector Organization

A visioning exercise was completed with neighborhood residents and stakeholders. A location was identified for development. However, the economy was terrible and the nonprofit was having a difficult time finding an investor and was afraid the project would fall apart. The private-sector partner was persistent. The collaboration successfully approached State Farm as an investor (this was State Farm's first investment in this type of deal anywhere in the nation). When the collaboration reported back to the neighborhood, "it was like they had amnesia that they had told us to do the development here . . . they were up in arms." All the partners attended the community meetings, "and we all took the bullets" but were able to persuade the neighbors. The project was supported by a majority of the residents; however, a small group of residents stood against the project. So, the nonprofit partner made funders feel comfortable and reached out to public officials and the media to convey the message that it was just a handful of neighbors that did not support the project.

Profile 4: Government, Nonprofit Organization, and Private-Sector Organization

A for-profit developer partnered with a community-based nonprofit housing developer. They have partnered in the past, and the for-profit wants the same deal structure negotiated in previous transactions. The for-profit has developed a system where they have multiple line items in the construction budget (e.g., construction, architectural, planning) because the for-profit is a vertically integrated development company. The nonprofit wanted to take a larger role and a larger developer fee. The for-profit did not believe that the nonprofit brought real "value to the deal" and felt the deal was fair. The for-profit had to put up the guarantees and was "taking all the risks" and refused to renegotiate a profit split that was acceptable to the nonprofit. The nonprofit walked away from the deal, and the for-profit found another nonprofit organization with no housing development experience, but a valid 501c3 and housing mission to replace the disgruntled nonprofit.

Profile 5: Government and Private-Sector Organization

Because of their perception, community residents did not want more affordable housing in their neighborhood. A for-profit developer who created housing that looked and felt exactly like market-rate housing, made a proposal. Residents don't understand the affordable-housing strategy proposed by the developer. The for-profit developer held meetings with community council members and the larger community with information showing proposed work, and the impact of similar work in other cities. The developer identified community leaders and met with them individually to answer detailed questions and is open about intentions with development. The developer conducted tours when construction started, did not displace any residents, employed minority contractors, and made local hires. Community detractors became supporters.

The state-financing agency would not approve the two deals submitted by the developer because they were in the same submarket. The developer proposed a case outlining the importance of the critical mass and comprehensive neighborhood revitalization needed with both deals. Based upon the information and potential impact, the state agency changed its policy, adopting neighborhood revitalization as a criterion for future funding. The state funded both deals. Because of the economic conditions, the developer can't sell tax credits for original pricing, creating a financing gap. The developer contacted the city, requesting additional assistance. The developer also goes after stimulus funds to fill the gap. The project secured additional funding from both sources to complete the project.

2.4.3 Data Collection

Semi-structured interviews (see Appendix A for interview protocol) were conducted over four months. Thirty-one interviews, ranging from 45 to 80 minutes in length, were conducted. Nine interviews were conducted face-to-face and 22 by telephone. Thirty respondents consented for their interview to be recorded, one declined. (Detailed notes were taken during the nonrecorded interview.) Digitally recorded interviews were transcribed by a professional service. Field notes were also taken during interviews to capture early ideas (Maxwell, 2004; Spradley, 1979) and note points for clarification.

An interview protocol consisting of six open-ended questions designed to elicit detailed narratives about respondents' actual experiences was used. Respondents were asked to provide a detailed personal background, along with a rich background of the project so as to probe for perspectives about project impetus, strategy and implementation as well as examples of decision-making and problem-solving. Respondents were invited to describe, in great detail, an instance of when the project was going exceptionally well, and the interviewer probed for what was going on, who was involved, and what made it "feel" right. Then respondents were asked to reflect and think of a specific time when things were not going well and to describe in as much detail as possible the particular event. Respondents from successful collaborations were asked to compare this successful experience with a less successful collaboration in their experience, probing for contrasts. Conversely, respondents from less successful collaborations were asked to compare this less-successful experience to a successful collaboration. The final question asked respondents to reflect on their experiences with collaborations, with an inquiry about lessons learned. The probes were useful in eliciting detail and clarification. Many respondents expressed pleasure at having the opportunity to reflect on experiences.

2.4.4 Data Analysis

Data analysis began immediately after the first interview and continued simultaneously with data collection. Each audio recording was listened to and each transcript read several times. Then, following recommendations of Corbin and Strauss (2008), transcripts were analyzed using open, axial, and selective coding protocols. Open coding involved a rigorous line-by-line reading of each transcript to identify phenomena of possible interest.

Coding was conducted manually. Segments of text were identified, categorized, and labeled, which produced the first level of codes. Iterative reviews of the audio recordings and repeated readings of the interview transcripts yielded 2,873 segments of text with potential significance. As meanings were identified they were labeled and grouped with fragments with similar meaning that had been captured in previous transcripts. These first levels of codes were assigned to 166 labeled categories. These categories of data were continuously refined and relabeled throughout the open-coding process.

In the second phase of analysis (axial coding), relationships, themes, and basic-level concepts were observed among the data and abstracted to higher-level categories (Corbin & Strauss, 2008). This continual refinement included constant comparison, relabeling of categories, and making connections. In the third phase of coding (selective coding), core categories were identified, codes were refined and re-categorized, and high-level concepts articulated. This process facilitated the identification of 63 codes and 10 key themes.

This process directed me back to the literature to identify connections between the data and existing theory, and the major themes and selected codes reconfirmed extant research on collaboration (e.g., trust). As trust is extensively studied, I decided to go back to the transcript data and begin again. In the initial data analysis, "not by a priori hypotheses, but by ongoing interpretation of data and emerging conceptual categories" (Suddaby, 2006, p. 634) from constant comparison, diagramming, and mapping, second order themes of phenomenon experienced by all informants did emerge. I decided to further analyze the data according to these categories. I transferred the narrative interviews to Atlas.ti (Muhr & Friese, 2004), a software specifically designed to conduct thematic coding and data management, to explore themes. A code scheme was developed a priori. I discussed codes with other researchers, which resulted in the identification of 10 "manifest level (directly observable in the information)" (Boyatzis, 1998, p. vii) themes—funding barriers/actions, site barriers/actions, partner barriers/actions, government barriers/actions, and resident barriers/actions—observed in the initial data analysis.

Thematic analysis is a "form of pattern recognition within the data, where emerging themes become the categories for analysis" (Fereday & Muir-Cochrane, 2006, p. 82). The content of what was said in the interview narratives was reexamined and recoded using the coding scheme as the categories for analysis. The recoding in Atlas.ti generated 780 codes. Through constant comparison, codes were continually modified and reexamined and then grouped into similar categories (Corbin & Strauss, 2008). As meanings were identified, they were labeled and grouped with fragments with similar meaning captured in previous interview transcripts. These categories of data were continuously refined and relabeled throughout the open-coding process. In a second phase of interpretation (axial coding), categories were continually refined and relabeled to create finer distinctions among categories, and patterns in themes and concepts began to emerge from the data (Corbin & Strauss, 2008).

Throughout the interpretation process, the research moved between the data and the new literature that informed the emerging theory (Glaser & Strauss, 2009; Maxwell, 2004). Analysis and continued review of the literature informed a revision of the initial conceptual model in support of discovered themes. From a heuristic approach (i.e., tacking back and forth among the data, research materials, the literature, and the original conceptual model), a grounded theory about the observed phenomena emerged. In a third stage—selective coding—key ideas were prioritized, and the key constructs were identified. The final analysis yielded 82 codes and four key themes that led to the findings for this study.

2.5 Findings

The data revealed that most affordable-housing collaborations encounter a common set of barriers that impose challenges to the success of their partnership and/or affordable-housing development. The interview data suggest leaders of successful and less successful collaborations react differently to these barriers. The findings from the data are summarized in Table 2.2.

Regardless of size, experience, or if the collaboration was successful or less successful, collaborations for affordable housing encountered four common barriers: a) lack of funds or uncertainty with tax credits (funding barriers); b) conflict with partners (partner barriers); c) affordable housing wanted or needed in the community but a challenge to build because of place-based issues (e.g., site contamination, inferior soil, land assembly, location) or people-based issues such as opposition from community residents (community barriers); and/or d) conflicts with government mandates or government opposition (government barriers). The barriers to collaboration and actions that emerged from the data are outlined in Table 2.3.

Table 2.2 Summary of Findings

1	Successful and less successful inter-organizational collaborations encountered similar barriers.
2	Leaders of successful and less successful inter-organizational collaborations take different actions when barriers to collaboration are encountered.
	2.1 When facing obstacles, leaders of successful collaborations tended to exercise heightened emotional and social competencies.
	2.2 Leaders of less successful collaborations lack conflict resolution or conflict management competence.
3	When facing obstacles, leaders of successful collaborations tended to take actions for creating a better future. Less successful collaborations focused on short-term viability.
4	More successful collaborations tended to focus on mission and community development whereas less successful collaborations were focused on the deal.
5	Successful collaborations consistently adapted to changes, while less successful collaborations failed to do so.

Table 2.3 Collaboration Barriers and Actions

Barrier Category	Barriers Experienced by Inter-Organizational Collaborations	Actions Taken by Inter-Organizational Collaborations
COMMUNITY	Affordable Housing a Challenge Affordable Housing Wanted/Needed Authentic Dialogue Challenges from Poverty/Lack of Skills Deteriorated/Obsolete Housing Stock Displacement of Residents Limited Resources/ Opportunities Project Not Wanted Soil/Zoning Trust Building	Active Listening and Dialogue Affordable Housing Developed Affordable Housing Planned Build Relationships Communicate and Engage Confirm Detractors Are Few Convene Meetings Creative Approach to Barrier Develop a Master Plan/Plan of Action Focus on Bigger Picture Focus on Mission/Make and Keep Promises Give Up Imagine Possibilities to Overcome Barrier Negotiate Show Possibilities Show Possibilities as a Way to Overcome Barrier Stay the Course Take Risks
FUNDING	Funding Gap Funding Guidelines Not Met Funding Not Awarded Tax Credit Investor Tax Credit Timing Tax Credit Values Decline	Communicate and Engage Convene Meetings Funding for Bigger Picture Project Give Up Question Policy Secure Additional Funds Secure Other Funds Seek Funding Sell Tax Credits Show Possibilities as a Way of Securing Additional Funding
GOVERNMENT	Mandates Opposition Zoning/Permits	Communicate and Engage Compromise Confront Convene Meeting Focus on Mission/Move Forward Give Up Imagine Possibilities to Overcome Barrier Leverage Partner New Idea Organize Politic Show Big Picture/Long Term Goal Show Mutual Wins

Barrier Category	Barriers Experienced by Inter-Organizational Collaborations	Actions Taken by Inter-Organizational Collaborations
PARTNER	Capacity Concessions Sought Different Approaches Different Cultures Different Goals/ Mission New Partnership Restrictions Risk Concern	Additional Projects Agree to Build Capacity Build Trust Communicate Compromise Convene Meetings Different Approach End Partnership Find Common Ground Focus on Mission Focus on Residents/Community Imagine Possibilities Interact Leverage Partner Mitigate Risk Negotiate Outline Mou/Roles Resent Partner Seek New Partner Show Strength Stay the Course

Finding 1: Successful and Less Successful Inter-Organizational Collaborations Encountered Similar Barriers

All the collaborations experienced funding barriers. In 4 of the 10 successful collaborations (and 2 of the 5 less successful collaborations) financing challenges stemmed from the traditional affordable-housing finance tool: the Low Income Housing Tax Credit (tax credits). Difficulties included: a) shortfall (value decline) in credits; b) loss of tax credits; or c) difficulty securing an investor to purchase tax credits. A leader from a successful collaboration explained the potential impact of a value decline of tax credits:

> our tax credit price fell from about 94 cents on the dollar down to about 60 cents on the dollar and there was just no way to get this deal done at those levels so we were pretty sure a number of times that the deal was dead. Likewise, a leader from a less successful collaboration explained the impact of an inability to secure an investor: I got these credits, but then I can't do nothing with them. So credit without an investor is worthless.

In the remaining collaborations, the financing challenges resulted from additional funding needed for the housing development (e.g., to structure the deal, as a result of failed grant applications [grant applied for and not received], shortfall in expected funding [funding awarded less than amount requested] or unexpected cost increases). A leader from a successful collaboration discussed the overall funding challenge associated with affordable housing: "it's very difficult to be able to build new construction with today's construction costs and still provide affordable rent. It's a very tough task. Even if the land is free." A leader from a less successful collaboration discusses additional financing needed to continue the development: "all of our resources were being tied up into doing the project."

Leaders of both successful and less successful collaborations experienced conflict with partners in working through their partnerships. Several leaders reported intense negotiations with partners. Even in the successful collaborations, results were mixed, with some pleased with the outcomes of the negotiations, and others displeased. A leader from a successful collaboration discussed negotiations with a partner:

> We didn't feel like we could say this deal point is a crummy deal point for my organization therefore we're going to bail on this thing if we don't get a better deal. . . . I didn't feel like I had a leg to stand on to do that . . . we did fight back on a number of deal points but . . . we might have lost the whole thing if we had of taken a really strong stand and said we're just not going to do these things and if that had happened that would have not been an acceptable outcome for us.

Likewise, a leader of a less successful collaborations discussed challenges with partner negotiations:

> It's not just like we're any other developer. I mean, we're a fairly large developer with some significant capacity. We want to control the deal. We want to be able to make the decisions that affect the financial ramifications of the deal. . . . And so it's easy to sort of say that, and it may be even easy to document it, but it is not easy to work through. And so we had to sort of struggle through that.

Leaders of both successful and less successful collaborations reported struggling with their partners' personnel problems, including turnover and limited experience: "they've had the challenge . . . keeping . . . key personnel in place . . . it makes our work challenging." Most of the less successful collaborations reported conflict over profit sharing and splitting the developer fee: "at the end of the day, they're trying to make money. That's it. There's no other way to say it."

Finally, all the collaborations included in the study experienced community and/or political barriers in the early stages of development—prior to construction of any housing. In addition, 5 of the 10 successful collaborations continued to experience community and/or political challenges while their housing developments were underway. A leader of a successful collaboration reported community opposition:

> There was a vocal opposition . . . from the neighbors because it was . . . more poor people coming into their neighborhood. So, they would never say that. They would couch it in other terms such as transportation, crowding . . . those kinds of issues. But that's code for . . . not in my backyard . . . that was the real issue.

Likewise, a leader from a less successful collaboration remarked that

> residents did not want to see more public housing in the community. A leader of a successful collaboration commented on opposition from the local government and the local community: the city planning commission voted us down. And it [was] truly NIMBYism, it was neighbors standing up and shaking their heads, and you know, calling the people we work with the scum of the earth . . . at [a] public meeting on public television.

A leader from a less successful collaboration describes mandates put in place by their local government: "Since the award was going to a nonprofit, [the city] wanted to see the nonprofit play a more active role."

Although they encountered similar barriers, clear differences emerged in the actions taken to address the relevant barriers.

Finding 2: Leaders of Successful and Less Successful Inter-Organizational Collaborations Take Different Actions When Barriers to Collaboration Are Encountered

2.1 When Facing Obstacles, Leaders of Successful Collaborations Tended to Exercise Heightened Emotional and Social Competencies

The research revealed that leaders of successful collaborations took on detractors, difficult populations, and government, demonstrating capabilities involving management of self (e.g., transparency, adaptability, initiative, and optimism) and others (e.g., empathy, service, developing others, and conflict management). Some reported an intense willingness to resolve disagreements with the community and resolve political opposition to ensure that housing for those in need was built. Others adopted "out-of-the-box" strategies for solutions. One organization devised an innovative strategy for a land swap to facilitate an affordable-housing project, thus overcoming a site and community barrier. The executive director of a mixed-use (i.e., commercial space and residential) affordable-housing development demonstrated adaptability when facing a funding barrier. As a result of the economic downturn, some of the commercial space remained vacant, affecting the organization:

> we're actually moving our office there because. . . . I can't afford to keep renting my current office and paying the mortgage over there so we're moving our office and, well, it's going to cost us a lot more money to have an office than it is now, but I have to deal with this issue.

These competencies produced results that improved conditions for the targeted population through the development of housing (and, in many cases, supportive services), won design awards, captured the attention of the HUD secretary, and changed policy. The approaches taken by the successful collaborations enabled them to move forward. For example, taking the initiative to hold community meetings for project detractors resulted in design changes that made for a more attractive building. The coding structure leading to this finding is mapped in Figure 2.2 where quotes from leaders of successful collaborations are connected to the competency cluster that emerged from the data of the social or emotional competency.

2.2 *Leaders of Less Successful Collaborations Lack Conflict Resolution or Conflict Management Competence*

Conversely, less successful collaborations unanimously reported unresolved conflict in their partnerships or were unable to move forward to complete the affordable-housing development: "We sat down multiple times and discussed potential roles for both of our organizations, and it sort of just became clear that through our discussions that [the partner] was going to be very uncomfortable playing that leadership role." Alternately, the partners were unyielding in their negotiations: "they were controlling everything; they did the pro formas, they looked at the house, they did the spec, they did everything. They just wanted me to bring the money and not ask questions." Some simply made less optimal decisions as a result of poor communication, or were unable to move forward to complete the development. For example, the leader of the nonprofit organization reported the funding gap at $55,000: "So, if the city was just giving 45 then [the nonprofit] had to go out and find financing for the other 55." The private-sector partner tells the same story: "The city . . . was only advancing about $45,000 for acquisition Rehab. We tried to structure a project that could be completed with $65,000 per asset, but we needed that $20,000 bridge loan as additional financing as a loan source." The real gap was $20,000, but the nonprofit partner believed the gap was $55,000. Further, the nonprofit revealed, "[w]e have a grant of $600,000 which we were willing to put on the table, but I wasn't willing to share in any fees." However, the information about the grant allocation was not shared with the private-sector partner for fear of lost revenues or

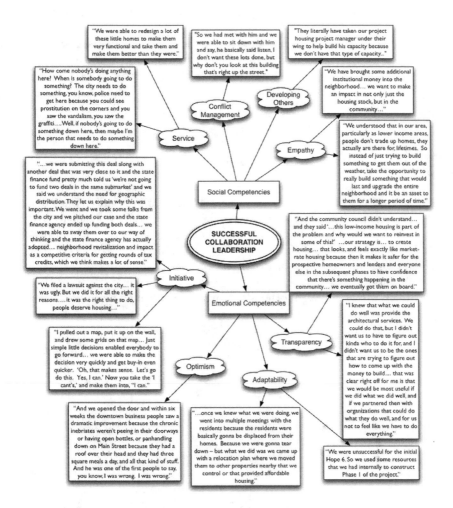

"We were able to redesign a lot of these little homes to make them very functional and take them and make them better than they were."

"So we had met with him and we were able to sit down with him and say, he basically said listen, I don't want these lots done, but why don't you look at this building that's right up the street."

"They literally have taken our project housing project manager under their wing to help build his capacity because we don't have that type of capacity..."

"How come nobody's doing anything here? When is somebody going to do something? The city needs to do something, you know, police need to get here because you could see prostitution on the corners and you saw the vandalism, you saw the graffiti....Well, if nobody's going to do something down here, then maybe I'm the person that needs to do something down here."

"We have brought some additional institutional money into the neighborhood... we want to make an impact in not only just the housing stock, but in the community..."

"We understood that in our area, particularly as lower income areas, people don't trade up homes, they actually are there for, lifetimes. So instead of just trying to build something to get them out of the weather, take the opportunity to really build something that would last and upgrade the entire neighborhood and it be an asset to them for a longer period of time."

"...we were submitting this deal along with another deal that was very close to it and the state finance fund pretty much told us 'we're not going to fund two deals in the same submarket' and we said we understand the need for geographic distribution. They let us explain why this was important. We went and we took some folks from the city and we pitched our case and the state finance agency ended up funding both deals... we were able to sway them over to our way of thinking and the state finance agency has actually adopted... neighborhood revitalization and impact as a competitive criteria for getting rounds of tax credits, which we think makes a lot of sense."

"And the community council didn't understand... and they said '...this low-income housing is part of the problem and why would we want to reinvest in some of this?' ...our strategy is... to create housing... that looks, and feels exactly like market-rate housing because then it makes it safer for the prospective homeowners and lenders and everyone else in the subsequent phases to have confidence that there's something happening in the community... we eventually got them on board."

SUCCESSFUL COLLABORATION LEADERSHIP

Conflict Management

Developing Others

Service

Empathy

Social Competencies

Initiative

Emotional Competencies

Transparency

Optimism

Adaptability

"We filed a lawsuit against the city... it was ugly. But we did it for all the right reasons.... it was the right thing to do, people deserve housing..."

"I pulled out a map, put it up on the wall, and drew some grids on that map... Just simple little decisions enabled everybody to go forward... we were able to make the decision very quickly and get buy-in even quicker. 'Oh, that makes sense. Let's go do this. Yes, I can.' Now you take the 'I can't's,' and make them into, "I can."

"I knew that what we could do well was provide the architectural services. We could do that, but I didn't want us to have to figure out kinda who to do it for, and I didn't want us to be the ones that are trying to figure out how to come up with the money to build... that was clear right off for me is that we would be most useful if we did what we did well, and if we partnered then with organizations that could do what they do well, and for us not to feel like we have to do everything."

"And we opened the door and within six weeks the downtown business people saw a dramatic improvement because the chronic inebriates weren't peeing in their doorways or having open bottles, or panhandling down on Main Street because they had a roof over their head and they had three square meals a day, and all that kind of stuff. And he was one of the first people to say, you know, I was wrong, I was wrong."

"...once we knew what we were doing, we went into multiple meetings with the residents because the residents were basically gonna be displaced from their homes. Because we were gonna tear down – but what we did was we came up with a relocation plan where we moved them to other properties nearby that we control or that provided affordable housing."

"We were unsuccessful for the initial Hope 6. So we used some resources that we had internally to construct Phase 1 of the project."

Figure 2.2 Emotional and Social Competencies of Successful Collaborations

fee sharing. In short, the funding gap could have been closed with the grant dollars, and the project could have moved forward had there been greater transparency and improved communication.

In some cases, inflexibility resulted in not using funding potentially available for the development. For example, one leader returned one million dollars to their city because a deal could not be agreed upon by the partners. Some partners simply felt resentful,

> I feel like I've been played in a lot of negotiations, and that's because I feel like I've been negotiating from a position of weakness. And when you negotiate from weakness, you're not going to push and fight

because you feel like, 'I have to get it done.' So you become the person that compromises.

Others just gave up and reported: "[we] didn't really sit down and hammer out the details." or argued, "I wasn't in charge of this."

Finding 3:   *When Facing Obstacles, Leaders of Successful Collaborations Tended to Take Actions for Creating a Better Future. Less Successful Collaborations Focused on Short-Term Viability.*

Despite the pressing challenges of deteriorated buildings and obsolete housing stock, funding losses, or government or resident opposition, the actions of successful collaborations demonstrated a commitment to focusing on the positive outcomes that would result from overcoming barriers. This attitude is demonstrated as a leader of a successful collaboration talks about changing the legacy of a community barrier:

> there was these neighborhoods . . . where people didn't necessarily cross boundaries to do projects . . . we've been able to . . . connect these two communities together, not just individually or organizationally, but also us going out to South L.A., participating in a lot of their events, them doing the same thing in Little Tokyo. A lot of their young people never having left South L.A. before ever in their lifetime, and experiencing a new culture, new communities.

Leaders of successful collaborations moved beyond the typical solutions available for resolving their problems in an effort to complete the affordable-housing development. Leaders of successful collaborations were inspired or inspirational as they imagined and demonstrated future possibilities. One leader in particular proclaimed his work "divine inspiration;" "I tell people this and sometimes they don't quite get it, but I tell it just the way it is that God played a strong role in this."

In contrast, leaders of less successful collaborations were often preoccupied with day-to-day management of their organizations, keeping their doors open, and managing the "overwhelming" challenges of the current economy: "this is a house that we put in $100,000 worth of work that in 2007 would appraise for $105,000. Today it's appraising at about $15,000. I've had two offers—one of $15,000 and one of $12,000. And I have a line of credit against it for like $35,000."

Some leaders of less successful collaborations sacrificed long-term viability because of short-term discomfort. For example, one leader decided within a few months to forego numerous development opportunities in an adjacent neighborhood where the partner nonprofit was located. The reason for the decision: "I am not interested in building their capacity." Many leaders of less successful collaborations felt their partners had "hidden agendas" and were mistrustful. One leader felt that it was not a collaboration and that takeover was imminent. Leaders reported not feeling respected or that their partners did not take their work seriously. Leaders of less successful collaborations were not mindful of the long-term viability of the collaboration, but only considered the immediate "value" that their partnerships could leverage. Successful inter-organizational collaborations create the theme of Actions for a Better Future as illustrated by the following supporting quotes from the data:

> you're coming back and you've just survived a storm. . . . You see nothing but despair, heartache, pain. . . . They were just paralyzed . . . when you go in and you rip all of that out and throw it out on the curb, you tear out all the sheetrock, you empty it and when they walk back into that house, there's nothing but 2 x 4's and some walls. A strange thing happens is that now you get this, 'You know? I always wanted to open this room up.' Simple little acts changed them from, 'I'll never be able to recover,' to 'You know, I see hope. I see possibilities,' and that lifts the spirit.

> As we got to know these folks, the houses were in pretty disrepair, as you can imagine, but they were owned, and the value was anywhere from $6,000 to $7,500 . . . They lived there all their lives, so they were born there, and the question was what was going to happen? They didn't want to go anywhere and . . . it's most likely folks would try to buy them out at a very low price . . . and then what are they going to do? If they chose to sell, they would probably be moving to an apartment and, despite the condition of the home, they owned it, so if they couldn't pay their rent, they don't get evicted. So we came up with the crazy idea . . . of building a house . . . and then individuals can move into that house while we work on their house, then it allows a transitional nature where we can improve those homes that are owned, try to stabilize the street though existing homeowners, and then maybe new development can occur. . . . The first one was LEED gold, and since then they're all LEED platinum.

> we're doing something that really makes sense in terms of improving people's quality of life, but people like, again, the governor, liked this model because it saves taxpayers money . . . all those people that are living in the building that are the chronic alcoholics, their detox admissions have gone down by about 90%, and those detox admissions cost $275 to $300 a day. Our people's involvement with law enforcement and the court system has gone down by 90%, and we've saved hundreds of thousands of dollars in emergency room visits. We literally have people that were getting drunk and getting so drunk that they go to the emergency room so they had a warm place to stay at night.

Less successful inter-organizational collaborations create the theme of Short-Term Viability as illustrated by the following supporting quotes from the data:

> I needed a partner that was bringing money to the table.
>
> The other times where we would have disagreements, they would be generally about what the value of services provided by each party were.
>
> They felt that we did not have the capacity to get houses done. That what they were bringing to the collaboration is that they have contractors—they can get the work done.
>
> I can go find another not-for-profit that's like a service-oriented not-for-profit, and say, listen, you provide housing for people with disabilities. I can provide you with five units or ten units in a building. You'll be a partner in the development, and we'll go from there.
>
> What they wanted me to do was to fund their staff, and my issue was I never saw the principal of the company. I always saw someone who worked at the company. So, my question each time was who am I working with? Who are the investors that you stand in front of?

Finding 4: More Successful Collaborations Tended to Focus on Mission and Community Development Whereas Less Successful Collaborations Were Focused on the Deal

Nonprofit organizations included in this study are tax-exempt, community-based organizations governed by neighborhood residents and stakeholders with missions around improving economic and social conditions. Leaders of successful collaborations remained mission driven, keeping the community connection by convening meetings and engaging funders, partners, government representatives, and the community. The data revealed that partners with relationships with the local communities targeted for development were critical to decrease opposition and were a sought-after characteristic by private-sector partners. For example, the president of a private-sector development company from a successful collaboration summarized the nonprofit partner: "they have their pulse on the community." Even with less successful collaborations, neighborhood connections were valued:

> But the real benefit that [partner] provided were all the existing relationships . . . [The partner] had really established a lot of community relationships with the local aldermen, with some of the local not-for-profit service providers, local schools . . . [the partner] was really engaged in the neighborhood immediately surrounding these projects, and . . . had some very good political contacts with the people at the city and decision-makers in the government, both locally and in the state level, and so that was important to us.

Unfortunately, leaders of less successful collaborations were more concerned with the transaction, focusing on the specifics of the deal (e.g., "fees" and "money"). The same leader of a less successful collaboration who touted the value of a partner with neighborhood connections (above) revealed what he considered most important in a conversation with a partner:

> I always would say to [partner], at some point this is about money. This is a business relationship . . . and you need to learn that lesson that you get compensated for what you bring to the table, and we can have a disagreement about what your value is that you're bringing to the table, but that's what it's about. And clearly, [the partner] wasn't getting these projects off the ground without some capacity, and that's what we brought to the table. We're financing relationships that [partner] didn't have and the ability to personally guarantee stuff that was worthwhile, and we moved these projects forward. . . . The investors, with all due respect, they really don't care about the minority partner.

Additional evidence in support of a Mission and Community Focus theme in successful inter-organizational collaborations is the following supporting quotes from the data:

> we started talking about possibly joining together to do a project. . . . They would work with a new organization. They would help to build our capacity to do housing in the future, and they would support our work and lend their experience to help us secure properties . . . and since 2007, we now have four projects that we're jointly working on together. . . . The bottom line for them is the community at the end of the day.
>
> We didn't have any money. We literally floated it on credit cards till we could raise the money, but we had to keep going because if we stopped we could lose momentum. We had to take some risks, and one of the things people ask me a lot is "So what do these families have? What's their skin in the game?" and I'm like, Guys, they've had skin in the game for 50 years.
>
> it's easy to come into a distressed neighborhood and simply take away from the neighborhood . . . you bring in your own crews and . . . all the money that's made on the job is taken out of the neighborhood. You know, basically people, contractors, subcontractors who come in from the suburbs or whatever, and they're doing their work. They're not going to spend it there locally. They're going to take it out of the neighborhood . . . we have been very conscientious in hiring as best as possible, some of the locals . . . they're typically used to "I work for a day. I'm going to get paid at the end of the day, and I'm going to get paid in cash." We pay them on Fridays, and I pay by check. [But most of the people do not have bank accounts.] I have gone to some of the local check-cashing facilities and/or convenience stores, introduced myself,

tell them what I'm doing, that we're helping build and renovate houses in their neighborhood. Once they meet me, the storeowners . . . they have a very easy feeling about cashing my checks. Because prior to that, they don't know who I am . . . we're actually working, not only with some of our subcontractors, but even with our tenants, to get them to open a bank account if [they] don't have one.

It was just meeting after meeting after meeting and just being completely open about what our intentions were.

affordable housing is a really tough nut to crack. It's hard to find land. . . . So here is an opportunity . . . we just don't normally get, and 90 units of affordable housing is a big deal for us.

Evidence in support of a Deal Focus theme in less successful inter-organizational collaborations is illustrated by the following supporting quotes from the data:

we start to talk about new transactions, my conversation is generally listen, the first time this whole arrangement was mutually beneficial. We were looking to make an entrée into this market and make some relationships, and you've helped us do that. We hope that we've added to your capacity and your knowledge about development and the building of your understanding of development. But yeah, going forward, those are not as valuable as they once were.

We can make the money off of urban deals, but we can't be invested long-term with the urban deals.

it was not a good business deal for us to take all the risk with acquiring 22 houses and not being able to sell them and not knowing when we can sell them but have to have them in our inventory. . . . The . . . developer wanted me to take all the risk.

I ended up meeting this church group who had this land, and they had plans, and they wanted to do some development, and [the for-profit (FP) partner said], "That's really not a good fit for our company. You know, you . . . need to do more deals, but I don't need to do stuff like this."

The bad part is the only deal that we'll do together is those deals that I bring. They don't . . . get me involved in any transactions. Simple as that . . . this is business. . . . There is no reciprocity when it comes to little helps big, but big never helps little, and it's because they don't have to, and it's just that simple.

Finding 5: Successful Collaborations Consistently Adapted to Changes, while Less Successful Collaborations Failed to Do so

Without exception, successful inter-organizational collaborations encountered significant barriers that could have caused their projects to fail.

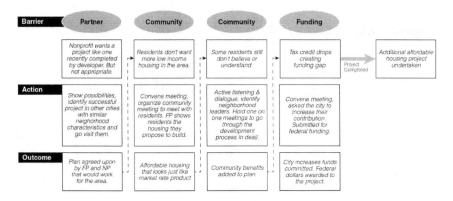

Figure 2.3a Successful Collaborations Adapt

Successful collaborations constantly overcame the barriers that challenged their success. Less successful collaboration partners were either unable to move beyond the first or second barrier before the collaboration completely failed or was severely strained, despite the fact that all the less successful collaborations included in the study had previous development experience, were established organizations, and two of the five collaborations had previous experience working with their partners.

Examples of a successful collaboration adapting to barriers (Figure 2.3a) and a less successful collaboration failing to do so (Figure 2.3b) are mapped. In the successful collaboration, the partners moved through four major barriers that could have derailed the project. Instead of failing, the partners worked through each of the challenges and completed the project. The first major barrier was that the nonprofit wanted the private developer to build a project similar to a recently completed project in a different area. The requested housing model was not an appropriate fit for the neighborhood. Instead of failing, the for-profit identified more appropriate housing developments in other cities with similar neighborhood characteristics. So the nonprofit and for-profit visited these developments, and what they learned ultimately informed the housing developed in their community. The collaboration moved forward, but encountered opposition from residents. Residents did not want to see more "low-income housing" in their already depressed community. Community meetings were convened, and renderings of the housing planned for construction were shared. Residents learned that the housing had "amenities and fixtures and things that you don't find in affordable housing typically. You walk in and you don't know if you're in a market-rate apartment or a condo." In the less successful example, the partnership fails in the early stages of the collaboration with the first barrier.

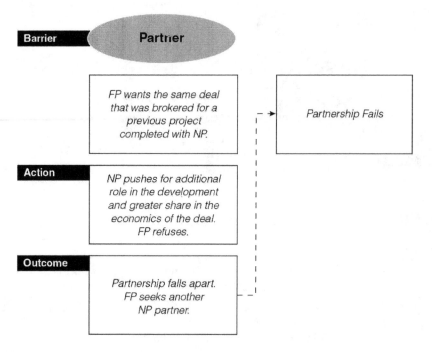

Figure 2.3b Less Successful Collaborations Fail Early

2.6 Power, Leadership and Design in Collaboration

Several literature streams inform inter-organizational collaboration. Power, leadership, and organizational hierarchies also affect collaboration outcomes. How design can influences power and leadership, along with the well-established role of these factors in collaboration, is discussed below.

2.6.1 Power

"A has power over B to the extent that he can get B to do something that B would not otherwise do" (Dahl, 1957, pp. 202–203). Power is a recurring theme, "causing anxiety or reward in collaboration" (Vangen & Huxham, 2003b, p. 7). A common characteristic of collaboration is a power imbalance (Ansell & Gash, 2007; Berger et al., 2004), which can result in misuse of leverage, imposed strategy or style, patronization, or dominance leading to mistrust (Ansell & Gash, 2007; Berger et al., 2004). Power imbalance is problematic for partners lacking organizational infrastructure (Ansell & Gash, 2007), i.e., planned processes and systems, skills, and the expertise to engage in technical discussions (Lasker, Weiss, & Miller, 2001; Warner,

2006), or time, energy, and/or freedom to be engaged (Yaffee & Wondolleck, 2003). The dominance of well-intentioned, more powerful partners does not always yield the best outcomes because underestimating the power of the weaker partner (Berger et al., 2004) or underrepresented groups (Ansell & Gash, 2007) can result in collaboration inertia (Huxham, 2003). Organizational hierarchies can also cause challenges within organizations that prove to be detrimental to subsequent collaborations between organizations (Schein, 2010).

Power between partners need not be equal (Selsky & Parker, 2005), though partners should each recognize the influence of the other. Three aspects of power that affect collaboration are: formal authority (i.e., the recognized right to make a decision), the control of critical resources (e.g., information, expertise, dollars, equipment), and discursive legitimacy (i.e., the recognized right to speak on the issues) (Hardy & Phillips, 1998, p. 219). Thus, power may be unilaterally situated (e.g., by government mandate; Mattessich, Murray-Close, & Monsey, 2001), accrued to those with financial resources or correlated to assets brought to the collaboration (Berger et al., 2004; Huxham, 2003), or discursively claimed (Hardy & Phillips, 1998). It is often anticipated that the private-sector partner will be more powerful, but this is not always the case (Berger et al., 2004).

Design alters this power dynamic. For breakthrough innovations, a variety of attitudes and skills are needed (Verganti, 2008). Instead of a focus on a power imbalance, a team-based approach to innovation unlocks the collaboration's creative power (Brown, 2009). In the design paradigm, the solutions to complex problems come from the creative work of the team (Brown, 2009), which is a different approach than analytical thinking. As Brown (2009, p. 67, quoting Nobel Prize laureate Linus Pauling) observes, "[t]o have a good idea, you must first have lots of ideas" or, as expressed by Pisano and Verganti (2008, p. 83), "interesting innovative solutions can come from people or organizations you might never have imagined had something to contribute." Design suggests that co-creation should replace hierarchy, "affording all stakeholders the possibility to influence and bring forth meaningful and relevant solutions in a collaborative environment" (Kirah, 2009, p. 3).

2.6.2 Leadership

Leaders, the collaboration literature suggests, contribute to the success of collaboration by engaging partners (Armistead, Pettigrew, & Aves, 2007), bridging the differences in organizational cultures (Berger et al., 2004; Huxham, 1996), and guiding partners through the "rough patches of the collaboration process" (Ansell & Gash, 2007, p. 554). Leaders that embrace, empower, involve, and mobilize members (Vangen & Huxham, 2003a) will promote effective collaboration outcomes. According to Lasker et al.

(2001), the skills required to lead partnerships are different from those of traditional leaders:

> Traditional leaders frequently have a narrow range of expertise, speak a language that can be understood only by their peers, are used to being in control, and relate to the people with whom they work as followers or subordinates rather than partners. Partnerships, by contrast, need boundary-spanning leaders who understand and appreciate partners' different perspectives, can bridge their diverse cultures, and are comfortable sharing ideas, resources, and power.
>
> (p. 193)

Leaders and designers are "meaning makers" (Bevan, Robert, Bate, Maher, & Wells, 2007). A design attitude encourages leaders to move beyond responding to the presented alternatives to engage in a decision-making process that involves collecting and interpreting evidence, designing possibilities, and testing multiple ideas (Boland, Collopy, Lyytinen, & Yoo, 2008). This approach suggests the design of effective collaborations may depend on the particular mindsets, skills, and perspectives of their leaders. A design attitude by a leader facilitates the collaborative process, "where all members of the organization are given the opportunity to create meaningful and relevant changes" within it (Kirah, 2009, p. 4). Kirah also states that design-minded leaders empower others to become agents of change. An inquiry about how and to what extent leaders influence the actual design and redesign of inter-organizational collaborations must necessarily appreciate the facilitative function of leadership described by Lasker and Weiss (2003). A leader with a "design mindset" has been described as having, "the ability to think holistically and to abstract meaning and value in multidisciplinary collaboration" (Kirah, 2009, p. 2).

Not all leaders, however, are "design minded." Goold and Campbell (2002, p. 117) contend "organizational structures evolve in fits and starts, shaped more by politics than by policies." When an organizational design is not working well, leaders may sense it, but "few take meaningful action" despite the fact that "design flaws can turn into disasters."

Another "determining factor in excellent leadership" is emotional intelligence (Boyatzis & McKee, 2005, p. 28). Grounded in individual psychological theory (Boyatzis, 2009; Goleman & Boyatzis, 2008), emotional intelligence is an essential condition, the "sine qua non of leadership" (Goleman, 1998, p. 38). Further, competency clusters that differentiate outstanding and average leaders include emotional intelligence competencies and social intelligence competencies (Boyatzis, 2008; Boyatzis & McKee, 2005). Emotional intelligence competencies cluster around self-awareness and self-management. Self-awareness is defined as knowing one's personal limits and strengths, self-confidence (knowing one's worth and capabilities), understanding personal emotions, their impact, and utilizing instinct to guide decisions (Boyatzis & McKee, 2005; Goleman, Boyatzis, & McKee, 2002). Key components of self-management include:

- transparency ("displaying honesty, integrity, and trustworthiness"),
- adaptability ("demonstrating flexibility in adapting to changing situations or overcoming obstacles" Boyatzis & McKee, 2005, p. 29),
- initiative ("readiness to act and seize opportunities"),
- optimism ("seeing the upside in events"),
- emotional self-control, and
- achievement (Goleman et al., 2002, p. 39).

Social intelligence competencies cluster around social awareness and relationship management. Social awareness includes:

- empathy ("sensing others' emotions, understanding their perspective, and taking interest in their concerns");
- service ("recognizing and meeting follower, client, or customer needs"); and
- organizational awareness

Relationship management includes:

- inspirational leadership ("guiding and motivating with a compelling vision"),
- conflict resolution,
- developing others,
- influence,
- change catalyst,
- conflict management,
- building bonds,
- and teamwork/collaboration (Boyatzis & McKee, 2005, p. 29).

Most of the specific literature on the relationship between leaders' design attitude and organizational effectiveness has focused on firms (Michlewski, 2008). Only a few scholars of inter-organizational collaborations have addressed the topic, and those have done so only tangentially. This research may discern if there are differences in the design attitudes and characteristics of leaders of inter-organizational collaborations with contrasting outcomes (i.e., more or less effective) and how that attitude affects successful affordable-housing inter-organizational collaborations.

2.7 Discussion

The literature is clear that the initial environment or preconditions for the partnership can enable or constrain collaboration (Ansell & Gash, 2007;

Peters, 1998) and identifies power imbalance among the partners (Berger et al., 2004; Gray, 1989) as a key variable. Leadership was also critical because leaders are central in making collaborations work (Ansell & Gash, 2007; Armistead et al., 2007; Crosby & Bryson, 2005) and molding the cultural values of their organizations in favor of collaboration (Armistead et al., 2007).

In contrast to previous research on collaboration, the initial environment, the collaboration process, and the structure of the collaboration, although important, did not emerge as the most salient determinants of success or failure in the affordable-housing inter-organizational collaborations in the study. Referring back to the literature on developing a theory of why some collaborations are successful and others less successful, the data revealed sharp differences among leader competencies, focus, and attitudes from successful collaborations and less successful collaborations when facing a barrier. Further, the ability of the collaboration to adapt to changes was paramount to its success. Most important, there was evidence of neighborhood rejuvenation and examples of innovation in each of the successful collaborations.

According to respondents, opposition to affordable housing is commonplace. The less successful affordable-housing developments occurred in the same turbulent economy as the successful collaborations. The findings suggest that less successful collaborations faced the same barriers as successful collaborations (Finding 1). The qualities of the leadership operating in the successful collaborations, however, are likely a contributing factor to success. Leaders of successful collaborations demonstrate emotional and social competencies associated with emotional intelligence (Boyatzis & McKee, 2005), suggesting that a degree of emotional intelligence is associated with leaders of successful collaborations. The emotional competencies exhibited by leaders of successful collaborations included adaptability, initiative, transparency, and optimism. The social competencies included empathy, service, conflict management, and developing others. Further, their partners recognize these competencies in successful collaborations. For example, one leader informed his[her] partner that they "really, really wanted a green and sustainable development." To achieve this goal, the partner took the initiative by writing a number of grants to supplement the "limited amount of money that was available for the project." As a result of the partner's efforts, funding was secured for the project, and a green roof was built for each of the townhomes in the development. An example of supporting optimism is provided as a partner recounts making "the right decision" in selecting another partner:

> There were a few times when we felt like the project might fall apart. But . . . [the partner's] sense of humor . . . persistence and the upbeatness of . . . attitude, made me . . . affirm that we had made the right decision when we were going over those rough waters. That yes, even though we

have invested all this money to date, and we could lose everything in just a couple weeks if we don't find an investor, that we will persist, and we will find an investor. And we did. And that was an amazing thing in this economy.

One leader of a successful collaboration (for-profit president) expressed empathy when recounting the challenges associated with the poverty encountered by neighborhood residents:

The more I stay invested in the distressed community, the area where we're working, the more I feel I'm becoming a social worker, in a sense, in that I spend a lot of time listening, and it also occurred to me that a lot of the folks that are living in this part of [the city] have a very, very tough life; transportation's an issue. Obviously, money's an issue. Housing, they live in substandard housing, many of them. They have to wait in line for everything. They've got to wait at the bus stop. They go buy their groceries. They get back and have got to wait for the bus stop. If they have to go to the doctor, they go to the county hospital, and they've got to wait in line, sometimes literally hours, to see a doctor. You know, nothing comes easy, and so it just takes on an added sense of being, just to be as nice as possible to everyone. Not that I would ever intentionally be rude to anybody, but it's just—there's an awareness that I can make or break somebody's day in how I treat them.

Research has shown that emotional intelligence is required for effective leadership (Goleman, 1998; Higgs & Aitken, 2003). "Even if they get everything else right if leaders fail in this primal task of driving emotions in the right direction, nothing they do will work as well as it could or should" (Goleman et al., 2002, p. 3).

A focus on mission and community also emerged as a potentially critical success factor because partners can be mismatched with respect to mission, structure, goals, organizational culture, decision-making style, motives, and desired constituents to serve. A focus on mission and community can serve as the driver behind the strength of each sector in a collaborative setting. If mutual gains are to be achieved, there needs to be some alignment among the partners because mismatched partners can strain collaboration (Berger et al., 2004). A focus on mission and community can provide necessary alignment, preempting problems of fit and structure, which will help avoid the misallocation of costs/benefits and/or mismatched partnerships (Berger et al., 2004) and foster renewal (Le Ber & Branzei, 2009). An example of the misallocation of costs/benefits is when the nonprofit partner's contribution is undervalued by the for-profit partner (Berger et al., 2004). This was an issue for less successful collaborations.

Although power imbalance was an issue for less successful collaborations, a design attitude appeared to transform the power dynamic for successful collaborations. A "design attitude" moves beyond commonplace solutions and ordinary systems of logic based upon how things are (Boland & Collopy, 2004) and instead focuses on human interaction and phenomenon aimed at changing an existing situation into a preferred one (Simon, 1996). Michlewski (2008), in his research on design attitude of professional designers, attributes empathy, authentic listening, bringing ideas to life, and engaging change and uncertainty as key characteristics of design attitude. When taking action in response to challenges, a leader's design attitude may affect his or her ability to move beyond usual solutions and move towards a successful collaboration. For example, a nonprofit builds a "holding house"—a house built on a vacant lot on the block—that families could move into while their home was being demolished and rebuilt so no one would be displaced. The holding house was completely designed and presented to the community. According to the nonprofit partner, neighborhood residents

> looked at it and said we don't like it. . . . From an efficiency standpoint, use of space, the kitchen was smaller and tighter and culturally within that street and that place, kitchens are really important. They wanted it to be done in a different layout because that's the way they cook and the way they live, and so we respected that, redesigned the entire house and there's nothing in the original design that's in that house.

Without exception, successful collaborations encountered significant barriers that could have caused their projects to fail. Successful collaborations, however, consistently overcame these barriers. Less successful collaboration partners were unable to move beyond the first or second barrier before the collaboration completely failed or was severely strained. Organizations are constantly being designed and redesigned as they seek a design gestalt (i.e., the ability to approach problems creatively and individually while maintaining unity across outcomes) through design intent, environmental constraints and capabilities, and purpose (Yoo, Boland, & Lyytinen, 2006). The findings support the organizational design literature, which suggests the importance of redesign and organizational reconfiguration. The process revealed by respondents is depicted in Figure 2.4, where a leader's emotional intelligence and focus on mission and goals affects the collaboration. A leader's design attitude strengthens the collaboration, although redesign can also have an effect.

2.7.1 *Implications for Practice*

Considerable research has been conducted on inter-organizational collaborations concerned with economic development, education, health care, the alleviation of poverty, capacity building, and environmental sustainability (Selsky & Parker, 2005), but there are few field-based studies on collaborations concerned with affordable housing, and no research has

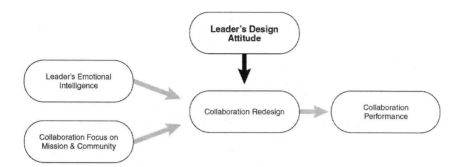

Figure 2.4 Conceptual Model

been conducted on the impact of emotional intelligence, design attitude, and redesign on affordable-housing inter-organizational collaborations. Nonprofit agencies and private developers may find the results useful for responding to the barriers that commonly confront inter-organizational collaborations.

2.7.2 Limitations

There are several limitations to this qualitative investigation. The sample was small, heavily concentrated in the Midwest, and not representative of all inter-organizational collaborations for affordable housing. Further, interviewing leaders may have introduced self-reporting bias. Interviewees were required to recount past experience, and some recollections may have been incomplete or compromised by the effect of time on memory creating the potential for recall bias.

Finally, qualitative data analysis depends heavily on the interpretations of the researcher. I have worked in the field of housing and community development for over 15 years. The potential for researcher bias, despite a conscious effort to control for this through the use of rigorous methods in designing and implementing this study, is acknowledged.

This chapter presents an understanding of success in the inter-organizational collaborations through qualitative inquiry. It stimulates further inquiry, particularly quantitative confirmation of the emerging constructs. The next chapter is the first of two quantitative studies validating those emerging constructs.

Note

1. Two papers were developed from this chapter. The first was presented at the Academy of Management 2011 Annual Conference and selected for publication in the *Best Paper Proceedings* (Madden, 2011). The second was for the *Journal of Nonprofit Education and Leadership* (Madden, 2017).

References

Ansell, C., & Gash, A. (2007). Collaborative governance in theory and practice. *Journal of Public Administration Research & Theory, 18*(4), 543–571.

Armistead, C., Pettigrew, P., & Aves, S. (2007). Exploring leadership in multi-sectoral partnerships. *Leadership, 3*(2), 211–230.

Asian Development Bank (ADB). (2008). *Public-private partnership handbook.* Manila, Philippines: Asian Development Bank.

Babbie, E. (2010). *The practice of social research.* Belmont, CA: Wadsworth.

Berger, I., Cunningham, P., & Drumwright, M. (2004). Social alliances. *California Management Review, 47*(1), 58–90.

Bevan, H., Robert, G., Bate, P., Maher, L., & Wells, J. (2007). Using a design approach to assist large-scale organizational change: "10 high impact changes" to improve the National Health Service in England. *Journal of Applied Behavioral Science, 43*(1), 135–152.

Bockmeyer, J. L. (2003). Devolution and the transformation of community housing activism. *Social Science Journal, 40*(2), 175–188.

Boland, R., Jr., & Collopy, F. (2004). Toward a design vocabulary for management. In R.J. Boland, F. Collopy, (Eds.), *Managing as designing.* Stanford University Press, Stanford, CA, 265–276.

Boland, R., Jr., Collopy, F., Lyytinen, K., & Yoo, Y. (2008). Managing as designing: Lessons for organization leaders from the design practice of Frank O. Gehry. *Design Issues, 24*(1), 10–25.

Boyatzis, R. E. (1998). *Transforming qualitative information: Thematic analysis and code development.* Thousand Oaks, CA: Sage.

Boyatzis, R. E. (2008). Competencies in the 21st century. *Journal of Management Development, 27*(1), 5–12.

Boyatzis, R. E. (2009). Competencies as a behavioral approach to emotional intelligence. *Journal of Management Development, 28*(9), 749–770.

Boyatzis, R. E., & McKee, A. (2005). *Resonant leadership: Renewing yourself and connecting with others through mindfulness, hope, and compassion.* Boston, MA: Harvard Business School Press.

Bratt, R. G. (2008). Nonprofit and for-profit developers of subsidized rental housing: Comparative attributes and collaborative opportunities. *Housing Policy Debate, 19*(2), 323–365.

Bratt, R. G. (2009). Challenges for nonprofit housing organizations created by the private housing market. *Journal of Urban Affairs, 31*(1), 67–96.

Bratt, R. G., & Rohe, W. M. (2007). Challenges and dilemmas facing community development corporations in the United States. *Community Development Journal, 42*(1), 63–78.

Brown, T. (2009). *Change by design: How design thinking transforms organizations and inspires innovation.* New York, NY: HarperCollins.

Bryson, J., Crosby, B., & Stone, M. (2006). The design and implementation of cross-sector collaborations: Propositions from the literature. *Public Administration Review, 66*(Special Issue), 44–55.

Bryson, J. M., & Crosby, B. C. (2008). *Failing into cross-sector collaboration successfully: Big ideas in collaborative public management.* Armonk, NY: M. E. Sharpe.

Chung, A. (2004). *Bridging sectors: Partnerships between nonprofits and private developers.* Cambridge, MA: Joint Center for Housing Studies, Harvard University, & NeighborWorks America.

Corbin, J. M., & Strauss, A. L. (2008). *Basics of qualitative research: Techniques and procedures for developing grounded theory*. Thousand Oaks, CA: Sage.

Cowan, S. M., Rohe, W., & Baku, E. (1999). Factors influencing the performance of community development corporations. *Journal of Urban Affairs, 21*(3), 325–339.

Crosby, B. C., & Bryson, J. M. (2005). *Leadership for the common good: Tackling public problems in a shared-power world*. San Francisco, CA: Jossey-Bass.

Dahl, R. (1957). The concept of power. *Behavioral Science, 2*(3), 201–215.

Das, T., & Teng, B. (1998). Between trust and control: Developing confidence in partner cooperation in alliances. *Academy of Management Review, 23*(3), 491–512.

Davidson, N. M. (2009). The value of lawyering in affordable housing transactions. In N. M. Davidson & R. P. Malloy (Eds.), *Affordable housing and public-private partnerships* (pp. 35–50). Burlington, VT: Ashgate.

Dirks, K., & Ferrin, D. (2001). The role of trust in organizational settings. *Organization Science, 12*(4), 450–467.

Euchner, C. C., & McGovern, S. J. (2003). *Urban policy reconsidered: Dialogues on the problems and prospects of American cities*. New York, NY: Routledge.

Fereday, J., & Muir-Cochrane, E. (2006). Demonstrating rigor using thematic analysis: A hybrid approach of inductive and deductive coding and theme development. *International Journal of Qualitative Methods, 5*(1), 80–92.

Finkenstaedt, R. L. (2009). *Organizational Capital: A new approach to lending in nonprofit affordable housing*. Cambridge, MA: Joint Center for Housing Studies, Harvard University, & NeighborWorks America.

Frisch, M., & Servon, L. (2006). CDCs and the changing context for urban community development: A review of the field and the environment. *Community Development Society, 37*(4), 88–108.

Galster, G., Levy, D., Sawet, N., Temkin, K., & Walker, C. (2005). *The impact of community development corporations on urban neighborhoods*. Washington, DC: The Urban Institute.

Glaser, B. G., & Strauss, A. L. (2009). *The discovery of grounded theory: Strategies for qualitative research*. Piscataway, NJ: Aldine Transaction.

Glickman, N. J., & Servon, L. J. (1999). More than bricks and sticks: Five components of community development corporation capacity. *Housing Policy Debate, 9*(3), 497–540.

Goleman, D. (1998). *Working with emotional intelligence*. Bantam.

Goleman, D., & Boyatzis, R. (2008). Social intelligence and the biology of leadership. *Harvard Business Review, 86*(9), 74–81.

Goleman, D., Boyatzis, R. E., & McKee, A. (2002). *Primal leadership: Realizing the power of emotional intelligence*. Boston, MA: Harvard Business School Press.

Goold, M., & Campbell, A. (2002). Do you have a well designed organization? *Harvard Business Review, 80*(3), 117–124.

Graddy, E. A., & Bostic, R. W. (2009). The role of private agents in affordable housing policy. *Journal of Public Administration Research & Theory, 20*(Special Issue), 81–99.

Gray, B. (1989). *Collaborating: Finding common ground for multiparty problems*. San Francisco, CA: Jossey-Bass.

Hardy, C., & Phillips, N. (1998). Strategies of engagement: Lessons from the critical examination of collaboration and conflict in an interorganizational domain. *Organization Science, 9*(2), 217–230.

Higgs, M., & Aitken, P. (2003). An exploration of the relationship between emotional intelligence and leadership potential. *Journal of Managerial Psychology, 18*(8), 814–823.

Ho, W. (2008). Community benefits agreements: An evolution in public benefits negotiation processes. *Journal on Affordable Housing & Community Development Law, 17*(1–2), 7–34.

Huxham, C. (1996). *Creating collaborative advantage*. London, England: Sage.

Huxham, C. (2003). Theorizing collaboration practice. *Public Management Review, 5*(3), 401–423.

Katz, B., Turner, M. A., Brown, K. D., Cunningham, M., & Sawyer, N. (2003). *Rethinking local affordable housing strategies: Lessons from 70 years of policy and practice*. Washington, DC: The Urban Institute & the Center on Urban and Metropolitan Policy.

Kirah, A. (2009). Co-creation and the design mindset. Paper presented at the Copenhagen conference, Co-creation designing for change. Retrieved from http://copenhagencocreation.com/files/upload/20090812_115736_cocreation_andthedesignmindset.pdf

Knotts, H. G. (2006). Sticks, bricks, and social capital: The challenge of community development corporations in the American Deep South. *Community Development Journal, 41*(1), 37–49.

Kroopnick, M. (2008). Affording Baltimore: Public-private approaches to workforce housing. *Urban Lawyer, 40*, 331–373.

Lane, C., & Bachmann, R. (1998). *Trust within and between organizations: Conceptual issues and empirical applications*. New York, NY: Oxford University Press USA.

Lasker, R., Weiss, E., & Miller, R. (2001). Partnership synergy: A practical framework for studying and strengthening the collaborative advantage. *Milbank Quarterly, 79*(2), 179–205.

Lasker, R., & Weiss, E. (2003). Broadening participation in community problem solving: A multidisciplinary model to support collaborative practice and research. *Journal of Urban Health, 80*(1), 14–47.

Le Ber, M., & Branzei, O. (2009). (Re)forming strategic cross-sector partnerships: Relational processes of social innovation. *Business & Society, 49*(1), 1–33.

Local Initiatives Support Corporation. (2014). Building sustainable communities by the numbers, 2013. Retrieved from www.lisc.org

Madden, J. (2011, January). Overcoming collaboration barriers in affordable housing public-private partnerships. In *Academy of Management Proceedings* (Vol. 2011, No. 1, pp. 1–6). Academy of Management.

Madden, J. (2017). Reimagining collaboration: Insight from leaders of affordable-housing cross-sector Collaborations on successful collaboration design, performance, and social innovation. *Journal of Nonprofit Education and Leadership, 7*(3), 182–196.

Mattessich, P. W., Murray-Close, M., & Monsey, B. R. (2001). *Collaboration: What makes it work: A review of research literature on factors influencing successful collaboration*. St. Paul, MN: Amherst H. Wilder Foundation.

Maxwell, J. A. (2004). *Qualitative research design: An interactive approach*. Thousand Oaks, CA: Sage.

Michlewski, K. (2008). Uncovering design attitude: Inside the culture of designers. *Organization Studies, 29*(3), 373–392.

Muhr, T., & Friese, S. (2004). *User's manual for ATLAS. ti 5.0*. Berlin, Germany: Scientific Software Development.

Myerson, D. L. (2002). *Community development corporations working with for-profit developers: The ULI/Charles H. Shaw Forum on Urban community issues.* Washington, DC: Urban Land Institute.

NeighborWorks America. (2014). NeighborWorks impact, national results in 2013. Retrieved from www.neighborworks.org

National Congress for Community Economic Development (NCCED). (2005). *Reaching new heights: Trends and achievements of community-based development organizations.* Washington, DC: National Congress for Community Economic Development. Retrieved from http://community-wealth.org/content/reaching-new-heights-2005-ncced-census-trends-and-achievements-community-based-development

Nooteboom, B., Berger, H., & Noorderhaven, N. (1997). Effects of trust and governance on relational risk. *Academy of Management Journal, 40*(2), 308–338.

Peters, B. (1998). With a little help from our friends: Public-private partnerships as institutions and instruments. In J. Pierre (Ed.), *Partnerships in urban governance: European and American experience* (pp. 11–33). London, England: Macmillan.

Pisano, G. P., & Verganti, R. (2008). Which kind of collaboration is right for you. *Harvard Business Review, 86*(12), 79–86.

Reuter, G. N. (2014, June). *Self-evaluation and community development corporations: The utility of robust management information systems* (Unpublished manuscript). Massachusetts Institute of Technology, Cambridge, MA.

Roberts, N. (2000). Wicked problems and network approaches to resolution. *International Public Management Review, 1*(1), 1–19.

Rohe, W. M., & Bratt, R. G. (2003). Failures, downsizings, and mergers among community development corporations. *Housing Policy Debate, 14*(1–2), 1–46.

Schein, E. H. (2010). *Organizational culture and leadership* (Vol. 2). San Francisco, CA: John Wiley & Sons.

Schwarz, L. M. (2008). 2007 National Affordable Housing Trust Fund Act: A national fund for a national need. *Journal on Affordable Housing & Community Development Law, 17*, 395–422.

Selsky, J., & Parker, B. (2005). Cross-sector partnerships to address social issues: Challenges to theory and practice. *Journal of Management, 31*(6), 849–873.

Silverman, R. M. (2009). Perceptions of nonprofit funding decisions: A survey of local public administrators and executive directors of community-based housing organizations (CBHOs). *Public Organization Review, 9*(3), 235–246.

Simon, H. (1996). The sciences of the artificial. Cambridge, MA: MIT Press.

Snavely, K., & Tracy, M. (2002). Development of trust in rural nonprofit collaborations. *Nonprofit & Voluntary Sector Quarterly, 31*(1), 62–83.

Spradley, J. P. (1979). *The ethnographic interview.* New York, NY: Holt, Rinehart & Winston.

Steffen, B.L., Carter, G.R., Martin, M., Pelletiere, D., Vandenbroucke, D.A., Yao, Y-G. D. (2015, April). *Worst case housing needs: 2015 report to Congress.* U.S. Department of Housing and Urban Development, Office of Policy Development and Research.

Stoecker, R. (2003). Understanding the development-organizing dialectic. *Journal of Urban Affairs, 25*(4), 493–512.

Suddaby, R. (2006). From the editors: What grounded theory is not. *Academy of Management Journal, 49*(4), 633–642.

U.S. Department of Housing & Urban Development (HUD). (2009). www.hud.gov

U.S. Department of Housing & Urban Development (HUD). (2012). *NSP laws and federal register notices: Community planning and development, neighborhood stabilization program, November 27*. Washington, DC: U.S. Government Printing House.

U.S. Department of Housing & Urban Development (HUD). (2015). *Worst case housing needs 2014: A report to Congress*. Washington, DC: U.S. Government Printing House.

Vangen, S., & Huxham, C. (2003a). Enacting leadership for collaborative advantage. *British Journal of Management, 14*, S61–S76.

Vangen, S., & Huxham, C. (2003b). Nurturing collaborative relations: Building trust in interorganizational collaboration. *Journal of Applied Behavioral Science 39*(1), 5–31.

Verganti, R. (2008). *Design driven innovation*. Boston, MA: Harvard Business School Press.

Vidal, A. C. (1992). *Rebuilding communities: A national study of urban community development corporations*. Community Development Research Center, Graduate School of Management and Urban Policy. New York, NY: New School for Social Research.

Vidal, A. C. (1997). Can community development re-invent itself? The challenges of strengthening neighborhoods in the 21st century. *Journal of the American Planning Association, 63*(4), 429–438.

Vidal, A. C., & Keating, W. D. (2004). Community development: Current issues and emerging challenges. *Journal of Urban Affairs, 26*(2), 125–137.

Von Hoffman, A. (2013). Calling upon the Genius of Private Enterprise: The Housing and Urban Development Act of 1968 and the Liberal Turn to Public-Private Partnerships. *Studies in American Political Development, 27*(2), 165–194.

Walker, C. (2002). *Community development corporations and their changing support systems*. Washington, DC: The Urban Institute, Metropolitan Housing and Communities Policy Center.

Walker, C., Gustafson, J., & Snow, C. (2002). *National support for local system change: The effect of the national community development initiative on community development systems*. Washington, DC: The Urban Institute, Metropolitan Housing and Communities Policy Center.

Warner, J. F. (2006). More sustainable participation? Multi-stakeholder platforms for integrated catchment management. *International Journal of Water Resources Development, 22*(1), 15–35.

Yaffee, S. L., & Wondolleck, J. M. (2003). Collaborative ecosystem planning processes in the United States: Evolution and challenges. *Environments: A Journal of Interdisciplinary Studies, 31*(2), 55–72.

Yin, J. S. (1998). The community development industry system: A case study of politics and institutions in Cleveland, 1967–1997. *Journal of Urban Affairs, 20*, 137–158.

Yoo, Y., Boland, R. J., Jr., & Lyytinen, K. (2006). From organization design to organization designing. *Organization Science, 17*(2), 215–229.

3 The ABCDS (Autonomy, Boundary Spanning, Common Vision, and Design Attitude) of Successful Collaboration[1]

In the previous chapter, key findings from the qualitative research suggest leaders of successful collaborations take actions intended to create a better future and remain mission-focused. Design also emerged, where leaders exhibit a design attitude and continuously redesign to meet ongoing challenges. Further, successful collaborations were innovative—creating solutions that rejuvenated their communities.

This chapter is the first quantitative study, designed to empirically validate the effect of autonomy, boundary spanning, common (or shared) vision on collaboration, and the mediating role of design attitude in successful collaboration performance. This research proposes a theoretical perspective for collaborators to adopt design science, the language of designers, and a design attitude as an empirically informed pathway for better managing the complexities inherent in collaboration. This study is also the first to empirically develop and quantitatively attempt to validate a design attitude scale for building better inter-organizational collaborations. Additionally, this work contributes research on successful collaboration performance, as well as evidence-based and research-informed strategies for creating viable practitioner tools in order to more effectively bridge research and practice.

This chapter is structured to summarize key insight from collaboration literature and design science first. I then present a research model and hypotheses. The section that follows outlines the research methods in detail. The chapter concludes with study findings, discussion, and implications for practice.

3.1 Insight from Research on Collaboration

Collaborations range from a one-time transaction to a full legal merger of two organizations based on formality, information sharing, facility sharing, and the offering of joint programs (Guo & Acar, 2005). Collaboration structure can be ambiguous, complex, and dynamic (Huxham, 2003): ambiguous from a lack of clarity on partner roles and expectations, complex from the identity of individual partners or because partners may be engaged in other collaborations, and dynamic because partners (or their purposes) may shift due to internal or external influences.

Collaboration literature outlines that the initial environment (or pre-conditions) for the partnership can enable or constrain collaboration (Ansell & Gash, 2007; Peters, 1998). In addition, leadership is critical in making collaborations work (Ansell & Gash, 2007; Armistead, Pettigrew, & Aves, 2007; Crosby & Bryson, 2005), and shaping the cultural values of their organizations in favor of collaboration (Armistead et al., 2007). The literature is replete with process models for collaboration. According to Gray (1989), the process involves problem solving, direction setting, and implementation, and, as described by Gajda (2004), follows the "simple stages" of assemble, order, perform, transform, and adjourn. Collaborations can follow the "stage models" (Tuckman, 1965) of form, storm, norm, perform, and adjourn (Tuckman & Jensen, 1977). Waddock (1989) sees the process as evolutionary, requiring partnership, issue crystallization, establishment, and maturity whereas Huxham (2003) views it as a cyclical process involving communication, trust, commitment, understanding, and outcomes. The general literature on collaboration is vast, and much of it is applicable to, and useful for, understanding how to build effective collaborations.

From a practitioner perspective, inter-organizational collaborations have benefits and challenges. For example, in theory, cross-sector inter-organizational collaborations should combine the best of what each sector brings to the relationship (Rosenau, 1999). A shared commitment of partners across and within sectors to address complex social problems (Pasquero, 1991), a desire for collective action (Ostrom, 1990), collective impact (Kania & Kramer, 2011), mutual benefit and collaborative advantage (Huxham, 1996) should drive the desire for successful collaboration. For example, Chung (2004) found that both nonprofit and for-profit partners can leverage additional financing for affordable-housing development as a result of their collaboration.

Still, important differences between the sectors may challenge collaboration. Recurring themes in the literature note

- the nonprofit partner as mission driven and the for-profit partner as profit driven (Selsky & Parker, 2005),
- a large nonprofit partner dominating its smaller nonprofit partner (Brinkerhoff, 2002), and
- the nonprofit partner, unlike the government partner, as more flexible and, unlike the for-profit partner, involving residents in their governance, planning, and development activities (Galster, Levy, Sawet, Temkin, & Walker, 2005).

These themes pose potential conflict of interests and strain collaboration. An evaluation of collaboration through the design lens may reframe collaboration challenges. I now suggest that more recent literature on design may yield insights about building better collaborations.

3.2 Design Science

Bridging perspectives from theory with the results of research on practice through design science (Rethemeyer, 2005; Jelinek, Romme, & Boland, 2008) may help improve collaboration performance. Herbert Simon (1996, p. 133) highlighted the fundamental importance of design and management, noting "the natural sciences are concerned with how the things are" whereas design science "is concerned with how things ought to be" in order to attain goals. Further, design "involves inquiry into systems that do not exist—either complete new systems or new states of existing systems" (Romme, 2003, p. 558). For participants in inter-organizational collaborations intended for developing affordable-housing, an outcome of this new system design is the change from government and nonprofit organizations moving from competitors in social service delivery to collaborators examining barriers and benefits in these inter-organizational relationships (Kim, 2010). A second outcome is a shift by policymakers from the historical segregation and concentration of poverty in poorly maintained public housing to investing in mixed income housing developments (Joseph, 2008).

Moreover, designers, like collaborators, encounter wicked problems—a raft of ill-formulated and confusing social system problems, that are often symptoms of other problems, including multiple stakeholders and decision-makers with conflicting values (Buchanan, 1992; Rittel & Webber, 1973). The provision of affordable housing can be seen as a wicked problem. For example, despite the need for affordable housing, area residents may oppose it; a plan to develop affordable housing in such a way as to not concentrate poverty results in a reduction of needed affordable-housing units; given the density of urban areas, the affordable-housing construction process has the potential to break up existing communities; finally, affordable housing may cause gentrification by attracting higher income residents to the redeveloped area, involuntarily displacing lower income residents (Diamond, 2009).

Simon (1966) argued that natural sciences show complexity as a mask for simplicity with the goal of finding patterns hidden in apparent chaos, whereas complexity theory (embraced by design science) suggests well-chosen design rules can shape resilient and productive processes. In other words, effective design outlines a set of simple rules and processes that can be applied to multiple complex situations (Jelinek et al., 2008), and following these guidelines is a better strategy for achieving and sustaining desired change than the generic application of predetermined solutions. This suggests design can be used as a comprehensive approach to problem solving, transformation (Bevan, Robert, Bate, Maher, & Wells, 2007), and the creation of a larger sense of purpose (Weick, 2004). Design "helps to bring together people from different disciplines and practices to jointly pursue a vision and boldly experiment." (Avital & Boland, 2008, p. 2). Given the similarities between designers and collaborators, design can have considerable influence on inter-organizational collaboration.

3.2.1 Redesign

Organization design is not a "single event," but a continual process (Galbraith, 1977). Reconfiguration of plans, strategies, approaches, and structure can yield organizational improvements, opportunities, and learning, and allow collaborations to respond in a positive way to change and unpredictability (Galbraith, Downey, & Kates, 2002). Effective organizational design is achieved using "strategic fit" (Galbraith, 2002). Strategic fit matches resources and capabilities with external opportunities and occurs when policy and strategy are aligned and reinforced (Galbraith, 2002). As Bryson and Crosby (2006, p. 51) note, inter-organizational collaborations "are most likely to create public value when they are resilient and engage in regular reassessments." Galbraith notes that redesign, or organization reconfiguration, is important to ensure alignment. Redesign is a critical design strategy.

3.2.2 Design Attitude

Little research has addressed design (and more specifically "design attitude") as key to the collaboration process (Ansell & Gash, 2007). Research from the previous chapter involving interviews with leaders of successful and less successful collaborations revealed sharp differences among leader competencies, focus, and attitudes when facing obstacles. The study found design attitude affects successful collaboration performance. However, the concept of design attitude has mostly been the subject of qualitative analysis and discussion in the design and management literature. Additional empirical research is needed to define and measure the relationship between design attitude and successful collaboration performance.

To address this gap, a design attitude scale developed from qualitative research to test its role in collaboration empirically is operationalized. Specifically, this investigation explored the positive impact of autonomy, shared vision, and boundary spanning on design attitude and the positive impact of design attitude on collaboration performance. A quantitative survey with 452 conventional leaders and managers (i.e., not professional designers, or architects) involved in recently completed or established inter-organizational collaborations was conducted. To my knowledge, this is the first study with a quantitatively validated design attitude scale intended to build better collaborations. The principal aims of this study were to contribute to theory and to ground the study in emerging data that may be beneficial for practitioners who are responsible for designing and implementing collaborations.

3.3 Research Model and Hypothesis Development

This research, informed by the emerging data in Chapter 2, explores the impact of key elements on collaboration performance: autonomy, shared vision, boundary spanning, and design attitude. I sought to understand the

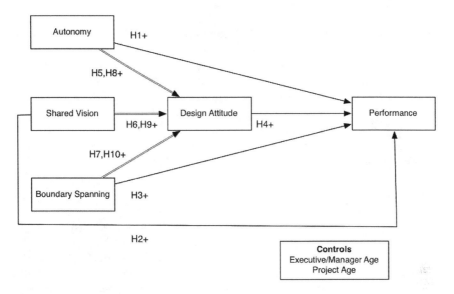

Figure 3.1 Research Model

effect of these elements and the mediating role of design attitude on successful collaboration performance. The research model is presented in Figure 3.1.

3.3.1 Collaboration Performance

According to Lui and Ngo (2004), perceived performance satisfaction is commonly used to measure the strategic performance of an alliance. This study utilizes perceived performance satisfaction as an indicator of collaboration performance. The literature provides additional research connecting the independent variables to collaboration performance and is cited in support of hypothesis formulation.

3.3.2 Autonomy

According to Barling, Kelloway, and Iverson (2003), autonomy is influence over one's job, a key component for high-quality work, and associated with an increase in participation with decision-making. Turner and Lawrence (1965) outline autonomy as discretion over one's ability to complete work assignments. From the purview of Hackman and Oldham (1975), autonomy is freedom to schedule work and determine procedures.

Despite the varying perspectives, autonomy is a key job characteristic (Rousseau, 1977) linked to performance and satisfaction with work (Sutton & Rousseau, 1979) and is important for individual success and growth

(Cola & Wang, 2017; Cola, 2015). Empirical research on job satisfaction suggests autonomy positively affects decision making, and supply-chain research suggests sharing decision making has a significant impact on collaboration performance (Kim & Oh, 2005). Further, without autonomy, passivity may occur resulting in an ineffective "response to opportunities and threats to performance" (Hughes & Morgan, 2007, p. 654). At the team level, autonomy is considered a critical element of team performance with high levels of task interdependence (Langfred, 2005). I expect autonomy to positively affect collaboration performance.

Hypothesis 1 Autonomy positively affects performance.

3.3.3 Shared Vision

Shared vision also refers to shared values and mutual goals (Morgan & Hunt, 1994). The concept of shared vision is important and is seen throughout the collaboration literature as "shared vision" (Manring & Pearsall, 2004; Rickards, Chen, & Moger, 2001; Walter & Petr, 2000; Wondolleck & Yaffee, 2000), "shared understanding" (Ansell & Gash, 2007; Tett, Crowther, & O'Hara, 2003), "shared goals" (Rickards et al., 2001), "common mission" (Alexander, Comfort, & Weiner, 1998; Roussos & Fawcett, 2000), and "common purpose" (Tett et al., 2003), to name a few.

A focus on the mission in collaborations emerged as a critical success factor in the qualitative research in Chapter 2. One route to creating this focus is the development of a shared vision because partners can be mismatched with respect to mission, structure, goals, organizational culture, decision-making style, motives, or desired constituents to serve. Further, "[a] clear shared goal can foster project team members from different functions to recognize their different needs, to think deeply, to stimulate information processing and to find creative solutions related to task issues" (Chen, Chang, & Hung, 2008, p. 26). For example, in a study of 418 project teams, a clearly stated goal was the only factor that predicted success (Pinto & Prescott, 1988). A shared goal also supports integration (i.e., combining of resources) across organizations and reduces inter-partner conflict (Tsai & Ghoshal, 1998). A shared goal also implies a shared meaning, and research suggests efficiency achievements (Inkpen & Tsang, 2005).

According to Rickards et al. (2001, p. 245), a key feature of shared vision is that "team members share a sense of purpose and responsibility that motivates and sustains team progress." Finally, successful collaboration performance is supported by inter-organizational coordinated action, and shared vision is necessary for this exchange (Dyer & Singh, 1998). I expect shared vision to positively and significantly impact collaboration performance.

Hypothesis 2 Shared vision positively affects performance.

3.3.4 Boundary Spanning

Organizational teams often have some, but not all of the needed resources within their boundaries. "Boundary spanning refers to actions a focal team undertakes to reach out into its environment to obtain important resources and support to respond to these demands, promote the team's work, and build goodwill among stakeholders. These activities help the team accomplish its objectives, thereby contributing to team performance" (Faraj & Yan, 2009, p. 606). Boundary spanning involves information acquisition, which in turns yields resources beneficial to team members (Ancona & Caldwell, 1992; Cross & Cummings, 2004). The work in boundary spanning also includes managing relationships (e.g., external stakeholders) and protecting resources (e.g., time, energy, external demands; Ancona & Caldwell, 1988; Hansen, 1999). Boundary spanning is also positively related to the success of the collaboration (Ancona & Caldwell, 1992). I expect boundary spanning to positively impact collaboration performance.

Hypothesis 3 Boundary spanning positively affects performance.

3.3.5 Design Attitude

Boland, Collopy, Lyytinen, and Yoo (2008, pp. 13–14) define "design attitude" as an "ongoing expectation that each project is a new opportunity to create something remarkable." A design attitude encourages moving beyond responding to the alternatives presented to engaging in a decision-making process that involves collecting and interpreting evidence, designing possibilities, and testing multiple ideas. For example, in Chapter 2 power imbalance was an issue for less successful collaborations. However, a design attitude appeared to change the power dynamic for successful collaborations, which supports the idea that a design attitude moves beyond default solutions and ordinary systems of logic based on how things are (Boland & Collopy, 2004) and instead focuses on human interaction and phenomenon intended to create a preferred situation (Simon, 1996). This concept suggests that effective collaborations may depend on particular mindsets, skills, and perspectives. I expect design attitude to positively impact performance.

Hypothesis 4 Design attitude positively affects performance.

Autonomy is also associated with higher intrinsic motivation, greater interest, and higher levels of trust (Deci & Ryan, 1987). Michlewski (2008), in his research on design attitude among professional designers, attributes empathy, authentic listening, the ability to bring ideas to life, and engaging change and uncertainty as key characteristics of design attitude. When inter-organizational collaborations are able to retain their autonomy, this has a positive impact on design attitude. For example, the nonprofit partner in one of the successful collaborations studied in Chapter 2 discusses never creating a formal memorandum of understanding, but describes the organizations as working "hand in hand" resulting in a "very productive partnership." The nonprofit partner further defines the inter-organizational collaboration as a "parallel collaboration" as opposed to a "hierarchical one" where it "was clear right off . . . that we would be most useful if we did what we did well, and if we partnered then with organizations that could do what they do well, and for us not to feel like we have to do everything." Further, there were examples of threatened autonomy in three of the less successful inter-organizational collaborations studied: the nonprofit partner who felt takeover was imminent, the nonprofit partner who wanted additional responsibilities as opposed to the same terms as a previous collaborative project, and the nonprofit partner who perceived a lack of control over any of the processes or funding secured. I expect autonomy to positively impact design attitude and design attitude to partially mediate the effect of autonomy on collaboration performance.

Hypothesis 5 Autonomy positively affects design attitude.
Hypothesis 6 Design attitude partially mediates the positive effect of autonomy on performance.

In thinking through research on shared vision and design attitude, Yoo, Boland, and Lyytinen (2006) discuss design gestalt—making things visible and bringing ideas to life. The study describes the design practice of renowned architect Frank O. Gehry as having "three interdependent elements: architectural vision, use of representational technologies, and a collaborative network for design and construction (Yoo et al. 2006, p. 217). In his discussion of design, Romme (2003) emphasizes creating something new. A senior consultant at Wolff Olins in Michlewski's study outlines "the ability to capture, not only to create the ideas, but to capture them simply into something visual that people relate to" (2008, p. 382). A connector of all these ideas is the importance of, and a commitment to making visible, a key characteristic of design attitude.

In Chapter 2, I discuss a successful collaboration adapting to overcome the barrier of community opposition when the private sector partner convened a community meeting to show neighborhood residents the affordable-housing product would be indistinguishable from market-rate housing (see Figure 2.3a). Neighborhood residents, the city, and the private sector developer had a shared vision about the type of housing desired for the community. During my interview, the for-profit developer stated,

> we want to create housing that looks and feels exactly like market-rate housing because then it makes it safer for the prospective homeowners and lenders and everyone else in the subsequent phases to have confidence that there's something happening in the community.

In a separate interview with the city official, when talking about the vision for the housing development for the city and the developer, he stated "[t]hey have a very good philosophy that affordable housing should not look different from market-rate housing. Their apartments that they rehab or build new have many upgrades that you don't find in affordable units" I expect shared vision to positively impact design attitude and design attitude to partially mediate the effect of shared vision on collaboration performance.

> **Hypothesis 7** Shared vision positively affects design attitude.
> **Hypothesis 8** Design attitude partially mediates the positive effect of shared vision on performance.

Design attitude is the ability to evaluate a situation from multiple perspectives. A quote from a senior director at Philips Design states, "[d]esigners themselves are actually managing all the constituent parts and therefore managing the connection and the connected contribution of all the constituent disciplines in solving any problem or creating a landscape for exploring further problems or further opportunities, further possibilities of growth" (Michlewski, 2008: 378). Kelley and VanPatter (2005) promote design as the glue for multidisciplinary teams. Further, in building his logic for design attitude Michlewski (2008) introduces the nexus concept advanced by Martin (2009). Nexus is an interaction point of internal and external influences. "The nexus model suggests that what some organizations perceive as unique to their culture is, in fact, non-unique and often attached to professional cultures which span many organizations" (Michlewski, 2008, p. 375). In considering all of these interconnections, I expect boundary spanning to positively impact design attitude.

Further, based upon inter-organizational collaborations studied in Chapter 2, I expect design attitude to partially mediate the effect of boundary spanning on collaboration performance. First, in the case where an inter-organizational collaboration was rebuilding after a natural disaster, the nonprofit partner discusses the chaos and disorganization of relief services. The nonprofit partner gives several examples of crossing boundaries to facilitate successful collaboration performance utilizing design attitude (e.g., creating solutions that did not previously exist, finding solutions and thinking outside of the box). In the first example, a potential donor informs the nonprofit partner that "typically" the international donor would deal with someone from the United Nations (U.N.) for disasters, however, there was neither an identified intermediary to give the funds to nor a local bank in operation because of the devastation. The local nonprofit partner responds, "Well, I'm not the U.N., but I never had a problem telling anybody what to do and where to go." The nonprofit partner then calls the Chief Executive Officer of a bank in a location not impacted by the storm to handle the transaction. The nonprofit partner admits he did not believe the donor would indeed make the contribution but contacted the bank later to learn funds were available. The nonprofit partner then takes on a procurement role using those donated funds to secure a generator and tables from Lowe's and computers and water from WalMart—all before power was restored to any of these businesses, writing down credit card numbers for later charging—while recruiting volunteers to facilitate opening a relief center the following day. In considering all of these interconnections, I expect boundary spanning to positively impact design attitude and design attitude to partially mediate the effect of boundary spanning on collaboration performance.

> **Hypothesis 9** Boundary spanning positively affects design attitude.
> **Hypothesis 10** Design attitude mediates the positive effect of boundary spanning on performance.

3.4 Methodology

To test the proposed hypotheses, I collected data using an online survey targeting an executive and management level population that had recently participated in an established or completed collaboration with another organization. Data analysis employed IBM SPSS Statistics (version 21) for basic statistical, EFA analysis and IBM SPSS AMOS (Analysis of Moment Structures, version 21) for covariance-based CFA and structural equation modeling. Analyses were completed in the following stages: confirmation of suitability of the data for multivariate analysis, a two-step structural equation modeling (SEM) strategy (Anderson & Gerbing, 1988) utilizing exploratory factor analysis (EFA), and confirmatory factor analysis (CFA) to build the SEM.

3.5 Construct Operationalization

Scale items for the independent variables (autonomy, shared vision, boundary spanning) and the dependent variable (collaboration performance) were adapted from the literature based upon their theoretical relevance and reliability. The scale for the mediator variable (design attitude) is developed based on previous design and management literature (Boland & Collopy, 2004; Gaskin & Berente, 2011) and the qualitative research in Chapter 2. All constructs were measured on a five-point Likert scale where 1 = strongly disagree and 5 = strongly agree. In the case of boundary spanning, the five-point scale meant that 1 = to a very small extent and 5 = to a very great extent.[2] A table of constructs is provided in Appendix B. The specification for all scales were reflective (Jarvis, MacKenzie, & Podsakoff, 2003).

3.5.1 Autonomy

In the choice of items for autonomy, a six-item scale was adapted from Hughes and Morgan (2007), which was based upon a theoretical framework grounded in entrepreneurial orientation and business performance literature. The authors describe autonomy as "the authority and independence given to an individual or team within the firm to develop business concepts and visions and carry them through to completion" (p. 652). The last three items were dropped from the analysis due to convergent validity issues. Cronbach's alpha for the three-item construct for my study was 0.78.

3.5.2 Shared Vision

In the choice of items for shared vision, a six-item scale was adapted by combining a three-item scale on shared vision adapted from Rickards et al. (2001) and a three-item scale on shared goals adapted from Chen et al. (2008). The Rickards study is based upon team dynamics and development, leadership, and performance relationships. The research describes shared vision as a shared sense of purpose and responsibility that sustains progress. The theoretical framing for the Chen study is based upon research on R&D project team members from a variety of disciplines regarding shared goals. Chen et al. (2008, p. 27) describe shared goals as "the cognitive capital developed by Rickards et al. (2001) to measure the clarity of shared goals within the team." I made the decision to combine these two three-item constructs in order to accurately measure shared vision because research supporting shared value is akin to shared goals (Morgan & Hunt 1994). Cronbach's alpha for the six-item construct for my study was 0.90.

3.5.3 Boundary Spanning

In the choice of items for boundary spanning, a four-item scale was adapted from Faraj and Yan's (2009) work on team research. As stated earlier, the authors describe boundary spanning as "actions a focal team undertakes to reach out into its environment to obtain important resources and support" (p. 606). Cronbach's alpha for the four-item construct for my study was 0.80.

3.5.4 Collaboration Performance

In the choice of items for collaboration performance, a five-item scale on performance satisfaction was adapted from Lui and Ngo's (2004) work on transaction cost theory. Their research sheds light on the roles of trust and contractual safeguards in relation to cooperation in non-equity alliances. The authors describe perceived performance satisfaction as a measure commonly used to gauge strategic performance of an alliance, which extends previous research by Saxton (1997) of perceived overall project satisfaction. As a dependent variable, items were kept as is to maintain the integrity of the construct based upon research conducted. Cronbach's alpha for the five-item construct for my study was 0.87.

3.5.5 Design Attitude

In the choice of items for design attitude, a six-item scale was developed from items proposed by Gaskin and Berente (2011) for measuring design attitude. I modified Gaskin and Berente's work in light of the qualitative research in Chapter 2. The modified six items included:

- We embrace an entrepreneurial spirit (finding new problems and solutions).
- We think outside the box (beyond past decisions and known solutions).
- We develop new solutions to old problems/decisions.
- We discover stakeholder/customer needs and requirements.
- We try new concepts given available resources.
- We iterate through trial and error driven by the belief that things can get better if we try more.

The fourth and sixth items were dropped from the analysis as a result of low loadings. The Cronbach alpha for the four-item construct for my study was 0.82.

3.5.6 Collaboration Checklist

A collaboration checklist was not included in the structural equation modeling but as a secondary tool to assess the collaborative process (Borden & Perkins, 1999). This self-evaluation tool examines 12 factors—catalysts, goals, history, understanding people served, leadership, roles and responsibilities, communication, connectedness, resources, sustainability, expanding the collaborative, and monitoring—that influence the collaborative process. The evaluation tool is measured on a five-point scale where 1 = strongly disagree, 2 = disagree, 3 = neither agree or disagree, 4 = agree, and 5 = strongly agree. The sum of the 12 items provides insight on another factor—a sense of the strength and progress of the overall collaboration. In this study, 60 is a perfect score, 0–20 describe collaborations experiencing a number of challenges, 21–40 describe collaborations demonstrating some strengths and progress, and 41–60 describe collaborations with strong components that are poised for growth. Borden and Perkins (1999, p. 1) note that "information gained from this tool can provide group members with an understanding of the strengths and challenges they face as they work to reach their goals." This tool served as an independent secondary examination of the success of the collaboration.

3.5.7 Controls

The two controls include the age of the respondent and the age of the project. Respondents were asked to indicate their age (1 = 30 or younger, 2 = 31 to 40, 3 = 41 to 50, 4 = 51 to 60, and 5 = 61 or older) and the length of time their project had been in existence (1 = less than three months and 5 = more than five years). Controlling for the age of respondent and the age of project serves as a proxy for experience that may be related to better collaboration performance (Yang, Huang, & Wu, 2011).

3.5.8 *Instrument Pretesting*

After developing the initial survey, "think-aloud/talk-aloud" exercises (Bolton, 1993) were conducted with selected respondents to identify any cognitive difficulties in forming survey responses. This effort resulted in survey adjustments and was repeated until content and face validity were achieved. The survey was then pretested with several additional respondents, resulting in some additional modifications to wording to ensure comprehension and clarity. Pretesting also included a q-sort (Hinkin, 1998) with 12 different respondents. A trial run of the online survey was completed where I requested six additional participants to complete the survey; then I followed up with respondents for another talk-aloud exercise. This effort resulted in additional wordsmithing; the development of a qualifier question to ensure survey participants are referencing participation in an established or recently completed collaboration; and some reordering of the survey questions so that the survey instrument was organized in sections, starting with a mix of both exogenous and endogenous factors. Finally, a pilot test (with 50 different respondents) was conducted prior to the launch of the survey with a review of outliers, item distributions, and preliminary EFA.

3.6 Data Collection

Two methods of survey delivery were utilized. In the first method, I leveraged both my personal contacts and social network resulting in about 400 contacts in executive or management positions in nonprofits, private sector organizations, or government organizations that engage in collaborations. These contacts were provided with a URL to the survey. Of these 400 connections, 199 started the survey and 67 qualifying surveys were utilized exceeding the 10–12% response and completion percentages of surveys involving executives (Hambrick, Geletkanycz, & Fredrickson, 1993). The balance of responses came from a screened professional research panel provided by Qualtrics.

3.6.1 *Characteristics of Respondents*

A total of 452 qualified respondents (i.e., they participated in an established or recently completed project involving a collaboration with another organization and held an appropriate management category position) contributed to the data analysis. Of this number, 58% were males and 42% were females from the private sector (74%), nonprofit sector (16%), and government

(10%). The management categories in the sample included executives (31%), senior vice president/vice president (11%), director (19%), manager (28%), officer (2%), coordinator (6%), and academic faculty (4%). Respondents self-reported that 96% of the collaborations were successful, and the collaboration checklist tool reported 92% in the "poised for growth" progress range with scores between 41 and 60 (out of a total of 60).

3.7 Data Analysis

3.7.1 *Exploratory Factor Analysis*

An exploratory factor analysis (EFA) was completed for this cross-sectional data (Anderson & Gerbing, 1988). The factor loading for design attitude items DA4 and DA6 was below the minimum threshold (Hair, Black, Babin, & Anderson, 2009, p. 117) and therefore these items were eliminated. Three autonomy items (AUT 4, AUT5, and AUT6) were also removed for validity reasons. The KMO and Bartlett's test were completed to ensure sample adequacy. The tests were significant, and communalities for each of the variables were greater than 0.3, further supporting adequate correlation for factor analysis. Further confirmation of the five-factor model was supported by the reproduced correlations matrix with 6% nonredundant residuals greater than 0.05. Beyond the conceptual definition of the unidimensional scale, reliability (i.e., the consistency between multiple variable measurements) is established with a Cronbach's alpha greater than 0.78 for all factors (see Table 3.1).

Sufficient convergent validity was achieved because factor loadings were above the minimum threshold of 0.350 for a sample size of 452 (Hair et al., 2009). The five-factor model did not have problematic cross loadings and therefore demonstrated sufficient discriminant validity. Finally, 57% of the total variance is explained by the five factors, and all factors had eigenvalues above 1.0.

Table 3.1 EFA Summary Statistics

Construct	Number of Items	Loadings	Cronbach's alpha
1. Performance	5	0.724; 0.793; 0.709; 0.792; 0.656	0.874
2. Shared Vision	6	0.736; 0.757; 0.835; 0.885; 0.720; 0.688	0.899
3. Boundary Spanning	4	0.729; 0.772; 0.646; 0.554	0.803
4. Design Attitude	4	0.643; 0.837; 0.693; 0.618	0.818
5. Autonomy	3	0.727; 0.723; 0.702	0.777

KMO = 0.918; Chi Square = 5217, df = 231, p = 0.000
Maximum Likelihood Estimation and Promax rotation with Kaiser Normalization

Table 3.2 Descriptive Statistics, Reliability, Correlations and Discriminant Validity

Construct	No. of Item	MSV	ASV	CA	CR	Construct				
						1.	2.	3.	4.	5.
1. Performance	5	0.526	0.385	.874	.875	.765	.396	.314	.526	.305
2. Shared Vision	6	0.396	0.293	.899	.893	.629	.763	.331	.300	.145
3. Boundary Spanning	5	0.393	0.337	.803	.806	.560	.576	.714	.393	.311
4. Design Attitude	4	0.526	0.396	.818	.820	.725	.548	.627	.730	.366
5. Autonomy	3	0.366	0.282	.777	.780	.553	.381	.558	.605	.737

MSV=maximum shared variance; ASV=average shared variance; CA=Cronbach's alpha; CR=composite reliability; square root of average variance extracted (AVE) are bolded values along the diagonal; values above the diagonal are squared correlations.

3.7.2 Confirmatory Factor Analysis

After consulting modification indices, three error terms within the shared vision factor were covaried resulting in a good fitting measurement model (χ^2 = 380.41, df = 194; GFI = 0.93; CFI = 0.96; RMSEA = 0.05; and PCLOSE = 0.82). The final test for validity reported average variance extracted (AVE) above 0.50 for all factors. The factors demonstrate convergent validity with diagonal values greater than the correlations. Composite reliability (CR) was also achieved with values above the 0.70 minimum threshold (see Table 3.2).

3.7.3 Common Method Bias

Data collection for both the independent and dependent variables were completed using a single survey instrument from the same individuals. A test for common method bias (CMB) was conducted to assess method bias affecting the measurement model (Podsakoff, MacKenzie, Lee, & Podsakoff, 2003). A common latent factor (CLF) was introduced to the model. A comparison of the standardized regression weights with and without the CLF showed no items with a difference in factor loadings greater than 0.20, which suggests common method bias is not a significant threat, therefore the CLF was not retained in the model.

3.7.4 Measurement Invariance

The good model fit of the CFA measurement model across gender indicates the model is configurally invariant. I also ran a metric invariance test across gender by constraining the factor loadings to be equal. In examining the nested model comparisons, the test for the Chi-square difference between the unconstrained and the equally constrained model was not significant (p = 0.977). Thus the measurement model meets the criteria for metric invariance across gender.

3.7.5 Structural Model

The controls [age of respondent (age) and age of project (time)] were tested for their effect on the endogenous variables. The control variables were found to have no influence on design attitude or collaborative performance (see Table 3.3). Mediation was tested using 2000 bias-corrected bootstrapping resamples in AMOS (with 95% bias corrected confidence intervals) to discover direct effects without mediation, then direct effects and indirect effects with mediation. The final model yielded excellent model fit (see Table 3.3).

3.8 Findings

3.8.1 Direct Paths

I predicted autonomy (H1) and shared vision (H2) would have a positive effect on performance. These hypotheses were supported with significant standardized estimates (beta = β) and p-values for autonomy (β = 0.16**) and shared vision (β = 0.32***). I was incorrect, however, about the hypothesis that boundary spanning (H3) would have a positive effect on performance (β = .004, p = 0.95). I correctly posited that design attitude (H4) would positively impact collaboration performance (β = 0.45***) as well that autonomy (H5), shared vision (H7), and boundary spanning (H9) would have a positive effect on design attitude. These hypotheses were supported and significant for autonomy (β = 0.35***), shared vision (β = 0.25***), and boundary spanning (β = 0.29***) on design attitude. The path analysis is presented in Table 3.3.

3.8.2 Mediation

I predicted that design attitude would partially mediate the independent variables autonomy (H6), shared vision (H8), and boundary spanning (H10) on collaboration performance. As shown in Table 3.3, design attitude partially mediates the effect of autonomy and shared vision on collaboration performance but fully mediates the effect of boundary spanning on collaboration performance.

3.9 Discussion and Implications for Practice

This study was conducted with the intent to provide empirical evidence on how collaborations can overcome challenges to successful performance. The findings are significant because they demonstrate the importance of autonomy (i.e., authority and independence; Hughes & Morgan, 2007), boundary spanning (i.e., linkages and interactions to leverage resources and support; Faraj & Yan, 2009), common or shared vision (i.e., a shared sense of purpose and responsibility that sustains and motivates; Rickards et al., 2001),

Table 3.3 Structural Model Results

Hypothesized Path	Regression Estimate	Standardized Estimate	Critical Ratio	Hypothesis Supported?
H1 Autonomy → Performance	0.15	0.16**	2.73	Yes
H2 Shared Vision → Performance	0.34	0.32***	5.91	Yes
H3 Boundary Spanning → Performance	0.00	0.00	0.06	No
H4 Design Attitude → Performance	0.44	0.45***	6.50	Yes
H5 Autonomy → Design Attitude	0.33	0.35***	5.49	Yes
H7 Shared Vision → Design Attitude	0.27	0.25***	4.21	Yes
H9 Boundary Spanning → Design Attitude	0.23	0.29***	3.94	Yes
Controls				
Design Attitude → Executive/Manager Age	0.000	0.000	−0.01	
Design Attitude → Project Age	0.025	0.048	1.16	
Performance → Executive/Manager Age	−0.016	−0.032	−0.92	
Performance → Project Age	0.016	0.031	0.88	

Squared Multiple Correlations:
R^2 Design Attitude = 0.53
R^2 Performance = 0.62

Goodness-of-fit statistics:
$\chi^2 = 380.41$, $df = 194$; GFI = 0.93; CFI = 0.96; RMSEA = 0.05; and PCLOSE = 0.82

Mediated Hypothesized Path	Direct Beta without Mediator	Direct Beta with Mediator	Indirect	Mediation
H6 Autonomy → Design Attitude → Performance	0.32***	0.16**	0.16***	Partial
H8 Shared Vision → Design Attitude → Performance	0.43***	0.32***	0.11***	Partial
H10 Boundary Spanning → Design Attitude → Performance	0.13*	0.00	0.13***	Full

Squared Multiple Correlations
R^2 Performance   0.52   0.62

* p < 0.05; ** p < 0.01; *** p < 0.001.

and design attitude (i.e., an opportunity to create something remarkable; Boland et al., 2008) as contributors to successful collaborations. I observed the positive impact of these key elements on collaboration and, more importantly, the mediating effects of design attitude. Further, although boundary spanning had no statistically significant impact on performance, design attitude fully mediated the effect of boundary spanning on performance.

In addition, there are four reasons why these findings are important. First, this study confirms previous research on the importance of shared vision for inter-organizational collaboration. For example, Huxham (2003, p. 404) explains that there is an abundance of "common wisdom" around the importance and necessity of clarity in aims and goals for collaboration, but this is not facilitated in "common practice" because of its difficulty.

Second, the idea of design attitude as a concept to be embraced by ordinary leaders and managers (i.e., not professional designers or architects) to increase successful collaboration performance is compelling. The findings support design attitude as critical to the collaboration process. This book explores successful inter-organizational collaboration from a design perspective and proposes there are important similarities between designers and collaborators. Weick (1993, p. 352) suggests designers are skillful at bricolage (i.e. the ability to utilize the resources available to perform necessary tasks), and bricoleurs (the persons involved in bricolage) are more effective because of these skills (Lévi-Strauss, 1966). Berger (2009, p. 3) explains design as

> a way of looking at the world with an eye towards changing it . . . that, a designer must be able to see not just what is, but what might be. . . . Designers are also makers. They sketch and build, giving form to ideas. They take a faint glimmer of possibility and make it visible and real to others.

Design scholar Buchanan (2004, p. 54) states that "[d]esign provides discipline in finding and solving problems in practical life" and outlines design in four broad areas of everyday existence: symbolic and visual communications, material objects, activities and organized services, and complex systems or living environments (Buchanan, 1992). This suggests that design "is desperately needed in, and applicable to, our most significant human activities," that design "make things right," and "creates things and places that work" (Caplan, 2005, pp. xv, 4). If collaborators adopted the language of designers and the idea of a design attitude to better manage the complexities inherent in collaboration, improving collaboration performance may be possible. "[L]anguage is crucial in constructing the situations we face, the ways we deal with them and the kinds of solutions we can expect to achieve. In short, language matters" (Boland & Collopy, 2004, p. 37).

Third, this research contributes validated scales to research. The shared-vision construct combined two three-item constructs from research on shared vision and shared goals to accurately measure shared vision for collaborations. This study also operationalized a design attitude scale developed from literature and qualitative research. This study is the first to empirically test, quantitatively develop, and validate a design attitude scale for building better collaborations. Testing of this scale involved 452 ordinary leaders and managers (i.e., not professional designers or architects) involved in recently completed or established inter-organizational collaborations.

Finally, this research contributes to the development of evidence-based strategies for creating practitioner tools for improving collaboration performance. For example, facilitated sessions (e.g., Collaboration Boot Camp—detailed in Chapter 6) could be developed between collaborators focusing on cultivating a culture of autonomy, boundary spanning, and the creation of a common vision in conjunction with activities to bring about sensemaking (Weick, Sutcliffe, & Obstfeld, 2009) and perspective taking (Boland & Tenkasi, 1995). This work can change collaborators into designers and bricoleurs, change existing situations into preferred ones (Simon, 1996) with a design attitude, and in this way, co-create strategies and design and redesign relevant solutions given available resources and conditions for successful collaboration performance.

This chapter suggests that design attitude can serve as an additional predictor of collaboration performance providing insight for building better collaborations. Adopting design strategies is important for building successful collaborations. Design attitude is not a concept reserved for professional designers and architects but has a significant use for executives and managers. The findings may be useful to public, private, and nonprofit organizations when designing and managing effective collaborations as well as the development of evidence-based practitioner tools and strategies.

3.9.1 Limitations

There are several limitations to this study. First, I observed some minor distributional nonnormality in a few of the measures (as noted in the data-screening section). Second, a third party collected data. Third, although perceptual performance measurements can be highly indicative of actual performance (Dess & Robinson, 1984), and the collaboration checklist served as a secondary source for evaluating collaboration performance, challenges remain in the absence of actual information on performance. Fourth, there is the possible existence of other equivalent models as a limitation of SEM. Finally, although testing showed no common method bias, no statistical test can guarantee that such bias does not exist (Podsakoff et al., 2003).

The next chapter is the second quantitative study, which examines additional emergent factors and antecedents and provides further understanding of team interaction components.

Notes

1. A paper was developed from this chapter and presented at the Academy of Management's 2014 Annual Conference (Madden, 2014).
2. In the case of boundary spanning, the five-point scale denoted 1 = to a very small extent and 5 = to a very great extent.

References

Alexander, J. A., Comfort, M. E., & Weiner, B. J. (1998). Governance in public-private community health partnerships: A survey of the Community Care Network: SM demonstration sites. *Nonprofit Management & Leadership, 8*, 231–332.

Ancona, D. G., & Caldwell, D. F. (1988). Beyond task and maintenance defining external functions in groups. *Group & Organization Management, 13*(4), 468–494.

Ancona, D. G., & Caldwell, D. F. (1992). Bridging the boundary: External activity and performance in organizational teams. *Administrative Science Quarterly, 37*(4), 634–665.

Anderson, J. C., & Gerbing, D. W. (1988). Structural equation modeling in practice: A review and recommended two-step approach. *Psychological Bulletin, 103*(3), 411–423.

Ansell, C., & Gash, A. (2007). Collaborative governance in theory and practice. *Journal of Public Administration Research & Theory, 18*(4), 543–571.

Armistead, C., Pettigrew, P., & Aves, S. (2007). Exploring leadership in multi-sectoral partnerships. *Leadership, 3*(2), 211–230.

Avital, M. & Boland, R.J (2008). Managing as Designing with a Positive Lens in M. Avital, R.J. Boland, and D.L. Cooperrider (Eds), *Designing Information and Organizations with a Positive Lens, Advances in Appreciative Inquiry Series*, Volume 2, 3–14. Elsevier Science: Oxford.

Barling, J., Kelloway, E. K., & Iverson, R. D. (2003). High-quality work, job satisfaction, and occupational injuries. *Journal of Applied Psychology, 88*(2), 276–283.

Berger, W. (2009). *Glimmer: How design can transform your life, your business, and maybe even the world.* New York, NY: Random House.

Bevan, H., Robert, G., Bate, P., Maher, L., & Wells, J. (2007). Using a design approach to assist large-scale organizational change: "10 high impact changes" to improve the National Health Service in England. *Journal of Applied Behavioral Science, 43*(1), 135–152.

Boland, R. N., Jr., & Collopy, F. (2004). Toward a design vocabulary for management. In R. J. Boland & F. Collopy (Eds.), *Managing as designing* (pp. 265–276). Stanford, CA: Stanford University Press.

Boland, R. N., Jr., Collopy, F., Lyytinen, K., & Yoo, Y. (2008). Managing as designing: Lessons for organization leaders from the design practice of Frank O. Gehry. *Design Issues, 24*(1), 10–25.

Boland, R. N., Jr., & Tenkasi, R. (1995). Perspective making and perspective taking in communities of knowing. *Organization Science, 6*(4), 350–372.

Bolton, R. N. (1993). Pretesting questionnaires: Content analyses of respondents' concurrent verbal protocols. *Marketing Science, 12*(3), 280–303.

Borden, L. M., & Perkins, D. F. (1999). Assessing your collaboration: A self-evaluation tool. *Journal of Extension, 37*(2), 67–72.

Brinkerhoff, J. M. (2002). Assessing and improving partnership relationships and out-comes: A proposed framework. *Evaluation & Program Planning, 25*(3), 215–231.

Bryson, J., Crosby, B., & Stone, M. (2006). The design and implementation of cross-sector collaborations: Propositions from the literature. *Public Administration Review, 66*(Special Issue), 44–55.

Buchanan, R. (1992). Wicked problems in design thinking. *Design Issues, 8*(2), 5–21.

Buchanan, R. (2004). Management and design: Interaction pathways in organiza-tional life. In R. Boland & F. Collopy (Eds.), *Managing as designing* (pp. 54–63). Stanford, CA: Stanford University Press.

Caplan, R. (2005). *By design: Why there are no locks on the bathroom door in the Hotel Louis XIV, and other object lessons* (2nd ed.). New York, NY: Fairchild.

Chen, M. H., Chang, Y. C., & Hung, S. C. (2008). Social capital and creativity in R & D project teams. *R & D Management, 38*(1), 21–34.

Chung, A. (2004). *Bridging sectors: Partnerships between nonprofits and private developers.* Cambridge, MA: Joint Center for Housing Studies, Harvard Univer-sity, & NeighborWorks America.

Cola, P. A. (2015). *Helping Top Talent to Thrive: The Significance of Relational Capacity, Teamwork and Organizational Support* (Doctoral dissertation, Case Western Reserve University).

Cola, P. A., & Wang, Y. (2017). *Discovering factors influencing physician scien-tist success in academic medical centers* (Unpublished manuscript). Case Western Reserve University, Cleveland, OH.

Crosby, B. C., & Bryson, J. M. (2005). *Leadership for the common good: Tackling public problems in a shared-power world.* San Francisco, CA: Jossey-Bass.

Cross, R., & Cummings, J. N. (2004). Tie and network correlates of individual per-formance in knowledge-intensive work. *Academy of Management Journal, 47*(6), 928–937.

Deci, E. L., & Ryan, R. M. (1987). The support of autonomy and the control of behavior. *Journal of Personality & Social Psychology, 53*(6), 1024–1037.

Dess, G. G., & Robinson, R. B. (1984). Measuring organizational performance in the absence of objective measures: The case of the privately-held firm and conglomer-ate business units. *Strategic Management Journal, 5*(3), 265–273.

Diamond, M. (2009). Affordable housing and the conflict of competing goods: A policy dilemma. In N. M. Davidson & R. P. Malloy (Eds.), *Affordable housing and public-private partnerships* (pp. 1–10). Burlington, VT: Ashgate.

Dyer, J. H., & Singh, H. (1998). The relational view: Cooperative strategy and sources of interorganizational competitive advantage. *Academy of Management Review, 23*(4), 660–679.

Faraj, S., & Yan, A. (2009). Boundary work in knowledge teams. *Journal of Applied Psychology, 94*(3), 604–617.

Galbraith, J. (1977). *Organizational design.* Reading, MA: Addison-Wesley.

Galbraith, J. (2002). *Designing organizations: An executive guide to strategy, struc-ture, and process.* San Francisco, CA: Jossey-Bass.

Galbraith, J., Downey, D., & Kates, A. (2002). *Designing dynamic organizations: A hands-on guide for leaders at all levels.* New York, NY: Amacom Books.

Gajda, R. (2004). Utilizing collaboration theory to evaluate strategic alliances. *American Journal of Evaluation, 25*(1), 65–77.

Galster, G., Levy, D., Sawet, N., Temkin, K., & Walker, C. (2005). *The impact of community development corporations on urban neighborhoods.* Washington, DC: The Urban Institute.

Gaskin, J., & Berente, N. (2011). Video game design in the MBA curriculum: An experiential learning approach for teaching design thinking. *Communications of the Association for Information Systems, 29*(1), 103–121.

Gray, B. (1989). *Collaborating: Finding common ground for multiparty problems.* San Francisco, CA: Jossey-Bass.

Guo, C., & Acar, M. (2005). Understanding collaboration among nonprofit organizations: Combining resource dependency, institutional, and network perspectives. *Nonprofit & Voluntary Sector Quarterly, 34*(3), 340–361.

Hackman, J. R., & Oldham, G. R. (1975). Development of the job diagnostic survey. *Journal of Applied Psychology, 60*(2), 159–170.

Hair, J. F., Black, B. C., Babin, B. J., & Anderson, R. E. (2009). *Multivariate data analysis* (7th ed.). Upper Saddle River: Prentice Hall.

Hambrick, D. C., Geletkanycz, M. A., & Fredrickson, J. W. (1993). Top executive commitment to the status quo: Some tests of its determinants. *Strategic Management Journal, 14*(6), 401–418.

Hansen, M. T. (1999). The search-transfer problem: The role of weak ties in sharing knowledge across organization subunits. *Administrative Science Quarterly, 44*(1), 82–111.

Hinkin, T. R. (1998). A brief tutorial on the development of measures for use in survey questionnaires. *Organizational Research Methods, 1*(1), 104–121.

Hughes, M., & Morgan, R. E. (2007). Deconstructing the relationship between entrepreneurial orientation and business performance at the embryonic stage of firm growth. *Industrial Marketing Management, 36*(5), 651–661.

Huxham, C. (1996). *Creating collaborative advantage.* London, England: Sage.

Huxham, C. (2003). Theorizing collaboration practice. *Public Management Review, 5*(3), 401–423.

Inkpen, A. C., & Tsang, E. W. (2005). Social capital, networks, and knowledge transfer. *Academy of Management Review, 30*(1), 146–165.

Jarvis, C. B., MacKenzie, S. B., & Podsakoff, P. M. (2003). A critical review of construct indicators and measurement model misspecification in marketing and consumer research. *Journal of Consumer Research, 30*(2), 199–218.

Jelinek, M., Romme, A., & Boland, R. (2008). Introduction to the special issue: Organization Studies as a science for design: Creating collaborative artifacts and research. *Organization Studies, 29*(3), 317–329.

Joseph, M. L. (2008). Early resident experiences at a new mixed-income development in Chicago. *Journal of Urban Affairs, 30*(3), 229–257.

Kania, J., & Kramer, M. (2011). Collective impact. *Stanford Social Innovation Review*, (Winter 2011), 1(9), 36–41.

Kelley, D., & Van Patter, G. K. (2005). Design as glue. Understanding the Stanford D. School. *NextD Journal Conversation, 21*, 1–9.

Kelley, D., & G. VanPatter. (2005). *Design as glue: Understanding the Stanford school.* NextDesign Leadership Institute.

Kim, B., & Oh, H. (2005). The impact of decision-making sharing between supplier and manufacturer on their collaboration performance. *Supply Chain Management: An International Journal, 10*(3), 223–236.

Kim, J.-E. (2010). *Assessing the collaborations between government and nonprofit organizations for effective social service delivery* (Unpublished manuscript). Case Western Reserve University, Cleveland, OH.

Langfred, C. W. (2005). Autonomy and performance in teams: The multilevel moderating effect of task interdependence. *Journal of Management, 31*(4), 513–529.

Lévi-Strauss, C. (1966). *The savage mind* (John Weightman, trans.) Chicago, IL: University of Chicago Press.

Lui, S. S., & Ngo, H.-Y. (2004). The role of trust and contractual safeguards on cooperation in non-equity alliances. *Journal of Management, 30*(4), 471–485.

Madden, J. (2014, August). The ABCDs (autonomy, boundary spanning, common vision and design attitude) of successful collaboration. Paper presented at the Academy of Management 2014 Annual Conference, Philadelphia, PA

Manring, S. L., & Pearsall, S. (2004). Creating an adaptive ecosystem management network among stakeholders of the Lower Roanoke River, North Carolina, USA. *Ecology & Society, 10*(2), 16. Retrieved from www.ecologyandsociety.org/vol10/iss2/art16/

Martin, R. (2009). *The design of business: Why design is the next competitive advantage.* Boston, MA: Harvard Business School Press.

Michlewski, K. (2008). Uncovering design attitude: Inside the culture of designers. *Organization Studies, 29*(3), 373–392.

Morgan, R. M., & Hunt, S. D. (1994). The commitment-trust theory of relationship marketing. *Journal of Marketing, 58*(3), 20–38.

Ostrom, E. (1990). *Governing the commons: The evolution of institutions for collective action.* Cambridge, England: Cambridge University Press.

Pasquero, J. (1991). Supraorganizational collaboration: The Canadian environmental experiment. *Journal of Applied Behavioral Science, 27*(1), 38–64.

Peters, B. (1998). With a little help from our friends: Public-private partnerships as institutions and instruments. In J. Pierre (Eds.), *Partnerships in urban governance: European and American experience* (pp. 11–33). London, England: Macmillan.

Pinto, J. K., & Prescott, J. E. (1988). Variations in critical success factors over the stages in the project life cycle. *Journal of Management, 14*(1), 5–18.

Podsakoff, P. M., MacKenzie, S. B., Lee, J.-Y., & Podsakoff, N. P. (2003). Common method biases in behavioral research: A critical review of the literature and recommended remedies. *Journal of Applied Psychology, 88*(5), 879–903.

Rethemeyer, R. (2005). Conceptualizing and measuring collaborative networks. *Public Administration Review, 65*(1), 117–121.

Rickards, T., Chen, M. H., & Moger, S. (2001). Development of a self-report instrument for exploring team factor, leadership and performance relationships. *British Journal of Management, 12*(3), 243–250.

Rittel, H., & Webber, M. (1973). Dilemmas in a general theory of planning. *Policy Sciences, 4*(2), 155–169.

Romme, A. (2003). Making a difference: Organization as design. *Organization Science, 14*(5), 558–573.

Rosenau, P. V. (1999). Introduction: The strengths and weaknesses of public-private policy partnerships. *American Behavioral Scientist, 43*(1), 10–34.

Rousseau, D. M. (1977). Technological differences in job characteristics, employee satisfaction, and motivation: A synthesis of job design research and sociotechnical systems theory. *Organizational Behavior & Human Performance, 19*(1), 18–42.

Roussos, S. T., & Fawcett, S. B. (2000). A review of collaborative partnerships as a strategy for improving community health. *Annual Review of Public Health, 21*, 369–402.

Saxton, T. (1997). The effects of partner and relationship characteristics on alliance outcomes. *Academy of Management Journal, 40*(2), 443–461.

Selsky, J., & Parker, B. (2005). Cross-sector partnerships to address social issues: Challenges to theory and practice. *Journal of Management, 31*(6), 849–873.

Simon, H. (1996). *The sciences of the artificial*. Cambridge, MA: MIT Press.

Sutton, R. I., & Rousseau, D. M. (1979). Structure, technology, and dependence on a parent organization: Organizational and environmental correlates of individual responses. *Journal of Applied Psychology, 64*(6), 675–687.

Tett, L., Crowther, J., & O'Hara, P. (2003). Collaborative partnerships in community education. *Journal of Education Policy, 18*, 37–51.

Tsai, W., & Ghoshal, S. (1998). Social capital and value creation: The role of intrafirm networks. *Academy of Management Journal, 41*(4), 464–476.

Tuckman, B. W. (1965). Developmental sequence in small groups. *Psychological Bulletin, 63*(6), 384–399.

Tuckman, B. W., & Jensen, M. A. C. (1977). Stages of small-group development revisited. *Group & Organization Management, 2*(4), 419–427.

Turner, A. N., & Lawrence, P. R. (1965). *Industrial jobs and the worker*. Boston, MA: Harvard Business School Press.

Waddock, S. (1989). Understanding social partnerships: An evolutionary model of partnership organizations. *Administration & Society, 21*(1), 78–100.

Walter, U., & Petr, C. (2000). A template for family centered interagency collaboration. *Families in Society: The Journal of Contemporary Human Services 81*, 494–503.

Weick, K. (2004). Rethinking organizational design. In R. Boland & F. Collopy (Eds.), *Managing as designing* (pp. 36–53). Stanford, CA: Stanford Business Books.

Weick, K. E. (1993). Organizational redesign as improvisation. In G. P. Huber, & W. H. Glick, (Eds.), *Organizational Change and Redesign*, (pp. 346–379). New York, NY: Oxford University Press.

Weick, K., Sutcliffe, K., & Obstfeld, D. (2009). Organizing and the process of sensemaking. In P. C. Nutt & D. C. Wilson (Eds.), *Handbook of decision making*, (pp. 83–104). West Sussex, UK: John Wiley & Sons, Ltd.

Wondolleck, J. M., & Yaffee, S. L. (2000). *Making collaboration work: Lessons from innovation in natural resource management*. Washington, DC: Island Press.

Yang, L. R., Huang, C. F., & Wu, K. S. (2011). The association among project manager's leadership style, teamwork and project success. *International Journal of Project Management, 29*(3), 258–267.

Yoo, Y., Boland, R. J., Jr., & Lyytinen, K. (2006). From organization design to organization designing. *Organization Science, 17*(2), 215–229.

4 Mutually Beneficial Exploration as a Key Antecedent for Successful Collaboration

The previous chapter empirically validates the positive impact of autonomy, boundary spanning, common (or shared) vision and the mediating role of design attitude as a key to successful collaboration performance.

This chapter is a second quantitative study building from literature and the previous qualitative and quantitative research presented in this book. This chapter examines mutuality as a critical antecedent of successful collaboration performance and the importance of active listening in team interaction. This research uncovers the link between mutually beneficial exploration with the validated constructs from Chapter 3—boundary spanning, design attitude, shared vision and autonomy. While inter-organizational collaboration is an effective way to address complex social problems, the immensity of the collaboration literature often leaves practitioners disconnected from theory. These findings identify a starting point for successful collaboration, answering the critical question for practitioners of "Where do we start?" as well as guidance for designing and building better collaborations.

This chapter is structured very similarly to the previous chapter. First, key insight from team literature and mutuality are presented to support hypotheses development. Research methods are outlined, followed by the main findings, discussion, and implications for practice. Because this is the second quantitative study building from the same data as the previous chapter, protocols for hypotheses development, methodology, construct operationalization, data collection, screening, and analysis are the same or similar. For example, construct operationalization for autonomy, shared vision, boundary spanning, collaboration performance, and design attitude is outlined in Chapter 3 for the first quantitative study and is utilized again here for the second quantitative study in this chapter.

4.1 Insight From Research on Teamwork and Mutuality

In their study to develop an integrative theory of collaboration, Bedwell et al. (2012) outlines the foundation for a nomological network, beginning with an integration of the conceptualizations of collaboration grounded in a comprehensive definition. Bedwell et al. (2012), building on work by Marks,

Mathieu, and Zaccaro (2001) and Salas, Burke, and Cannon-Bowers (2000), suggests the construct most resembling "collaboration" is teamwork: "Both constructs are multidimensional and represent processes that involve two or more entities actively and reciprocally working towards achievement of a shared goal" (p. 135). Research and practice on inter-organizational collaboration demonstrates the significance of teamwork and its similarity to collaboration. Research on teams provides additional insight on collaboration.

Beyond the definitions of collaboration and teamwork, the research shows that teams are also critical to the collaborative process. For example, teamwork is required for collaborative work (Cappelli & Rogovsky, 1994) such that

- organizations complete work tasks via teamwork (Marks et al., 2001);
- organizations are more team-oriented than individual-oriented (Cohen & Bailey, 1997);
- teamwork skills are required for a range of new hires including MBAs (Dowd & Liedtka, 1994).

In addition, teamwork is required by procurement professionals (Chang & Bordia, 2001) and nonprofit managers (Waugh & Streib, 2006) because the team collaborative processes and collaboration outcomes are relied upon by managers (Bedwell et al., 2012). Also, like collaborations, teams are adaptive, dynamic, and complex systems (McGrath et al., 2000) with team performance theory tenets of "inputs," "processes," and "outcomes" (Kozlowski, Gully, Nason, & Smith, 1999), similar to the three areas in traditional collaboration theory: preconditions, process, and outcomes (Gray, 1985; Gray & Wood, 1991).

4.1.1 Experiential Learning & Team Learning

Building from developments in team literature and theory may address gaps in collaboration theory and practice. For example, there are four types of teams (parallel, work, project, and management; Cohen & Bailey, 1997; Edmondson, 1999). A key finding in the team literature from research on student project teams (Bowen, 1998) was frustration with team participation, a phenomena also identified in collaboration research (see Parker, 2000; Hamric & Blackhall, 2007) despite previous team-building exercises based upon communication (McIntyre & Salas, 1995). Like collaboration, the experience of teams can range from transformational to frustrating (Lingham, 2009). Research on teams shows that project teams cultivate teamwork skills through experiential learning (Kolb, 1984), an individual-level learning process involving the combination of two dimensions: grasping knowledge (i.e., knowing) and transforming knowledge (i.e., learning; Lingham, 2008). The two dimensions define where learning between the individual and the environment takes place (Kolb & Kolb 2012) to facilitate innovation (Gemmell, 2011), leadership (Robinson, 2005; Kayes, Kayes & Kolb, 2005), and strategy (Van der Heijden, 1996; Kolb, Lublin, Spoth, & Baker, 1986).

Experiential learning theory, using the concept of learning dimensions in conversational learning spaces, provides an empirically validated scale for team learning—the Team Learning Inventory (TLI; Lingham, 2004). Although responses are collected from individual members of teams, Lingham (2004) established Team Interaction as a group level construct. Validation is triangulated through:

(a) composition model characteristics (Schneider, Salvaggio, & Subirats, 2002),
(b) a Direct Consensus Model based upon appropriate compositional models outlined by Chan (1998) and given the within-group agreement in the appropriate range (James, Demaree, & Wolf, 1984, 1993), and
(c) intraclass correlations (ICCs) using the harmonic mean for analysis (Haggard, 1958) to achieve statistically significant values ($p < 0.000$) for each dimension of Team Interaction (Lingham, 2004, 2009).

The development of TLI and the Team Interaction group-level construct is critical for providing insights into building effective collaborations. Consider the robust theoretical framework grounding this research summarized by Lingham (2009, p. 7):

(a) it is developed from foundational team research (Lewin, 1951; Bales, 1949; 1979; Bion, 1959; Schutz, 1966);
(b) it includes work on group growth and development (Mills, 1967; Schein, 1993; Star, 1989; Engentrom & Middleton, 1996) and accepted trust (Rogers, 1970);
(c) it is developed from the established theory of Experiential Learning (Kolb, 1984), which also includes works from Dewey (1938, 1964), Lewin (1951), Piaget (1965), James (1977), Vygotsky (1978), and Friere (1992);
(d) it includes communities of practice to create or generate knowledge (Brown & Duguid, 1991; 2000; Nonaka, 1994; and Wenger, 1998); and
(e) the philosophical works of Habermas (1984), and Gadamer (1994).

Learning is described as "the process whereby knowledge is created through the transformation of experience" (Kolb, 1984, p. 38). The discipline of team learning focuses on dialogue where the meaning of complex issues is explored from multiple perspectives (Senge, 1990). Team learning builds upon team research, and the TLI provides a measurable and testable tool to better develop group dynamics and team interaction (Lingham, n.d.). In addition to team learning, this study proposes that mutuality is critical for collaboration.

4.1.2 *Mutuality*

Roschelle and Teasley (1995) define collaboration as the "mutual engagement of participants in a coordinated effort to solve a problem together" (cited in Dillenbourg, Baker, Blaye, & O'Malley, 1996, p. 2). Mutuality is an important function in successful collaboration (Brinkerhoff, 2002; Thomson, Perry, & Miller, 2009), and the concept is referred to throughout the collaboration literature. For example, mutuality, along with norms, governance, administration, and organizational autonomy are five key dimensions of collaboration studied by Thomson et al. (2009).[1] Ansell and Gash (2007 suggest that successful collaboration requires mutual recognition, whereas other scholars note that the realization of mutual benefits is important for reducing misunderstandings (Dwyer, Schurr, & Oh, 1987; Anderson and Narus, 1991; Mohr & Spekman, 1994), and that mutual dependency (Anderson & Weitz, 1992; Morgan & Hunt, 1994; Monckza, Peterson, Handfield, & Ragatz, 1998) and mutual commitment (Blankenburg, Eriksson, & Johanson, 1999) are key in strategic alliances. In partnerships, mutual respect is a key component (Brinkerhoff, 2002). Finally, in health care, mutual trust and respect is identified as one of seven essential elements for successful collaboration (Way, Jones, & Busing, 2000).

Mutuality or interdependence is also a key dimension of collaboration (Thomson, 2001). Mutuality is further characterized as a win-win solution that can present specifically as synergistic value creation (Lindgreen & Swaen, 2010) or, more generally, as complementarity (Powell, 1996; Nohria & Garcia-Pont, 1991) or shared interest (Lax & Sebenius, 1986). The idea of mutuality is supported in inter-organizational literature (Van de Ven, Emmett, & Koenig, 1975; Warren, Burgunder, Newton, & Rose, 1975; Levine & White, 1961), organizational behavior literature (Hellriegel, Slocum & Woodman, 1986, Gordon, 1993; Robbins, 1996); and collaboration literature (Gray, 1989; Pasquero, 1991; Wood & Gray, 1991; Bardach, 1998; Huxham & Vangen, 2000b; Selsky, 1991).

4.2 Additional Discovery from Qualitative Research

Semi-structured interviews were conducted with 31 leaders of inter-organizational collaborations concerned with affordable housing. Beyond the five findings reported in the qualitative study (Chapter 2), two additional discoveries are presented in this chapter. First the concept of exploring mutual benefit emerged from the lived experiences of leaders of successful collaborations, prompting the development and testing of a mutually beneficial exploration scale (see Table 4.1). Second, in addition to mutual benefit, innovative solutions that rejuvenated communities were actualized in all of the successful collaboration case studies. These solutions were far-ranging, building upon the local strengths and opportunities of the inter-organizational collaboration.

Table 4.1 Summary of Constructs from Chapter 3

Construct	Adapted/ Developed	Research	(For this research)	
			Number of Items	Cronbach's Alpha
Performance	Adapted	Lui and Ngo (2004); Saxton (1997)	4 items	0.87
Shared Vision	Adapted	Rickards, Chen, and Moger (2001); Chen, Chang, and Hung (2008)	6 items	0.90
Design Attitude	Developed	Gaskin and Berente (2011); Chapter 2	4 items	0.82
Autonomy	Adapted	Hughes and Morgan (2007)	3 items	0.78
Boundary Spanning	Adapted	Faraj and Yan (2009)	4 items	0.80

In my study, neighborhoods were rejuvenated through innovation and innovative ideas. Design scholars and design practitioners have noted design as central to innovation (Kimbell, 2011). This idea is applicable to all sectors and reinforces the empirical research presented in this book, suggesting design may be a critical success factor for inter-organizational collaboration. Although many private-sector firms, such as McDonalds, Apple, Steelcase, Research in Motion (the creators of the Blackberry), Proctor & Gamble, and Cirque du Soleil (Martin, 2009; Verganti, 2009) have benefited from design thinking and design-driven innovation, the concept has not penetrated to other sectors. While some design firms are making inroads (i.e., Luma Institute), the average nonprofit organization has limited access to and knowledge of design expertise, and collaborations between NGOs and design firms are neither affordable nor routine (Rockefeller Foundation, 2008). Brown and Wyatt (2010, p. 31) observed,

> [d]esigners have traditionally focused on enhancing the look and functionality of products. Recently, they have begun using design tools to tackle more complex problems, such as finding ways to provide low-cost healthcare throughout the world. Businesses were first to embrace this new approach—called design thinking—now nonprofits are beginning to adopt it too.

Outside the United States, IDEO, a design and innovation consulting firm, collaborated with an NGO working in Kenya, Tanzania, and Mali to develop new technologies that have created viable products for local entrepreneurs, generated jobs, and moved nearly a half million people out of poverty. Elsewhere, "One Laptop per Child," a collaboration between several design firms and the Massachusetts Institute of Technology (MIT) Media Lab, is improving education for children in developing countries (Rockefeller Foundation, 2008). Also, several workshops bringing NGO

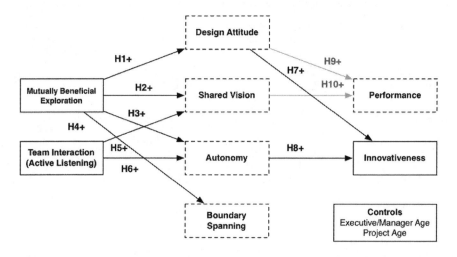

Figure 4.1 Research Model

decision-makers, foundation and corporate leaders, and social-design activists to "design summits" have been staged in the last several years to promote "human centered solutions to problems that challenge the quality of life" (American Institute of Graphic Arts [AIGA], 2009, p. 4). In the following section, the research model and hypotheses development provides greater insight and evidence towards advancing this research.

4.3 Research Model and Hypotheses Development

The research presented is informed by the previous qualitative (Chapter 2) and quantitative (Chapter 3) analysis that show autonomy, boundary spanning, shared vision, and design attitude positively affect collaboration performance. Building upon the idea of mutuality, and understanding the importance of active listening in team interaction (Lingham, 2004), this study examines mutually beneficial exploration and active listening as key antecedents to autonomy, boundary spanning, shared vision, and design attitude. This study also examines the impact of design attitude on innovation. The conceptualized research model is presented in Figure 4.1. The hashed boxes in Figure 4.1 represent constructs (i.e., design attitude, shared vision, autonomy, boundary spanning, and performance) previously defined in Chapter 3.

4.3.1 Mutually Beneficial Exploration

In strategic alliances, mutual dependency (Anderson & Weitz, 1992; Morgan & Hunt, 1994; Monckza et al., 1998) and mutual commitment (Blankenburg et al., 1999) are critical. The idea of exploring mutual benefit emerged from the lived experiences of leaders of successful inter-organizational collaborations in Chapter 2. Mutually beneficial exploration is defined as exploration of new possibilities (March, 1991) where an advantage is gained for all members of the collaboration (Madden, 2011). As outlined in the previous chapter, a design attitude encourages individuals to move beyond "default solutions" to engage in a decision-making process involving the collection and interpretation of evidence, designing possibilities, and testing multiple ideas—towards "creating new possibilities for the future" (Boland & Collopy, 2004, p. 4). One example of exploring mutual benefit impacting design attitude is illustrated when the "holding house" solution emerges from collaborative partners wanting to get the project completed and neighborhood residents—who are also key partners—not wanting to be displaced, "If we build a house and then individuals can move into that house while we work on their house. . . . Holding house, as they deemed it." I expect mutually beneficial exploration to positively and significantly affect design attitude.

Hypothesis 1 Mutually beneficial exploration strongly and positively affects design attitude.

Also from the qualitative interviews were examples of exploring mutual benefit impacting shared vision. When inter-organizational collaborations achieve shared vision through exploring mutual benefit, the shared vision can carry the collaboration through the inherent difficulties associated with collaboration. As the nonprofit partner stated, "there were definitely times when the project could have just crashed and burned and there was a lot of really tough negotiations to the point where people were really upset. But we did get through it . . . there really was that sort of drive from all parties to make it happen." I expect mutually beneficial exploration to positively and significantly affect shared vision.

Hypothesis 2 Mutually beneficial exploration positively affects shared vision.

According to Thomson (2001, p. 87), "collaboration, to be collaboration, must include partners who maintain their own distinct identities and organizational authority separate from (though simultaneously with) the collaborative effort." Thomson also suggests a tension between "self-interest" and "collective interest." This idea is connected with Liedtka, Haskins, Rosenblum, and Weber's (1997) discussion of the mutual development of individual and collective capabilities. When inter-organizational collaborations can explore mutual benefit, autonomy can be supported even when organizations have to work closely. One example of from the qualitative research outlines how. The more experienced nonprofit partner states:

Especially in terms of how we help mentor or help build the capacity for other organizations. So they approached us with the idea of working with them to help develop their capacity and do projects . . . So this was before we even had a site. So the plan was they would, if they were serious about developing the capacity, they would then hire a project manager, who would then meet with our director of real estate on a regular basis, typically weekly . . . our director of real estate would basically work with this person like he would any of our project managers in our organization . . . help mentor them, get them moving along.

I expect mutually beneficial exploration to positively and significantly affect autonomy.

Hypothesis 3 Mutually beneficial exploration positively affects autonomy.

I also expect mutually beneficial exploration to positively impact boundary spanning. One example from the qualitative research: "there was a need for groups of color to work together more closely . . . we started talking about possibly joining together to do a project . . . where all of those goals would be met."

Hypothesis 4 Mutually beneficial exploration positively affects boundary spanning.

4.3.2 Team Interaction (Active Listening)

The team interaction aspect of active listening emphasizes team members taking the time to listen and examine all sides of an issue prior to taking action. This aspect of team interaction highlights the importance of being aware of member perspectives and of reflection on the team perspective. Active listening demonstrates an appreciation and valuing of team members, which helps develop trust and bonding. Active listening also supports high levels of sensitivity and social integration for team members (Lingham, n.d.). I expect the active listening aspect of team interaction to positively affect shared vision. I also expect the active listening aspect of team interaction to positively affect autonomy.

Hypothesis 5 Team interaction (active listening) positively affects shared vision.
Hypothesis 6 Team interaction (active listening) positively affects autonomy.

4.3.3 Innovativeness

According to Garcia and Calantone (2002), innovativeness can create a paradigm shift and influence resources, skills, knowledge, capabilities, or strategy. Innovativeness articulates both the flexibility and the willingness to create knowledge and solutions (Liu & Phillips, 2011) and implies constant innovation (Wang & Ahmed, 2004). Further, as Kimbell (2011, p. 287) outlines, "since organizations are under pressure to maintain or grow market share, or if in the public sector, increase user satisfaction and effectiveness, then designers and their thinking have something important to offer."

In the qualitative research, there were several examples of innovativeness. One example from each of the ten successful inter-organizational collaborations studied illustrates innovativeness and neighborhood rejuvenation:

- the holding house to make it possible for local families not to be displaced during their housing renovation process,
- a community benefits agreement developed to secure neighborhood residents an economic benefit from neighborhood revitalizations,
- a land swap to facilitate the development of affordable-housing units in an area where available land and property are difficult to find,
- dynamic compaction used for soil remediation to ensure project completion and reduced project costs,
- a green roof on an affordable housing development to realize sustainability, energy savings, and stormwater management and contribute to improved health through pollution reduction,
- a grid system to coordinate critical disaster relief services,
- a lawsuit against the local municipality to guarantee housing for chronic inebriates,
- an externship program to complement housing and provide critical skills for persons aging out of foster care,
- a training program for residents to incubate business skills and develop pathways into the construction trades, and
- a social service exchange program to leverage needed services for residents.

Entrepreneurial teams are assets for innovativeness (Carpenter, 2002). I expect design attitude and autonomy to positively affect innovativeness.

Hypothesis 7 Design attitude positively affects innovativeness.
Hypothesis 8 Autonomy positively affects innovativeness.

4.3.4 Performance

Building from the results from Chapter 3, I again expect design attitude and shared vision to positively affect performance.

Hypothesis 9 Design attitude positively affects performance.
Hypothesis 10 Shared vision positively affects performance.

4.4 Methodology

To test the proposed hypotheses, I collected data using an online survey targeting an executive and management level population with recent participation in an established or recently completed project in collaboration with another organization. Specifics regarding the sample are provided (see Table 4.3). Scale items for the autonomy, shared vision, boundary spanning, collaboration performance, design attitude, innovativeness, and the active listening attribute of team interaction were adapted from existing literature (see sections below for details). Data analysis employed IBM SPSS Statistics (version 21) for basic statistical analysis and IBM SPSS AMOS (version 21) for covariance-based structural equation model analysis. Analyses were completed in the following stages: confirmation of suitability of the data for multivariate analysis, a two-step structural equation modeling (SEM) strategy (Anderson & Gerbing, 1988) utilizing exploratory factor analysis (EFA), and confirmatory factor analysis (CFA) to build the SEM.

4.5 Construct Operationalization

Scale items for autonomy, shared vision, boundary spanning, collaboration performance, design attitude, innovativeness, and the active listening attribute of team interaction were adapted from literature based upon their theoretical relevance and reliability. The mutually beneficial exploration construct had not been empirically tested, but scale development was based upon the qualitative analysis in this research. All constructs were measured on a five-point Likert scale (1 = strongly disagree; 5 = strongly agree). The constructs used from Chapter 3 are summarized in Table 4.1 below. A full table of constructs (including survey items) is provided in Appendix C. The specifications for all scales were reflective (Jarvis, Mackenzie, & Podsakoff, 2003).

4.5.1 Innovativeness

In the choice of items for innovativeness, a three-item scale was adapted from Hughes and Morgan (2007). According to the authors, "[i]nnovativeness captures a bias toward embracing and supporting creativity and experimentation, technological leadership, novelty, and R&D in the development of products, services, and processes" (p. 652). As a dependent variable, items were kept as is to maintain the integrity of the construct based upon the research conducted. Cronbach's alpha for the three-item construct was 0.83.

4.5.2 Team Interaction (Active Listening)

In the choice of items, a three-item scale was adopted from the Team Learning and Development Inventory (TLI) active listening attribute (Lingham, 2004). According to the author, TLI measures "real" (i.e., experienced) and "ideal" (i.e., would like to experience) conversational spaces in teams. Capturing this information provides a "common language but also increase knowledge of the team experience and skills to deal with what is important (and unique) for the team" promoting "team-directed learning" (p. 3). Cronbach's alpha for the three-item construct was 0.79.

4.5.3 *Mutually Beneficial Exploration*

Based upon the interviews described in Chapter 2 and a review of the collaboration literature, a mutually beneficial exploration scale was developed in this study. The scale items and examples of supporting quotes from the interviews are presented in the following section. The three items included: "This collaboration explored possibilities beneficial for all members," "This collaboration was successful through partnerships," and "This collaboration strategy was very successful." Cronbach's alpha for the three-item construct was 0.78.

Scales were developed from supporting quotes. Examples of supporting quotes of the three scale items are provided.

This Collaboration Explored Possibilities Beneficial for All Members

We also committed that if we make money on these deals we're going to give back to the community and we did make money and we put a $50,000 scholarship fund that is controlled by the . . . youth council to promote education in the neighborhoods.

They let us explain why this was important. We went and we took some folks from the city and we pitched our case and the state finance agency ended up funding both deals . . . because the real magic is getting some critical mass and visible impact and we were able to sway them over to our way of thinking and the state finance agency has actually adopted . . . neighborhood revitalization and impact as a competitive criteria for getting rounds of tax credits, which we think makes a lot of sense.

No, we had some ideas and it turns out some of our ideas were right but some of them—some of the ideas that we found down the road were better than the ones we had so really it was a mixture of some of our quote conventional wisdom with an infusion of some new ideas.

They have an annual picnic that they'll invite us to and we'll show up. They've done community events, like they've had a tofu fest. We have the Central Avenue Jazz Fest. Staff from both sides go and support each other's event. So we thought of non-formal ways to pull people together.

We had a property that we developed about 20 years ago . . . which was 24 older, rental apartment units located in close proximity to the . . . Metro Corridor . . . and it is one of the most desirable locations to live in the Metropolitan area because of the proximity of transportation . . . we wanted to tear down the buildings and build a high-rise development. We then got into an extensive negotiation, collaboration with . . . a major developer in this area . . . who was redeveloping a larger parcel of land near us—adjacent to us, where they wanted to build several high-rise office complexes and also build some town-houses. Our property was set back . . . from the Metro where theirs was a little closer. In this collaboration and negotiation . . . [we developed] a solution that was better . . . we would swap our land, trade it, for a parcel . . . [they] owned closer to the Metro so that we could do our high-rise building. And they would then build their townhouses on our older parcel . . . So that the highest density would be closest to the Metro and the lowest density would be furthest from the Metro and closer to the residential neighborhoods . . . County is investing a significant amount of their resources in the project . . . the for-profit developer, in return for higher density for their office building is investing some funds into our affordable-housing project . . . So that it's a win-win for all involved.

This Collaboration Was Successful Through Partnerships

And then also, when it comes down to external relationships, we all share in that. And we all—each group brings something different to the table on that level. . . . One way was to go back to the city to ask them to help fill that gap. But the way you would do it is work through your local city council person and all the different agencies. So we got together. We identified what the problem was. It was this gap. What are some possible solutions? We identified what those were, what the parts we would be hitting up. And then collectively we said, "Okay, well, how should we approach it?" And rather than say, "Who has the best relation with the city council person?" in this example, we both did. So we both opted to go together to meet with her and lay out the situation and the problem, and then make them ask jointly.

But the real benefit that [the partner] provided were all the existing relationships. . . . [The partner] had really established a lot of community relationships with the local aldermen, with some of the local not-for-profit service providers, local schools . . . [the partner] was really engaged in the neighborhood immediately surrounding these projects, and . . . had some very good political contacts with the people at the city and decision makers in the government, both locally and in the state level.

we filled our first project in 2007. And since 2007, we now have four projects that we're jointly working on together. It is a model partnership. You tend to want all of your partnerships to be that way

Well, it was more of a mentoring scenario because they've never done a project before. So I would be assisting them in putting all the financing, selling the equity, assisting in the design of the project. And they were hopefully kind of learning from what we're doing there as well.

This Collaboration Strategy Was Very Successful

We have brought some additional institutional money into the neighborhood. . . . we want to make an impact in not only just the housing stock, but in the community.

We've had 3500 people apply for this 97 units . . . a lot of the vision of the project was really realized . . . we're very proud of it . . . was an incredible accomplishment.

You look at it as more than just a real estate project. There's a variety of different things that you need to accomplish when you do this, like job creation, long-term viability of the project. If you're doing a project that you may not be involved with for 5 years or 15 years it's much different. So you want to make sure that the project would last. You want to make sure that you don't have any issues with not having people that live in the area work on the project. So all that kind of stuff is much different than just getting the lowest bid or doing a project that would not have other spinoff benefits.

And so we just proposed it and had a clear-cut strategy on being able to execute, and they supported it.

We were able to redesign a lot of these little homes to make them very functional and take them and make them better than they were.

4.5.4 Controls & Instrument Pretesting

The same controls from Chapter 3 (section 3.5.7) were utilized and include the age of the respondent and the age of the project. Again, controlling for the age of respondent and the age of the project serves as a proxy for experience that may be related to better collaboration performance (Yang, Huang, & Wu, 2011).

The protocol for instrument pretesting is detailed in Chapter 3 (section 3.5.8) and include "think-aloud/talk-aloud" exercises (Bolton, 1993) with practitioners resulting in survey adjustments until content and face validity were achieved. Preliminary online testing resulted in additional wordsmithing, and qualifier questions were added. Finally, the survey was pilot tested with 50 different respondents prior to a full launch of the survey with a review of outliers, item distributions, and preliminary EFA.

4.6 Data Collection

Data was collected via an online survey using Qualtrics. As outlined in Chapter 3 (section 3.6), two methods of survey delivery were utilized. In the first method, I leveraged both my personal contacts and social network, and the balance of responses came from a screened professional research panel provided by Qualtrics.

4.6.1 *Characteristics of Respondents*

A total of 452 qualified respondents (i.e., people who had participated in an established or recently completed project involving a collaboration with another organization and held an appropriate management category position) contributed to the data analysis. Table 4.2 summarizes the demographics of the sample.

Table 4.2 Sample Characteristics

	Number	*Percentage*
Gender		
Males	261	58%
Females	191	42%
Management Category		
Executive	139	31%
Senior Vice President/VP	48	11%
Director	88	19%
Officer	11	2%
Manager	125	28%
Coordinator	25	6%
Academic Faculty	16	4%
Successful Collaboration		
Yes	436	96%
No	16	4%
Collaboration Checklist		
0–20: Number of Challenges	0	0%
21–40: Strength and Progress	35	8%
41–60: Poised for Growth	417	92%
Sector		
Nonprofit	73	16%
Private/For-Profit	333	74%
Government	46	10%
Age		
30 or younger	40	9%
31–40	111	25%
41–50	137	30%
51–60	112	25%
61 or older	52	12%
Project Age		
Less than 3 months	60	13%
4–12 months	183	40%
13 months to 2 years	115	25%
25 months to 5 years	59	13%
More than 5 years	35	8%

4.7 Data Screening

Incomplete survey responses were not included, resulting in no missing data in the survey. A box plot was examined for outliers. There were a few responses with exceptionally high values, but no theoretical basis for removing them, and no reason to believe them incorrect, so they were not deleted. I tested all of the variables for kurtosis. Four of the six shared vision (SV) items have kurtosis issues with SV1, SV3 and SV4 greater than 3. Also three of the five performance (PERF) items have kurtosis issues, but all less than 3. Curve estimation regressions were completed for all direct effects in the model. Relationships were sufficiently linear. The Variable Inflation Factors (VIFs) were also less than 2.0 for all relationships, which suggests no multicollinearity issues for the model.

4.8 Data Analysis

A two-step approach (Anderson & Gerbing, 1988) was completed for this cross-sectional data. The KMO and Bartlett's test were completed to ensure sample adequacy. The tests were significant and communalities for each of the variables were greater than 0.3, which further supported adequate correlation for factor analysis. Further confirmation of the model was supported by the reproduced correlations matrix with 6% nonredundant residuals greater than 0.05. Beyond the conceptual definition of the unidimensional scale, reliability—the consistency between multiple variable measurements—was established with a Cronbach's alpha greater than the lower limit of acceptability (0.70).

4.8.1 Exploratory Factor Analysis

I used SPSS for the EFA with Principal Axis Factoring, and Promax rotation with Kaiser Normalization was completed with the mutually beneficial exploration and the active listening attribute of team interaction. The factor loading for two mutually beneficial exploration items (MBE1 and MBE2) were eliminated, as well as additional items based upon validity issues. The KMO and Bartlett's test were completed to ensure sample adequacy. The tests were significant and communalities for each of the variables were greater than 0.30, which further supported adequate correlation for factor analysis. Beyond the conceptual definition of the unidimensional scale, reliability was established with a Cronbach's alpha greater than the lower limit of acceptability (0.70).

From the EFA, Cronbach's alpha greater than 0.70 were reported for shared vision (six-items, alpha = 0.90), design attitude (four-items, alpha = 0.82), boundary spanning (five-items, alpha = 0.80), autonomy (three-items, alpha = 0.78), team interaction (active listening; three-items, alpha = 0.79), mutually beneficial exploration (three-items, alpha = 0.78), performance (five-items, alpha = 0.87), and innovativeness (three-items, alpha = 0.83). Sufficient convergent validity was achieved because factor loadings were

Table 4.3 Descriptive Statistics, Reliability, Correlations and Discriminant Validity

Construct	No. of items	AVE	CR	Construct							
				1.	2.	3.	4.	5.	6.	7.	8.
1. Autonomy	3	0.54	0.78	**0.78**	0.14	0.31	0.12	0.09	0.03	0.01	0.00
2. Shared Vision	6	0.58	0.89	0.38	**0.90**	0.34	0.30	0.16	0.12	0.03	0.07
3. Boundary Spanning	5	0.51	0.81	0.56	0.58	**0.80**	0.40	0.34	0.18	0.27	0.05
4. Design Attitude	4	0.53	0.82	0.61	0.55	0.63	**0.82**	0.42	0.52	0.24	0.19
5. Team Interaction	3	0.55	0.79	0.70	0.63	0.58	0.65	**0.79**	0.49	0.44	0.62
6. Mutually Beneficial Exploration	3	0.55	0.79	0.61	0.59	0.56	0.72	0.70	**0.78**	0.79	0.59
7. Performance	5	0.58	0.87	0.57	0.63	0.56	0.74	0.66	0.89	**0.87**	0.53
8. Innovativeness	3	0.63	0.83	0.69	0.52	0.57	0.83	0.69	0.77	0.73	**0.83**

AVE=average variance extracted; CR=composite reliability; Cronbach's alpha reported on the diagonal; values above the diagonal are squared correlations.

above the minimum threshold of 0.35 for a sample size of 452 (Hair, Black, Babin & Anderson, 2009).

After consulting the modification indices, three error terms were covaried, which resulted in a good fitting measurement model (χ^2= 766.71, df = 401; GFI = 0.90; CFI = 0.95; RMSEA = 0.05 and PCLOSE = 0.96). The EFA solutions were then analyzed in a CFA model.

4.8.2 Confirmatory Factor Analysis

The final test for construct validity reported average variance extracted (AVE) above 0.50 for all factors. The factors demonstrated convergent validity with diagonal values greater than the correlations. Composite reliability (CR) was also achieved with values above the 0.70 minimum threshold (see Table 4.3). The measurement model was tested for invariance across management category with no significant differences between managers and leaders, therefore the measurement model meets the criteria for metric invariance across management category.

4.8.3 Common Method Bias

Data collection for both the independent and antecedent variables was completed using a single survey instrument. A test for common method bias (CMB) was conducted to determine common method bias affecting the measurement model (Podsakoff, MacKenzie, Lee, & Podsakoff, 2003). A common latent factor (CLF) was introduced to the model. A comparison of the standardized regression weights with and without the CLF showed items with a difference in Betas greater than 0.20 suggesting common method bias, therefore the CLF was retained in the model to account for the influence of the common method bias.

4.9 Findings

Mutually beneficial exploration was predicted to have a positive impact on design attitude (H1), shared vision (H2), autonomy (H3), and boundary spanning (H4). These hypotheses were supported with standardized estimates (beta= β) and p-values for design attitude (β = 0.65***), shared vision (β = 0.35***), autonomy (β = 0.34**), and boundary spanning (β = 0.73***). The active listening attribute of team interaction was also predicted to have a positive impact on shared vision (H5) and autonomy (H6). These hypotheses were supported with standardized estimates (beta = β) and p-values for shared vision (β = 0.2*) and autonomy (β = 0.32***). Both design attitude (H7) and autonomy (H8) were predicted to have a positive impact on innovativeness. These hypotheses were supported with standardized estimates (beta = β) and p-values for design attitude (β = 0.55***) and autonomy (β = 0.29***). Design attitude (H9) and shared vision (H10) were also predicted to have a positive impact on performance. These hypotheses were also supported for design attitude (β = 0.28*) and shared vision (β = 0.25***). None of the control variable paths were significant. Results and R^2 values of the endogenous variables are presented, along with results for the tested hypotheses, in Table 4.4.

4.10 Discussion and Implications for Practice

This study sought to identify key antecedents or preconditions that would affect previously validated factors having a positive and significant impact on successful collaboration performance. This research posited that mutually beneficial exploration would positively affect shared vision, design attitude, autonomy, boundary spanning, and that the active listening attribute of team interaction would positively affect shared vision and autonomy. The results revealed mutually beneficial exploration has a strong and significant impact on all of the factors, and the active listening attribute of team interaction has a positive impact on shared vision and autonomy. These findings are important because mutually beneficial exploration and active listening can serve as starting points for a successful collaboration.

The survey results for mutually beneficial exploration are consistent with the literature on corporate social performance, building upon components of win-win paradigms (Husted & de Jesus Salazar, 2006; Dentchev, 2004; Margolis & Walsh, 2003; Orlitzky, Schmidt, & Rynes, 2003; Burke & Logsdon, 1996), enlightened value maximization, and enlightened stakeholder theory (Jensen, 2010). Win-win paradigms are synergistic where there is mutual benefit for everyone involved (Lindgreen & Swaen, 2010; Eylon, 1998; Follett, 1918). However, there are limitations to win-win paradigms.

Table 4.4 Structural Model Results

	Hypothesized Path	Regression Estimate	Standardized Estimate	Hypothesis Supported?
H1	Mutually Beneficial Exploration → Design Attitude	1.07	0.65***	Yes
H2	Mutually Beneficial Exploration → Shared Vision	0.60	0.35***	Yes
H3	Mutually Beneficial Exploration → Autonomy	0.64	0.34**	Yes
H4	Mutually Beneficial Exploration → Boundary Spanning	1.97	0.73***	Yes
H5	Team Interaction → Shared Vision	0.15	0.18*	Yes
H6	Team Interaction → Autonomy	0.29	0.32***	Yes
H7	Design Attitude → Innovativeness	0.51	0.55***	Yes
H8	Autonomy → Innovativeness	0.23	0.29***	Yes
H9	Design Attitude → Performance	0.28	0.28*	Yes
H10	Shared Vision → Performance	0.24	0.25***	Yes

Squared Multiple Correlations

R^2 Design Attitude	0.42	R^2 Boundary Spanning	0.54
R^2 Shared Vision	0.22	R^2 Innovativeness	0.49
R^2 Autonomy	0.33	R^2 Performance	0.19

Goodness-of-fit statistics:
$\chi^2 = 766.71$, df = 401; GFI = 0.90; CFI = 0.95; RMSEA = 0.05 and PCLOSE = 0.96

* $p < 0.05$; ** $p < 0.01$; *** $p < 0.001$.

Hahn, Figge, Pinkse, and Preuss (2010, p. 219) illustrate two fundamental limitations for corporate sustainability. First, they suggest that "by following the win—win paradigm, scholars and practitioners do not take account of all potentially positive corporate contributions to sustainable development but restrict themselves—even if unconsciously—to win—win solutions." The second limitation is the limited analysis of various strategies and initiatives in favor of performing an evaluation through only a profit maximization lens. There is also great skepticism in win-win paradigms: some scholars view everyone winning as, "a rhetorical tool for placating local concerns in order to advance a single privileged agenda, while leaving certain populations by the wayside" (Simon, Bumpus, & Mann, 2012, p. 276).

Stakeholder theory also provides a critical theoretical foundation for corporate social performance research (Clarkson, 1995; Margolis & Walsh, 2003; Van der Laan, van Ees, & van Witteloostuijn, 2008). According to stakeholder theory,

> managers should make decisions that take account of
> the interests of all the stakeholders in a firm.
> Stakeholders include all individuals or groups who can
> substantially affect, or be affected by, the welfare of
> the firm—a category that includes not only the
> financial claimholders, but also employees, customers,
> communities, and government officials
> (Jensen, 2010, p. 32).

Adapting stakeholder theory, enlightened value maximization, and enlightened stakeholder theory hold greater insight for mutually beneficial exploration. Enlightened value maximization and enlightened stakeholder theory promote long-term value over short-term wins and motivation by vision and strategy (Jensen, 2010). Mutually beneficial exploration examines beneficial possibilities for all involved parties as well as success through partnerships and strategy.

The team interaction attribute of active listening is also critical because practitioners and scholars suggest that active listening is an important strategy for building group development (Rogers & Farson, 1957) and collaboration (Nugent & Halvorson, 1995). This is true across disciplines: active listening is identified as a key skill in initial interactions and is supported by researchers in nursing (Bryant, 2009), education (McNaughton, Hamlin, McCarthy, Head-Reeves, & Schreiner, 2007), social work (Rogers & Welch, 2009; Nugent & Halvorson, 1995), and leadership (Hoppe, 2007).

The study's findings show mutually beneficial exploration to be a significant positive antecedent to previously validated constructs (i.e., design attitude, shared vision, autonomy, and boundary spanning) that lead to successful collaboration performance and rejuvenative collaboration. These findings provide additional guidance for designing and building better collaborations and contribute to research on inter-organizational collaborations. The identification of key antecedents can serve as a starting point for a successful collaboration by answering the critical question for practitioners: "Where do we start?"

Collaborating is an effective way of addressing complex social problems, but the immensity of the collaboration literature can leave practitioners wondering if the focus should be on:

- preconditions, process, outcomes (Gray & Wood, 1991),
- structure (Huxham, 2003),
- design (Bryson, Crosby, & Stone, 2006),
- governance (Ansell & Gash, 2007),
- accountability (Tschirhart, Christensen, & Perry, 2005),
- leadership (Chrislip & Larson, 1994),
- power (Vangen & Huxham, 2003b),
- power imbalance (Berger, Cunningham, & Drumwright, 2004),
- networks (Agranoff, 2006),
- trust (Das & Teng, 2001),
- measurement and evaluation (Thomson et al., 2009) or
- sustainability (Kumar & van Dissel, 1996).

This research contributes to the development of an evidence-based starting point for designing and building better collaborations, particularly ones that are rejuvenative in nature. For example, collaborators in a facilitated session (e.g., Collaboration Boot Camp—detailed in Chapter 6) would explore mutual benefit as a first step for successful collaboration. In addition to mutually beneficial exploration, the work would build from the active listening process, which involves restating the ideas and position of the speaker to their satisfaction (Garland, 1981); maintaining high levels of nonverbal involvement with the speaker (also known as "back channeling"; McNaughton et al., 2007), and asking questions when appropriate (Weger, Castle Bell, Minei, & Robinson, 2014) in order to elaborate the speaker's beliefs (Paukert, Stanger, & Hope, 2004).

These findings may be useful for public, private, and nonprofit organizations interested in designing and building effective inter-organizational engagement and for practitioners seeking evidence-based practitioner tools and strategies for enabling effective rejuvenative collaboration.

4.10.1 Limitations

There are several limitations to this study. First, the data was collected from voluntary participants involved in an established or recently completed inter-organizational collaborations. Second, the qualitative data sample was heavily concentrated in the Midwest. Third, respondents were required to recount past experiences, which created the potential for recall bias. Fourth, this study relied upon a single method of obtaining self-reported data. In addition, a third party collected the quantitative data. To account for the common method bias, a common latent factor was retained in the analysis. Fifth, the study's generalizability may be limited and should be validated in other contexts. Finally, the data was not collected from members of intact teams.

Note

1. Thomson's 13-item mutuality scale assumes levels of mutuality based upon certain indicators (e.g., combining resources, sharing information, respect, goal attainment, win-win solutions) whereas my use of mutually beneficial exploration is based on the lived experiences of top leaders in relation to inter-organizational and cross-sector collaborations.

References

Agranoff, R. (2006). Inside collaborative networks: Ten lessons for public managers. *Public Administration Review, 66*(Special Issue), 56–65.

American Institute of Graphic Arts (AIGA). (2009). *Aspen design summit.* Aspen Meadows, CO: AIGA, the Professional Association for Design.

Anderson, E., & Weitz, B. A. (1992). The use of pledges to build and sustain commitment in distribution channels. *Journal of Marketing Research, 29,* 18–34.

Anderson, J. C., & Gerbing, D. W. (1988). Structural equation modeling in practice: A review and recommended two-step approach. *Psychological Bulletin, 103*(3), 411–423.

Anderson, J. C., & Narus, J. A. (1991). Partnering as a focused market strategy. *California Management Review, 33*(3), 96–97.

Ansell, C., & Gash, A. (2007). Collaborative governance in theory and practice. *Journal of Public Administration Research & Theory, 18*(4), 543–571.

Bales, R. F. (1949). *Interaction process analysis: A method for the study of small groups.* Cambridge, MA: Addison-Wesley.

Bardach, E. (1998). *Getting agencies to work together: The practice and theory of managerial craftsmanship.* Washington, DC: Brookings Institution Press.

Bedwell, W. L., Wildman, J. L., DiazGranados, D., Salazar, M., Kramer, W. S., & Salas, E. (2012). Collaboration at work: An integrative multilevel conceptualization. *Human Resource Management Review, 22*(2), 128–145.

Berger, I., Cunningham, P., & Drumwright, M. (2004). Social alliances. *California Management Review, 47*(1), 58–90.

Bion, W. R. (1959). *Experiences on groups and other papers.* New York, NY: Basic Books.

Blankenburg Holm, B., Eriksson, K., & Johanson, J. (1999). Creating value through mutual commitment to business network relationships. *Strategic Management Journal, 20*(5), 467–486.

Boland, R., Jr., & Collopy, F. (2004). Toward a design vocabulary for management. In R. J. Boland & F. Collopy (Eds.), *Managing as designing* (pp. 265–276). Stanford, CA: Stanford University Press.

Bolton, R. N. (1993). Pretesting questionnaires: Content analyses of respondents' concurrent verbal protocols. *Marketing Science, 12*(3), 280–303.

Bowen, D. D. (1998). Team frames: The multiple realities of the team. *Journal of Management Education, 22*(1), 95–103.

Brinkerhoff, J. M. (2002). Assessing and improving partnership relationships and outcomes: A proposed framework. *Evaluation & Program Planning, 25*(3), 215–231.

Brown, T., & Wyatt, J. (2010). Design thinking for social innovation. *Stanford Social Innovation Review, 8*(1), 31–35.

Brown, J. S., & Duguid, P. (1991). Organizational learning and communities-of-practice: Toward a unified view of working, learning and innovation. *Organization Science, 2*(1), 40-57.

Brown, J. S., & Duguid, P. (2000). *The social life of organization*. Boston, MA: Harvard Business School Press.

Bryant, L. (2009). The art of active listening. *Practice Nurse, 37*(6), 49–52.

Bryson, J., Crosby, B., & Stone, M. (2006). The design and implementation of cross-sector collaborations: Propositions from the literature. *Public Administration Review, 66*(Special Issue), 44–55.

Burke, L., & Logsdon, J. M. (1996). How corporate social responsibility pays off. *Long Range Planning, 29*(4), 495–502.

Cappelli, P., & Rogovsky, N. (1994). New work systems and skill requirements. *International Labour Review, 133*(2), 205–220.

Carpenter, M. A. (2002). The implications of strategy and social context for the relationship between top management team heterogeneity and firm performance. *Strategic Management Journal, 23*(3), 275–284.

Chan, D. (1998). Functional relations among constructs in the same content domain at different levels of analysis: A typology of composition models. *Journal of Applied Psychology, 83*(2), 234–246.

Chang, A., & Bordia, P. (2001). A multidimensional approach to the group cohesion-group performance relationship. *Small Group Research, 32*(4), 379–405.

Chen, M. H., Chang, Y. C., & Hung, S. C. (2008). Social capital and creativity in R & D project teams. *R & D Management, 38*(1), 21-34.

Chrislip, D. D., & Larson, C. E. (1994). *Collaborative leadership*. San Francisco, CA: Jossey-Bass.

Clarkson, M. B. (1995). A stakeholder framework for analyzing and evaluating corporate social performance. *Academy of Management Review, 20*, 92–117.

Cohen, S. G., & Bailey, D. E. (1997). What makes teams work: Group effectiveness research from the shop floor to the executive suite. *Journal of Management, 23*(3), 239–290.

Das, T. K., & Teng, B. S. (2001). Trust, control, and risk in strategic alliances: An integrated framework. *Organization Studies, 22*(2), 251–283.

Dentchev, N. A. (2004). Corporate social performance as a business strategy. *Journal of Business Ethics, 55*(4), 397–412.

Dewey, J. (1938). *Experience and education*. New York, NY: Macmillan.

Dewey, J. (1964). The nature of method. In R. Archambault (Ed.), *John Dewey on education* (pp. 387–403). Chicago: University of Chicago Press. (Original work published 1916)

Dillenbourg, P., Baker, M., Blaye, A., & O'Malley, C. (1996). The evolution of research on collaborative learning. In E. Spada & P. Reiman (Eds.), *Learning in humans and machine: Towards an interdisciplinary learning science* (pp. 189–211). Oxford, England: Elsevier.

Dowd, K. O., & Liedtka, J. (1994). What corporations seek in MBA hires: A survey. *Magazine of the Graduation Management Admission Council, 10*(2), 34–39.

Dwyer, F. R., Schurr, P. H., & Oh, S. (1987). Developing buyer-seller relationships. *Journal of Marketing, 51*, 11–27.

Edmondson, A. (1999). Psychological safety and learning behavior in work teams. *Administrative Science Quarterly, 44*(2), 350–383.

Engentrom, Y., & Middleton, D. (1996). *Cognition and communication at work.* Cambridge, England: Cambridge University Press.

Eylon, D. (1998). Understanding empowerment and resolving its paradox: Lessons from Mary Parker Follett. *Journal of Management History, 4*(1), 16–28.

Friere, P. (1992). *Pedagogy of the oppressed.* New York, NY: Continuum.

Follett, M. P. (1918). *The new state: Group organization the solution of popular government.* University Park, PA: Penn State Press.

Gadamer, H. G. (1994). *Truth and method* (2nd rev. ed.). New York, NY: Crossroad.

Garcia, R., & Calantone, R. (2002). A critical look at technological innovation typology and innovativeness terminology: A literature review. *Journal of Product Innovation Management, 19*, 110–132.

Garland, D. R. (1981). Training married couples in listening skills: Effects on behavior, perceptual accuracy, and marital adjustment. *Family Relations, 30*, 297–307.

Gaskin, J., & N. Berente (2011). Video game design in the MBA curriculum: An experiential learning approach for teaching design thinking. *Communications of the Association for Information Systems, 29*(1), 103–121.

Gemmell, R. M. (2011). *Entrepreneurial innovation as a learning system* (Unpublished manuscript). Case Western Reserve University, Cleveland, OH.

Gordon, J. R. (1993). *A diagnostic approach to organizational behavior* (4th ed.). Needham Heights, MA: Allyn & Bacon.

Gray, B. (1985). Conditions facilitating interorganizational collaboration. *Human Relations, 38*(10), 911–936.

Gray, B. (1989). *Collaborating: Finding common ground for multiparty problems.* San Francisco, CA: Jossey-Bass.

Gray, B., & Wood, D. J. (1991). Collaborative alliances: Moving from practice to theory. *Journal of Applied Behavioral Science, 27*(1), 3–22.

Habermas, J. (1984). *The theory of communicative action*, volume 1: reason and the rationalization of society, translated by T. McCarthy, Boston, MA: Beacon Press.

Haggard, E. A. (1958). *Intraclass correlation and the analysis of variance.* Oxford, England: Holt.

Hair, J. F., Black, B. C., Babin, B. J., & Anderson, R. E. (2009). *Multivariate data analysis*, 7th edition. Upper Saddle River: Prentice Hall.

Hahn, T., Figge, F., Pinkse, J., & Preuss, L. (2010). Trade-offs in corporate sustainability: You can't have your cake and eat it. *Business Strategy & the Environment, 19*(4), 217–229.

Hamric, A. B., & Blackhall, L. J. (2007). Nurse-physician perspectives on the care of dying patients in intensive care units: Collaboration, moral distress, and ethical climate. *Critical Care Medicine, 35*(2), 422–429.

Hellriegel, D., Slocum, J. W., & Woodman, R. W. (1986). *Organizational behavior.* New York, NY: West.

Hoppe, M. H. (2007). Lending an ear: Why leaders must learn to listen actively. *Leadership in Action, 27*, 11–14.

Hughes, M., & Morgan, R. E. (2007). Deconstructing the relationship between entrepreneurial orientation and business performance at the embryonic stage of firm growth. *Industrial Marketing Management, 36*(5), 651–661.

Husted, B. W., & de Jesus Salazar, J. (2006). Taking Friedman seriously: Maximizing profits and social performance. *Journal of Management Studies, 43*(1), 75–91.

Huxham, C. (2003). Theorizing collaboration practice. *Public Management Review, 5*(3), 401–423.

Huxham, C., & Vangen, S. (2000b). Ambiguity, complexity and dynamics in the membership of collaboration. *Human Relations, 53*(6), 771–806.

James, L. R., Demaree, R. G., & Wolf, G. (1984). Estimating within-group interrater reliability with and without response bias. *Journal of Applied Psychology, 69*(1), 85–98.

James, L. R., Demaree, R. G., & Wolf, G. (1993). An assessment of within-group interrater agreement. *Journal of Applied Psychology, 78*(2), 306–309.

James, W. (1977). Percept and concept: The import of concepts. In J. McDermott (Ed.), *The writings of Williams James* (pp. 217–247). Chicago, IL: University of Chicago Press.

Jarvis, C. B., MacKenzie, S. B., & Podsakoff, P. M. (2003). A critical review of construct indicators and measurement model misspecification in marketing and consumer research. *Journal of Consumer Research, 30*(2), 199–218.

Jensen, M. C. (2010). Value maximization, stakeholder theory, and the corporate objective function. *Journal of Applied Corporate Finance, 22*(1), 32–42.

Kayes, A. B., Kayes, D. C., & Kolb, D. A. (2005). Experiential learning in teams. *Simulation & Gaming, 36*(3), 330–354.

Kimbell, L. (2011). Rethinking design thinking: Part I. *Design and Culture, 3*(3), 285–306.

Kolb, A. Y., & Kolb, D. A. (2012). Experiential learning theory. In N. M. Seel (Ed.), *Encyclopedia of the sciences of learning* (pp. 1215–1219). New York, NY: Springer.

Kolb, D. A. (1984). *Experiential learning: Experience as the source of learning and development*. Englewood Cliffs, NJ: Prentice Hall.

Kolb, D. A., Lublin, S., Spoth, J., & Baker, R. (1986). Strategic management development: Using experiential learning theory to assess and develop managerial competence. *Journal of Management Development, 5*(3), 13–24.

Kozlowski, S. W., Gully, S. M., Nason, E. R., & Smith, E. M. (1999). *Developing adaptive teams: A theory of compilation and performance across levels and time.* Pulakos (Eds.), *The changing nature of work performance: Implications for staffing, personnel actions, and development*, 240, 292.

Kumar, K., & van Dissel, H. G. (1996). Sustainable collaboration: Managing conflict and cooperation in interorganizational systems. *MIS Quarterly, 20*(3), 279–300.

Lax, D. A., & Sebenius, J. K. (1986). *The manager as negotiator: Bargaining for cooperation and competitive gain*. New York, NY: Free Press.

Levine, S., & White, P. E. (1961). Exchange as a conceptual framework for the study of interorganizational relationships. *Administrative Science Quarterly, 5*(4), 583–601.

Lewin, K. (1951). *Field theory in social science*. New York, NY: Harper Torchboooks.

Liedtka, J. M., Haskins, M. E., Rosenblum, J. W., & Weber, J. (1997). The generative cycle: Linking knowledge and relationships. *Sloan Management Review, 39*, 47–58.

Lindgreen, A., & Swaen, V. (2010). Corporate social responsibility. *International Journal of Management, 12*(10), 1–7.

Lingham, T. (2004). *Developing a measure for conversational spaces in teams* (Unpublished doctoral dissertation). Case Western Reserve University, Cleveland, OH.

Lingham, T. (2008). Experiential learning theory. In S. Clegg & J. R. Bailey (Eds.), *International encyclopedia of organization studies* (pp. 487–492). Thousand Oaks, CA: Sage.

Lingham, T. (2009, July). *An experiential approach to team interaction: Developing a measure to capture its diverse dimensions and aspects.* Paper presented at the Interdisciplinary Group Research Conference, Colorado Springs, CO.

Lingham, T. (n.d.). *Understanding, measuring and mapping team interaction: Team learning and development.* New York, NY: Routledge. (Manuscript submitted for publication.)

Liu, Y., & Phillips, J. (2011). Examining the antecedents of knowledge sharing in facilitating team innovativeness from a multilevel perspective. *International Journal of Information Management, 31*(1), 44–52.

Lui, S. S., & Ngo, H.-Y. (2004). The role of trust and contractual safeguards on cooperation in non-equity alliances. *Journal of Management, 30*(4), 471-485.

Madden, J. (2011, January). Overcoming collaboration barriers in affordable housing public-private partnerships. In *Academy of Management Proceedings* (Vol. 2011, No. 1, pp. 1–6). Academy of Management.

Margolis, J., & Walsh, J. (2003). Misery loves companies: Rethinking social initiatives by business. *Administrative Science Quarterly, 48,* 268–305.

Marks, M. A., Mathieu, J. E., & Zaccaro, S. J. (2001). A temporally based framework and taxonomy of team processes. *Academy of Management Review, 26*(3), 356–376.

Martin, R. (2009). *The design of business: Why design is the next competitive advantage.* Boston, MA: Harvard Business School Press.

McGrath, J. E., Arrow, H., & Berdahl, J. L. (2000). The study of groups: past, present, and future. *Personality & Social Psychology Review, 4*(1), 95–105.

McIntyre, R. M., & Salas, E. (1995). Measuring and managing for team performance: Emerging principles from complex environments. In R. Guzzo & E. Salas (Eds.), *Team effectiveness and decision making in organizations* (pp. 149–203). San Francisco: Jossey Bass.

McNaughton, D., Hamlin, D., McCarthy, J., Head-Reeves, D., & Schreiner, M. (2007). Learning to listen: Teaching an active listening strategy to pre-service education professionals. *Topics in Early Childhood Special Education, 27,* 223–231.

Mills, T. M. (1967). *The sociology of small groups.* Englewood Cliffs, NJ: Prentice Hall.

Mohr, J., & Spekman, R. (1994). Characteristics of partnership success: Partnership attributes, communication behavior and conflict resolution techniques. *Strategic Management Journal, 15,* 135–152.

Monckza, R. M., Peterson, K. J., Handfield, R. B., & Ragatz, G. L. (1998). Success factors in strategic supplier alliances: The buying company perspective. *Decision Sciences, 29*(3), 553–577.

Morgan, R. M., & Hunt, S. D. (1994). The commitment-trust theory of relationship marketing. *Journal of Marketing, 58*(3), 20–38.

Nohria, N., & Garcia-Pont, C. (1991). Global strategic linkages and industry structure. *Strategic Management Journal, 12*(S1), 105–124.

Nonaka, I. (1994). A dynamic theory of organizational knowledge creation. *Organizational Science, 5*(1), 14–37.

Nugent, W. R., & Halvorson, H. (1995). Testing the effects of active listening. *Research on Social Work Practice, 5*(2), 152–175.

Orlitzky, M., Schmidt, F. L., & Rynes, S. L. (2003). Corporate social and financial performance: A meta-analysis. *Organization Studies, 24*(3), 403–441.

Parker, H. (2000). Interfirm collaboration and the new product development process. *Industrial Management & Data Systems, 100*(6), 255–260.

Pasquero, J. (1991). Supraorganizational collaboration: The Canadian environmental experiment. *Journal of Applied Behavioral Science, 27*(1), 38–64.

Paukert, A., Stagner, B., & Hope, K. (2004). The assessment of active listening skills in helpline volunteers. *Stress, Trauma, & Crisis, 7*, 61–76.

Piaget, J. (1965). *The moral judgment of the child.* New York, NY: Free Press.

Podsakoff, P. M., MacKenzie, S. B., Lee, J.-Y., & Podsakoff, N. P. (2003). Common method biases in behavioral research: A critical review of the literature and recommended remedies. *Journal of Applied Psychology, 88*(5), 879–903.

Powell, W. W. (1996). Inter-organizational collaboration in the biotechnology industry. *Journal of Institutional and Theoretical Economics, 152*, 197–225.

Rickards, T., Chen, M. H., & Moger, S. (2001). Development of a self-report instrument for exploring team factor, leadership and performance relationships. *British Journal of Management, 12*(3), 243–250. Rockefeller Foundation. Design for Social Impact. Retrieved from http://www.rockefellerfoundation.org/blog/design-social-impact

Robbins, S. P. (1996). *Organizational behavior: Concepts, controversies, applications.* Englewood Cliffs, NJ: Prentice Hall.

Robinson, J. (2005). *Individual learning styles and their relationship to leadership styles* (Unpublished Ph.D. dissertation). Claremont Graduate School, Pomona, CA.

Rockefeller Foundation. *Design for Social Impact.* Retrieved from www.rockefellerfoundation.org/blog/design-social-impact

Rogers, A., & Welch, B. (2009). Using standardized clients in the classroom: An evaluation of a training module to teach active listening skills to social work students. *Journal of Teaching in Social Work, 29*, 153–168.

Rogers, C. (1970). *Carl Rogers on encounter groups.* New York, NY: Harper & Row.

Rogers, C. R., & Farson, R. E. (1957). *Active listening: Industrial relations center of the University of Chicago.* Chicago, IL: University of Chicago.

Roschelle, J., & Teasley, S. D. (1995). The construction of shared knowledge in collaborative problem-solving. In C. E. O'Malley (Ed.), *Computer-supported collaborative learning* (pp. 69–97). Berlin, Germany: Springer-Verlag.

Salas, E., Burke, C. S., & Cannon-Bowers, J. A. (2000). Teamwork: Emerging principles. *International Journal of Management Reviews, 2*(4), 339–356.

Saxton, T. (1997). The effects of partner and relationship characteristics on alliance outcomes. *Academy of Management Journal, 40*(2), 443–461.

Schein, E. (1993). On dialogue, culture, and organizational learning. *Organizational Dynamics, 22*(20), 40–51.

Schneider, B., Salvaggio, A. N., & Subirats, M. (2002). Climate strength: A new direction for climate research. *Journal of Applied Psychology, 87*(2), 220–229.

Schutz, W. C. (1966). *The interpersonal world.* Palo Alto, CA: Science & Behavior Books.

Selsky, J. W. (1991). Lessons in community development: An activist approach to stimulating interorganizational collaboration. *Journal of Applied Behavioral Science, 27*(1), 91–115.

Senge, P. M. (1990). *The fifth discipline: The art and science of the learning organization.* New York, NY: Doubleday.

Simon, G. L., Bumpus, A. G., & Mann, P. (2012). Win-win scenarios at the climate-development interface: Challenges and opportunities for stove replacement programs through carbon finance. *Global Environmental Change, 22*(1), 275–287.

Star, S. L. (1989). *Regions of the mind: Brain research and the quest for scientific certainty.* Stanford, CA: Stanford University Press.

Thomson, A. M. (2001). *Collaboration: Meaning and measurement* (Unpublished doctoral dissertation). Indiana University, Bloomington, IN.

Thomson, A. M., Perry, J., & Miller, T. (2009). Conceptualizing and measuring collaboration. *Journal of Public Administration Research & Theory, 19*(1), 23–56.

Tschirhart, M., Christensen, R. K., & Perry, J. L. (2005). The paradox of branding and collaboration. *Public Performance & Management Review, 29*(1), 67–84.

Van der Heijden, K. (1996). *Scenarios: The art of strategic conversation.* New York, NY: Wiley.

Van der Laan, G., van Ees, A., & van Witteloostuijn. (2008). Corporate social and financial performance: An extended stakeholder theory, and empirical test with accounting measures. *Journal of Business Ethics, 79,* 299–310.

Van de Ven, A. H., Emmett, D. C., & Koenig, R., Jr. (1975). Theoretical and conceptual issues in inter-organizational theory. In A. R. Negandhi (Ed.), *Inter-organizational theory* (pp. 19–38). Kent, OH: Kent State University Press.

Vangen, S., & Huxham, C. (2003b). Nurturing collaborative relations: Building trust in interorganizational collaboration. *Journal of Applied Behavioral Science, 39*(1), 5–31.

Verganti, R. (2008). *Design driven innovation.* Boston, MA: Harvard Business School Press.

Vygotsky, L. S. (1978). *Mind in society: The development of higher psychological process.* Cambridge, MA: Harvard University Press.

Wang, C. L., & Ahmed, P. K. (2004). The development and validation of the organizational innovativeness construct using confirmatory factor analysis. *European Journal of Innovation Management, 7*(4), 303–313.

Warren, R. L., Burgunder, A. F., Newton, J. W., & Rose, S. M. (1975). The interaction of community decision organizations: Some conceptual considerations and empirical findings. In A. R. Negandhi (Ed.), *Inter-organizational theory* (pp. 167–181). Kent, OH: Kent State University Press.

Waugh, W. L., & Streib, G. (2006). Collaboration and leadership for effective emergency management. *Public Administration Review, 66*(S1), 131–140.

Way, D., Jones, L., & Busing, N. (2000, May). *Implementation strategies: Collaboration in primary care-family doctors and nurse practitioners delivering shared care.* Paper presented at the Ontario College of family physicians, Toronto: Ontario.

Weger, H., Jr., Castle Bell, G., Minei, E. M., & Robinson, M. C. (2014). The relative effectiveness of active listening in initial interactions. *International Journal of Listening, 28*(1), 13–31.

Wenger, E. (1998). *Communities of practice: Learning, meaning, and identity.* New York, NY: Cambridge University Press.

Wood, D., & Gray, B. (1991). Toward a comprehensive theory of collaboration. *Journal of Applied Behavioral Science, 27*(1), 139–162.

Yang, L. R., Huang, C. F., & Wu, K. S. (2011). The association among project manager's leadership style, teamwork and project success. *International Journal of Project Management, 29*(3), 258–267.

5 Creating the Collaboration Blueprint
Connecting the Practical and Theoretical Perspectives

The aim of the previous two chapters was to quantitatively validate emerging constructs from the qualitative study, while beginning to show the causal relationships among the constructs. In this chapter, I diagram the connections of the practical perspective from the qualitative study (Chapter 2) to more theoretical levels based upon evidence from the two quantitative studies (Chapter 3 and Chapter 4). I then build from the results an evidence-based design plan (or blueprint) for successful inter-organizational collaboration. In conjunction with the blueprint, this chapter presents additional critical collaboration success factors (i.e., facilitated collaboration or a Collaboration Boot Camp—detailed in Chapter 6) and tools (i.e., training in design thinking, design attitude, and redesign; team and individual coaching; a team-building module such as the Team Learning Inventory (TLI); and building emotional intelligence through the Emotional and Social Competencies Inventory (ESCI)].

5.1 A Grounded Theory Approach

The goal of my qualitative research was to generate theory grounded in the real experiences of leaders from the nonprofit, private, and government sectors participating in affordable-housing collaborations in order to shed light into the complex and seemingly "black box" of collaboration (Thomson & Perry, 2006). The literature suggests the initial environment or preconditions of the partnership can enable or constrain collaboration (Ansell & Gash, 2007; Peters, 1998) and identifies power imbalance among partners (Berger, Cunningham, & Drumwright, 2004; Gray, 1989) as a key variable. A history of cooperation or conflict among partners is an important precondition. While high conflict is not always a collaboration barrier, a history of conflict creates low trust levels that foster manipulation and deters communication, which may create barriers (Ansell & Gash, 2007). If mutual gains are to be achieved, there needs to be alignment among the partners.

Leadership and partner experience are also critical: leaders are crucial for making collaborations work (Ansell & Gash, 2007; Armistead, Pettigrew, &

Aves, 2007; Crosby & Bryson, 2005) and molding the cultural values of their organizations in favor of collaboration (Armistead et al., 2007). Partner experience can be essential because partners can have differing organizational missions, structures, goals, desired constituents to be served, cultures, partner decision-making styles, and partner motives; in cases of severe difference, collaborative advantage is difficult to achieve (Huxham, 2003, Berger et al., 2004). However, partner experience can reduce or mitigate strains on inter-organizational collaboration like the lack of renewal necessary for continued commitment (Le Ber & Branzei, 2009); the engagement of new people in preparation for personnel turnover (Berger et al., 2004); and the conflict that emerges from different aims, expectations, strategies, and outcomes (Bryson, Crosby, & Stone., 2006). Experience also creates better design thinkers because a particular phenomenon may have been seen before, meaning experienced partners "don't have to interpret every sensation or input from scratch as a novice would" (Martin, 2009, p. 165).

Initial data analysis of my qualitative study merely confirmed previous extant research on collaboration, e.g., experience; leadership; the importance of aligning the goals, mission, vision, and values; mutual respect; and trust-building (in particular, my interviews indicated that collaborators should spend time together getting to know one another). As a result, I completed a subsequent reanalysis of my initial data based upon manifest level (Boyatzis, 1998) themes—the four common affordable- housing, inter-organizational collaboration barriers and subsequent actions taken. Specifically, the reanalysis of the data based upon what actions and behaviors were taken when inter-organizational collaborations faced:

(A) lack of funds or uncertainty with tax credits (i.e., funding barriers/ actions);
(B) conflict with partners (i.e., partner barriers/actions);
(C) affordable housing wanted or needed in the community, but a challenge to build (e.g., site contamination, inferior soil, land assembly, location— place based) or opposition from community residents—people based (i.e., community barriers/actions); and
(D) government mandates or government opposition (i.e., government barriers/actions).

The analysis of the data through this lens yielded six key findings (Table 5.1).

The most pivotal discoveries (bolded in Table 5.1) from the inter-organizational collaborations in my qualitative study (Chapter 2) were the sharp differences between successful and less successful collaborations regarding focus, the actions taken when facing a collaboration obstacle, and the ability to adapt to change for successful collaboration performance and innovation that actualized neighborhood rejuvenation. The qualitative findings were insightful. How the quantitative analysis builds is as follows.

Table 5.1 Summary of Qualitative Study Findings

1	Successful and less successful inter-organizational collaborations encountered similar barriers.
2	Leaders of successful and less successful inter-organizational collaborations take different actions when barriers to collaboration are encountered.
	2.1 When facing obstacles, leaders of successful collaborations tended to exercise heightened emotional and social competencies.
	2.2 Leaders of less successful collaborations lack conflict resolution or conflict management competence.
3	When facing obstacles, leaders of successful collaborations tended to **take actions for creating a better future.** Less successful collaborations focused on short-term viability.
4	More successful collaborations tended to **focus on mission and community development** whereas less successful collaborations were focused on the deal.
5	Successful collaborations consistently **adapted to changes,** while less successful collaborations failed to do so.
6	Successful collaborations demonstrated innovativeness, **rejuvenating neighborhoods.**

5.2 Practical Perspective

From my study on affordable-housing, inter-organizational collaborations (Chapter 2), the actions and behaviors of less successful collaborations created attractors that pushed toward silos masking as collaboration, that is, towards a more "perfunctory" role, whereas the actions/behaviors of successful collaborations created attractors that pulled toward collaboration performance and innovation, towards a more "rejuvenative" role. To build analytical scaffolding, behavioral labels were assigned to the collaboration based upon actions/behaviors when facing a collaboration barrier (Figure 5.1a).

The behavioral label (in parenthesis) is identified for the actions of successful and less successful collaborations. Less successful collaborations have short-term viability (exploitative), are deal focused (transactional), and fail early (rigid). Successful collaborations take actions for creating a better future (explorative), are mission and community development focused (relational), and adapt to change (adaptive). Figure 5.1b connects the (a) context of the collaboration barrier to the (b) actions/behaviors taken by the successful or less successful collaborations studied, and applies the (c) behavioral label. The model then connects the successful collaboration to (d) "rejuvenative" collaboration emerging through mutually beneficial exploration, active listening in team interaction, and design attitude.

As supported in literature these inter-organizational collaborations made choices—the less successful collaboration attractors were transactional, exploitative, and rigid; the successful collaborations attractors were relational, explorative, and adaptive (Lavie & Rosenkopf, 2006; Rothaermel & Deeds, 2004; March, 1991). The connection to the quantitative research follows.

5.3 Quantitative Research

To connect the qualitative research to quantitative analysis, a drilldown of concepts from the Chapter 2 findings is required. First, the resulting emergent constructs (i.e., autonomy, boundary spanning, shared vision, design attitude, collaboration performance, mutually beneficial exploration, innovativeness, and the team-learning attribute of active listening) were subjected to quantitative analysis over two studies (Figure 5.1c). Second, the findings from Chapter 3 (the first quantitative analysis) are significant because they demonstrate the importance of:

- autonomy (i.e., authority and independence; Hughes & Morgan, 2007),
- boundary spanning (i.e., linkages and interactions to leverage resources and support; Faraj & Yan, 2009),
- shared vision (i.e., a shared sense of purpose and responsibility that sustains and motivates; Rickards, Chen, & Moger, 2001),
- design attitude (i.e., an opportunity to create something remarkable; Boland et al., 2008; and
- design thinking concepts Gaskin & Berente, 2011) as contributors to a successful collaboration.

This study empirically validates the positive impact of these five key concepts on collaboration performance and the mediating effect of design attitude.

Chapter 4 (the second quantitative analysis) uncovers mutually beneficial exploration (i.e., exploring possibilities, successful partnerships, and strategy) as a key antecedent for autonomy, boundary spanning, shared vision, and design attitude that have a positive and significant impact on collaboration performance. Chapter 4 also reveals the strong positive relationship between mutually beneficial exploration and the team-learning attribute of active listening (i.e., awareness and reflection of perspectives with high levels of sensitivity and social integration; Lingham, 2009), as well as the positive and significant effect of design attitude and autonomy on innovativeness (Figure 5.1c).

5.4 Additional Tools

This research suggests a practitioner model for collaboration that focuses on phenomenon at the intersection of the practical (experiential learning) and the theoretical (teleological change) for rejuvenative collaboration (see Figure 1.2). Also emergent from this research are additional tools around design, teams, and emotional intelligence to assist practitioners with the difficulties inherent in collaboration. For design, training in design thinking, design attitude, and redesign can impact successful collaboration performance and innovation, facilitating project development through the design lens of inspiration, ideation, and implementation. For teams, individual

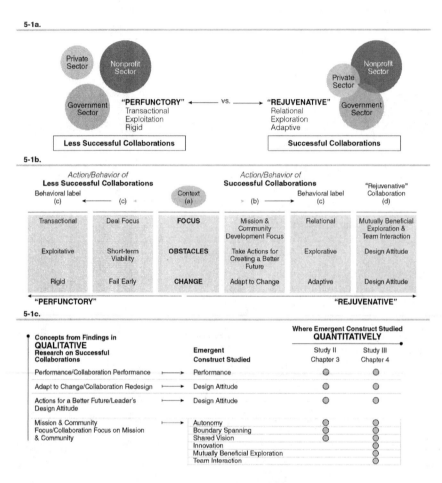

Figure 5.1 Conceptual Model of the Practical to Theoretical Framing

coaching, team coaching, and team-building modules such as the Team Learning Inventory (TLI) can also impact successful collaboration performance and innovation. For emotional intelligence, the Emotional and Social Competencies Inventory (ESCI) can impact successful collaboration performance by bolstering self-awareness, self-management, social awareness, and relationship management.

5.4.1 Design Thinking

Design thinking suggests experience assists with the reconciliation of analytical thinking ("to declare truths and certainties about the world") and intuitive thinking ("the art of knowing without reasoning") (Martin 2009,

p. 5–6). For example, "conventional business thinking said that a company could have innovation or it could have efficiency, but not both at once. There was, according to the received wisdom, always a trade-off," but design thinking makes both possible (Martin 2009, p. 82). Design thinking cultivates a design attitude and redesign.

Design inquiry can be thought of as a form of active research in which knowledge is created through action. The values that define the content dimension of design inquiry include (a) assuming each situation is unique; (b) focusing on purpose and ideal solutions; and (c) applying systems thinking (Romme, 2003). In general, design thinking is defined as "an analytic and creative process that engages a person in opportunities to experiment, create and prototype models, gather feedback, and redesign" (Razzouk & Shute, 2012, p. 330). Brown (2009) outlines the design framework as inspiration, ideation, and implementation. This framework is presented in Figure 5.2.

5.4.2 Team Learning Inventory

Teams are complex systems in which improved team interaction can be a critical success factor for successful collaboration and innovation. The TLI can map actual and desired interactions at the team level where coaching and team-directed learning significantly improves team performance (Lingham, 2009). Moreover, the TLI facilitates the development of a common language for team members that, in turn, facilitates team learning and interaction. This work can assist collaborators to communicate effectively and to generate and share knowledge, therefore supporting rejuvenative collaborating.

The learning needs assessment tool can identify the specific skills participants need to develop that will assist participants in improving collaborative interactions. Team coaching provides collaborators assistance for moving from their "actual" to their "desired" state (Lingham, 2009). In addition,

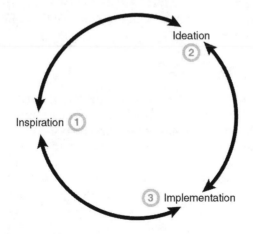

Figure 5.2 Design Thinking Framework

the coaching helps participants with developing their own leadership style. The TLI mapping system outlines 10 dimensions of team interaction along four major dimensions: (1) Non-task-related interactions (diverging dimension with the five aspects of engagement, active listening, individuality, relationality, solidarity); (2) task-related interactions (converging dimension with three aspects of understanding, action, and planning); (3) power and influence interactions; and (4) openness interactions (Lingham, n.d.). These four dimensions and 10 aspects provide teams with in-depth knowledge of interactions, which will help them actualize team learning and development. Team learning, interaction, and coaching are critical for building and sustaining effective collaboration and rejuvenative collaboration. As stated in the research and realized in practice, organizations know they need to collaborate but are seldom guided.

5.4.3 Emotional and Social Competency Inventory

The emotional and social competency inventory (ESCI) is based upon emotional intelligence and begins with a 360-degree survey. The ESCI survey assesses 12 competencies (Hay Group, 2011) in four distinct areas (i.e., self-awareness, self-management, social awareness, and relationship management). Emotional intelligence competencies and social intelligence competencies differentiate outstanding and average performers (Boyatzis, 2008; Boyatzis & McKee, 2005). Emotional intelligence competencies cluster around self-awareness and self-management. Self-awareness is defined as knowing one's personal limits and strengths, self-confidence (i.e., knowing one's worth and capabilities), understanding personal emotions (and their impact), and utilizing instinct to guide decisions (Boyatzis & McKee, 2005; Goleman, Boyatzis, & Mckee, 2002). Social intelligence competencies cluster around social awareness and relationship management. Providing feedback to the collaborators from the ESCI survey in conjunction with coaching would facilitate improved performance and effectiveness.

5.4 A Collaboration Blueprint

This research contributes to the development of evidence-based practitioner tools and strategies for designing and managing effective collaborations and improving collaboration performance. Paley (n.d.) begins his teleological argument with "just as the function and complexity of a watch implies a watch-maker, so likewise the functions and complexity of . . ." and I would conclude with the view that the functions and complexity of inter-organizational collaboration implies the need for a collaboration-maker. This research can serve as a training ground for collaborative partners interested in rejuvenative collaboration.

Building better collaborations can be an effective strategy for successful performance, innovation, and rejuvenation. First, the collaboration blueprint proposes an expansion of the traditional collaboration framework from preconditions, process and outcomes (Gray, 1989) to preconditions, process, outcomes, and impact. The rationale for adding an impact component emerges from grounded theory research (Chapter 2) in which successful collaboration performance led to innovation and rejuvenation as well as a quantitative validation of performance and innovation (Chapter 4). Extending the collaboration framework suggests a focus on impact over outcome. Second, the collaboration blueprint places empirically validated constructs from this book into the preconditions, process, outcomes, and impact framework to serve as a collaboration design plan or blueprint.

Reading the blueprint, inter-organizational collaborations are guided through (1) preconditions, (2) process, (3) outcomes, and (4) impact. For (1) preconditions, collaborators start with the mutually beneficial exploration of possibilities, successful strategy, and partnership through active listening. Next, collaborators would create a shared vision. Moving to (2) process, the collaborators then explore collaboration from a design perspective as a form of discipline for solution-finding with a design attitude for the co-creation, design, and redesign of relevant solutions using available resources. Next, collaborators bolster autonomy as well as boundary spanning capabilities for the move to (3) successful collaboration performance and innovation. Finally, moving to (4) impact, successful collaboration performance and innovation facilitates rejuvenative collaboration. The collaboration blueprint is presented in Figure 5.3.

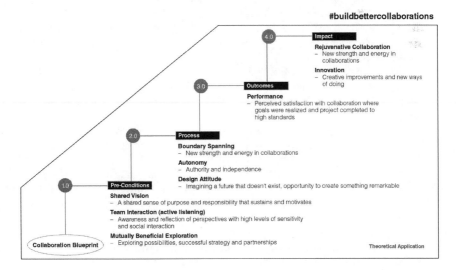

Figure 5.3 Collaboration Blueprint

5.5 Rejuvenative Collaboration

At the intersection of experiential learning theory and teleological process theory are the constructs studied in this book that contribute to rejuvenative collaboration and provide the framework for a collaboration blueprint. As noted above, rejuvenative collaboration is the combination of successful collaboration performance and innovation. The collaboration blueprint contributes to successful collaboration performance.

References

Ansell, C., & Gash, A. (2007). Collaborative governance in theory and practice. *Journal of Public Administration Research & Theory, 18*(4), 543–571.

Armistead, C., Pettigrew, P., & Aves, S. (2007). Exploring leadership in multi-sectoral partnerships. *Leadership, 3*(2), 211–230.

Berger, I., Cunningham, P., & Drumwright, M. (2004). Social alliances. *California Management Review, 47*(1), 58–90.

Boland, R., Jr., Collopy, F., Lyytinen, K., & Yoo, Y. (2008). Managing as designing: Lessons for organization leaders from the design practice of Frank O. Gehry. *Design Issues, 24*(1), 10–25.

Boyatzis, R. E. (1998). *Transforming qualitative information: Thematic analysis and code development.* Thousand Oaks, CA: Sage.

Boyatzis, R. E. (2008). Competencies in the 21st century. *Journal of Management Development, 27*(1), 5–12.

Boyatzis, R. E., & McKee, A. (2005). *Resonant leadership: Renewing yourself and connecting with others through mindfulness, hope, and compassion.* Boston, MA: Harvard Business School Press.

Brown, T. (2009). *Change by design: How design thinking transforms organizations and inspires innovation.* New York, NY: HarperCollins.

Bryson, J., Crosby, B., & Stone, M. (2006). The design and implementation of cross-sector collaborations: Propositions from the literature. *Public Administration Review, 66*(Special Issue), 44–55.

Crosby, B. C., & Bryson, J. M. (2005). *Leadership for the common good: Tackling public problems in a shared-power world.* San Francisco, CA: Jossey-Bass.

Faraj, S., & Yan, A. (2009). Boundary work in knowledge teams. *Journal of Applied Psychology, 94*(3), 604–617.

Gaskin, J., & Berente, N. (2011). Video game design in the MBA curriculum: An experiential learning approach for teaching design thinking. *Communications of the Association for Information Systems, 29*(1), 103–121.

Goleman, D., Boyatzis, R. E., & McKee, A. (2002). *Primal leadership: Realizing the power of emotional intelligence.* Boston, MA: Harvard Business School Press.

Gray, B. (1989). *Collaborating: Finding common ground for multiparty problems.* San Francisco, CA: Jossey-Bass.

Hay Group. (2011). *Emotional and social competency inventory: A user guide for accredited practitioners.* Prepared by L&T direct and the McClelland Center for Research and Innovation. Philadelphia, PA: Hay Group.

Hughes, M., & Morgan, R. E. (2007). Deconstructing the relationship between entrepreneurial orientation and business performance at the embryonic stage of firm growth. *Industrial Marketing Management, 36*(5), 651–661.

Huxham, C. (2003). Theorizing collaboration practice. *Public Management Review,* 5(3), 401–423.

Lavie, D., & Rosenkopf, L. (2006). Balancing exploration and exploitation in alliance formation. *Academy of Management Journal, 49*(4), 797–818.

Le Ber, M., & Branzei, O. (2009). (Re) forming strategic cross-sector partnerships: Relational processes of social innovation. *Business & Society, 49*(1), 1–33.

Lingham, T. (2009, July). *An experiential approach to team interaction: Developing a measure to capture its diverse dimensions and aspects.* Paper presented at the Interdisciplinary Group Research Conference, Colorado Springs, CO.

Lingham, T. (n.d.). *Understanding, measuring and mapping team interaction: Team learning and development.* New York, NY: Routledge. (Manuscript submitted for publication.)

March, J. G. (1991). Exploration and exploitation in organizational learning. *Organization Science, 2*(1), 71–87.

Martin, R. (2009). *The design of business: Why design is the next competitive advantage.* Boston, MA: Harvard Business School Press.

Paley, W. (n.d.). http://philosophy.lander.edu/intro/paley.shtml, retrieved January 6, 2015.

Peters, B. (1998). With a little help from our friends: public-private partnerships as institutions and instruments. In J. Pierre (Eds.), *Partnerships in urban governance: European and American experience* (pp. 11–33). London, England: Macmillan.

Razzouk, R., & Shute, V. (2012). What is design thinking and why is it important? *Review of Educational Research, 82*(3), 330–348.

Rickards, T., Chen, M. H., & Moger, S. (2001). Development of a self-report instrument for exploring team factor, leadership and performance relationships. *British Journal of Management, 12*(3), 243–250.

Romme, A. (2003). Making a difference: Organization as design. *Organization Science, 14*(5), 558–573.

Rothaermel, F. T., & Deeds, D. L. (2004). Exploration and exploitation alliances in biotechnology: A system of new product development. *Strategic Management Journal, 25*(3), 201–221.

Thomson, A. M., & Perry, J. L. (2006). Collaboration processes: Inside the black box. *Public Administration Review, 66*(S1), 20–32.

6 Leverage Point Development
Examples of Inter-Organizational Collaborations Utilizing the Collaboration Blueprint

The previous chapter proposes the collaboration design plan (or blueprint) and additional tools for successful collaboration performance. This final chapter connects theory to practice through a design lens. In 2009, I started my doctoral programs and began working with nonprofit organizations and local governments bringing knowledge and analytical and research skills from my educational experience to practitioners. I have utilized the findings from my research to create the collaboration blueprint. As an engaged scholar, I have infused design methods into the creation of solutions for nonprofit organizations. Strengthening the skills of nonprofit practitioners is done to ensure the continuous integration of problem solving and opportunity leveraging expertise. Integrating design into practitioner tools and training holds the possibility for increasing the skills and abilities of nonprofit managers and leaders, supporting the continued development of the nonprofit sector.

This final chapter is structured as follows: First, I use data to show the growth of the nonprofit sector and the need for teaching skills to nonprofit leaders and managers. Second, I propose building better collaborations as a critical leverage point for nonprofit organizations. In this same section, I reintroduce the collaboration blueprint and suggest delivery of the tool for practitioners through a design lens. I then provide details on the inspiration, ideation, and implementation (Brown, 2009) design framework for project development and discuss specific steps. My findings show how practice can change. In fact, my findings have changed practice already—I have used the collaboration blueprint to actualize funding, structure, strategy, and sustainability for inter-organizational collaborations engaged in community-focused work.

This work involves visioning, organizational assessment, environmental scanning, and research. The results inform a program design and implementation strategy building upon the strengths and opportunities of the organizations (while mitigating weaknesses and threats) and are grounded in research. The work culminates in the development of a strengths-based and research-informed logic-modeled program articulated in a grant proposal that actualizes rejuvenative collaboration and innovation. Examples of specific outcomes over four years include over 13.5 million in grant dollars secured for low-income communities to create opportunities for low-income individuals. This result also leveraged an additional $7.3 million in neighborhood investment; created 200 full-time jobs, 129 part-time jobs, and 50 entrepreneurial opportunities; enabled 400 job readiness, placement, and retention services for public assistance recipients; and provided employment training and work supports for over 1,000 public housing residents. In the final section I provide additional information of these examples from my work on inter-organizational collaboration by design. This work also informed the development of a new Master (MSc) of Business Design and Innovation[1] degree for business and nonbusiness majors to build design skills, lead and manage high performing cross-functional teams, and develop effective strategies and programs for private, nonprofit, and government sectors.

6.1 Growth of the Nonprofit Sector

The number of nonprofit organizations has been growing steadily, from 12,500 in 1940 to more than 2.3 million operating in the United States today (National Center for Charitable Statistics, 2013). Further, nonprofits organizations employ 10% of the workforce (Salamon, Sokolowski, Haddock, & Tice, 2013). This growth has stimulated a demand for nonprofit managers (Murdock, Tekula, & Parra, 2013; Salamon & Sokolowski, 2005), heightening the required skills for effective nonprofit management and intensifying the need for professional development and training (Mottner & Wymer, 2011). Research also suggests nonprofits will need to recruit and develop 640,000 new senior managers in the next decade to support the growth in the sector (Jiang, 2008). Finally, a sizable proportion of current nonprofit managers are nearing retirement. It is projected that, beginning in 2016, about 80,000 new executives will be needed each year in nonprofit organizations (Murdock et al., 2013; Tierney, 2006) in a variety of areas, including poverty alleviation, economic development, community development, healthy food access, health care, education, arts and culture, homelessness, and environmental sustainability.

Although this book may be useful for private, nonprofit, and government sectors collaborating across and within sectors, it is my hope this chapter will be particularly useful for nonprofit organizations. Given the growth of the sector, nonprofit leaders and managers need practical skills and tools (that are evidence-based and research-informed) because the existence of nonprofit organizations involves their being tasked to address complex social problems, often through inter-organizational collaboration.

6.2 Leverage Point Development

The aperture between research and practice creates critical leverage points for development and thriving for nonprofit organizations. Building better collaborations is one such strategy for leveraging opportunities, successful performance, innovation, and rejuvenation in community-focused work.

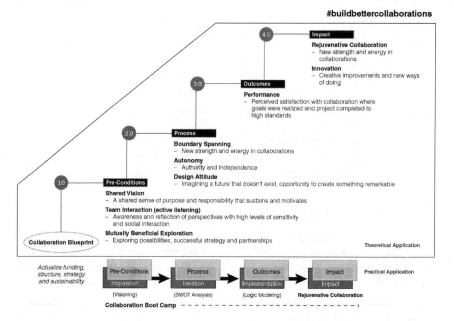

Figure 6.1 Collaboration Boot Camp[2]

However, there is a lack of training in collaboration and cooperative learning (Bossert, 1988) despite the fact that many researchers recommend instruction for the development of collaboration skills (Lai, 2011; Fall, Webb, & Chudowsky, 2000; Webb, 1995) and the need for structuring tasks that facilitate mastery (Dillenbourg, 1999; Mercer, 1996; Webb, 1995; Bossert, 1988).

Grounded in theory and experiential learning, rejuvenative collaboration is the result of successful collaboration performance and innovation. The collaboration blueprint is developed from qualitative research building from the lived experiences of leaders participating in collaborations and validated quantitatively. The collaboration blueprint contributes to successful collaboration. As stated in the previous chapter, the complexity of inter-organizational collaboration implies the need for a collaboration-maker.

The transition from theory to practice happens through the design lens of inspiration, ideation, and implementation. Delivering the blueprint can happen in what I call the Collaboration Boot Camp (see bottom of Figure 6.1). In the boot camp, inter-organizational collaborations learn to actualize funding, structure, strategy, and sustainability.

6.3 Through a Design Lens

The design thinking process proposed by Brown and Wyatt (2010, p. 33) is described as "a system of overlapping spaces" in which inspiration is "the problem or opportunity that motivates the search for solutions; ideation as the process of generating, developing, and testing ideas; and implementation as the path that leads from the project stage into people's lives." The Collaboration Boot Camp facilitator plays the role of the convener and provides expert intervention. According to Levitt and March (1988), adaptive learning is problematic and rare, making expert intervention necessary (Argyris & Schon, 1978). The role of the convener is critical for successful collaboration (Wood & Gray, 1991) and includes bringing legitimacy, procedural skill, and the ability to identify needed stakeholders (Gray, 1989). The specific components of inspiration, ideation, and implementation are described next.

6.3.1 Inspiration

The inspiration component of the Collaboration Boot Camp includes visioning. This facilitated process can be done in small and large group settings. Visioning asks participants to allow themselves to imagine that if time and resources were not an issue, what, for example, is the vision for their project, organization, or community. The visioning process is critical for allowing participants the cognitive space to imagine a future that may not exist. There is extant literature on the importance of visioning toward an ideal self in the leadership arena (Boyatzis & McKee, 2005), and this has shown to have neurological underpinnings (Jack, Boyatzis, Khawaja, Passarelli, & Leckie, 2013) as well as it being related to individual and organizational performance (Boyatzis, Rochford & Taylor, 2015).

6.3.2 Ideation

The ideation component of Collaboration Boot Camp includes idea generation and situational analysis. Following the visioning session, a list of ideas about what the future could look like is generated. Participants are guided through situational analysis in which they are prompted to generate ideas about current or near-future strengths, weaknesses, opportunities, and threats (SWOT). In this session, the facilitator can take notes (small groups), or provide participants with post-it notes on which they can write their ideas and post them (small or large groups).

The facilitator then reviews the information, starting with the vision, then moves through ideas from the SWOT analysis. Next, the facilitator asks the group to identify transitional ideas (or steps) that could move them from their existing SWOT (actual) situation towards their vision of the future (desired). Another list of ideas (or steps) is generated. Using the nominal group technique, participants prioritize the ideas and co-create a list of strengths-based steps to help them transition to their imagined future.

Sometimes during ideation, a reminder of mission is useful, and I build from my housing background noting that, similar to home building, a key tool in mission building is a 2x4 where inter-organizational collaborators are planning "to" have an impact (then articulating that impact), "by" committing to some fundamental work (then articulating that work), "for" a specific population or cause (then articulating that population or cause). The question then becomes: What is the "2x4" of the inter-organizational collaboration?

6.3.3 Implementation

The implementation component involves research, logic modeling, sustainable system design, and funding. To be effective in securing support for their work, inter-organizational collaborations must demonstrate their impact both qualitatively and quantitatively. Nonprofit organizations often secure and retain funding using anecdotal stories and images, but this qualitative information must also be anchored quantitatively. The research component is critical because it identifies evidence-based solutions that enable the nonprofit organization to thrive. In addition to the importance of data and research, the use of a logic model is critical.

The logic model can facilitate project implementation. The logic model is a visual representation of a pathway that enables support and course correction. The logic model is useful for designing evaluations and performance measurement, which are increasingly used in program design and management (they also facilitate shared responsibility for outcomes; McLaughlin & Jordan, 2004). Logic models can also be used to describe internal management functions. The five components of the logic model include resources/inputs, activities, outputs, outcomes, and impact. A facilitated logic modeling exercise allows participants to identify resources needed to complete specific activities. Outputs are generated based on the activities to be completed—outcomes are the resulting changes. For example, outputs can be thought of as numbers (e.g., number of community meetings, number of high school graduates); outcomes can be thought of as an increase/decrease or percentage change (e.g., increased civic engagement, a percentage reduction in teen pregnancy rates). Impact is the resulting fundamental change. Another key component of the logic model is the ability to begin anywhere in the logic model and move backward and forward to ensure the logic is solid. An example of how to read a logic model is presented in Figure 6.2.

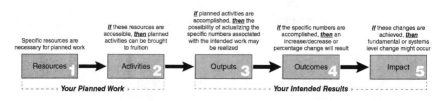

Figure 6.2 Logic Model

With the logic model in place, designing a sustainable system is possible. Participants can identify what resources and support are needed, and the logic model can serve as a guide for prioritizing and organizing investment and for promoting comprehensive, integrated, and collaborative strategic implementation to align stakeholders on objectives and impact. A conceptual map or infographic is also helpful.

Funding is the final part of the ideation component of the boot camp. It includes funding research at the local, national, and federal levels. Funding can include a grant proposal as well as a development strategy intended to reach a variety of potential funding sources (e.g., funding targets for special events; strategies for individual, corporate, and foundation sources).

6.4 Examples

Figures 6.3 through 6.14 illustrate my work with inter-organizational collaborations between 2011 and 2016. I use the collaboration blueprint through the design lens to guide my work, facilitating inspiration and ideation sessions with collaborators as outlined in the Collaboration Boot Camp. I assist organizations with the implementation component through the development of logic models, systems maps, and infographics for ongoing project and collaboration management, measurement and for designing sustainable systems. From this work, I conducted additional research and prepared grant proposals for funding innovative ideas. In the following section, I briefly describe several collaborative projects, providing detailed information for the creation of the logic models, conceptual models, or infographics I created and submitted with the projects or proposals that were subsequently funded.

My hope is that, in providing these examples, practitioners can benefit from this work, be motivated to focus on possibilities, and utilize evidence-based strategies outlined in my Collaboration Blueprint for overcoming barriers of inter-organizational collaboration. The results can lead to funding, innovation, and rejuvenative community solutions.

6.4.1 Urban Café and Community Kitchen (ca. July 2011—Awarded $759,374)

The Bridgeport Market, Cafe & Community Kitchen is a comprehensive intervention designed to create sustainable employment and business opportunities, improve access to healthy affordable foods, and promote education. This initiative is proposed for Kinsman, the poorest neighborhood in Cleveland, Ohio, which has a poverty rate of 35%. Area residents also suffer from acute food access challenges; for example, fast food is 4.5 times as accessible as supermarkets. The initiative proposes to eliminate local food deserts, build food security, and develop vibrant communities of opportunity. The effort is designed around developing a market, café, and community kitchen that will hire and train low-income persons from the community so that they can then find jobs and take advantage of opportunities for entrepreneurship. The approach is designed to create a variety of healthy food choice options, address or work around personal and community barriers, change attitudes towards healthy food through education and marketing, leverage the existing momentum of neighborhood revitalization, and harness the local food movement.

This collaborative effort created rejuvenative collaboration and innovation through the development of healthy food retail, specifically a café and small market, a fruit and vegetables truck for mobile distribution of healthy food options (imagine an ice cream truck in urban neighborhoods—with special stops at churches and residential high-rises housing senior citizens—but with fresh produce instead of ice cream), and a community kitchen with a training area for cooking classes for adults and youth. This impact is the result of the practical application of the collaboration blueprint (through a design lens). I facilitated a visioning exercise with collaborative partners to create shared vision, to ensure partners were actively listening, and for partners to explore mutual benefit in actualizing the project (inspiration). I then facilitated a SWOT analysis, identifying boundary spanning opportunities to mitigate project weaknesses and threats, demonstrating collaborative partners could retain autonomy by leveraging strengths and opportunities, and strengthening design attitude and design thinking capabilities to create possibilities and something remarkable (ideation). I then conducted additional research for the completion of the federal funding application, building a logic model to guide the work (implementation). A federal grant of $759,374 was awarded to fund this project. This was a significant achievement for a community-based organization and had a significant impact in the high-poverty neighborhood served. The details of the logic model are described next.

Burten, Bell, Carr Development, Inc. (BBC), a community development corporation, was the lead nonprofit in this work and the applicant for the federal funding. The mission of BBC is to enhance the quality of life for area residents by initiating and cultivating housing, retail, employment, and recreation opportunities through effective partnerships with residents, community groups, government, corporations and institutions.[3] The other collaborative partners for this project included Ohio State University Extension, Cuyahoga Community College, Rid-All Green Partnership, Green City Growers, Cuyahoga Metropolitan Housing Authority, and neighborhood residents. The logic model outlined the system's thinking and implementation plan for success.

Recall the five parts of the logic mode—resources/inputs, activities, outputs, outcomes, and impact. For this project the **Resources** harnessed from the partners to implement the project included human, financial, organizational, community outreach, and Burten, Bell, Carr Development, Inc. (BBC) experience. BBC has experience in commercial development and efficiently and effectively built out the space proposed for funding. BBC also has experience in fundraising, fiscal management and oversight, and garnering community support and buy-in. BBC facilitated the complicated land assembly process for market and community gardeners, and finding individuals seeking agriculture business development opportunities. BBC also served as the lead agency for recruitment, tracking and monitoring jobs, and business development. Additional resources included the Ohio State University Extension for agriculture entrepreneurial training and conducting workshops; Cuyahoga Community College also provided training through their Plant Science and Landscape Technology degree/certificate programs and classes and workshops through their Health & Wellness, Dietetic Technician, and Culinary Arts programs. Rid All Green Partnership taught the Will Allen urban agriculture model and is a Growing Power Environmental Science Commercial Urban Agriculture Training Center. Rid All Green Partners was a supplier and vendor with yield from their farm and aquaponic facility, conducted workshops, and provided training, jobs, and composting. Green City Growers provided lettuce and herbs year-round from their greenhouse and hired low-income local residents for the hydroponic greenhouse facility. Cuyahoga Metropolitan Housing Authority hosted the Farmers Market at their Administrative Headquarters and provided access to potential customers and volunteers. The Cleveland Food Terminal and other Local Food Producers served as an addition food source for year-round provision of affordable healthy produce. The Local Food Movement organizations served as potential customers, volunteers, and workshop presenters, and as a resource for additional strategic alliances, technical assistance, and promotion. Also, key resources included available Vacant Land to support future agriculture business opportunities and Vacant Commercial space at Bridgeport Place to house the café and market and support distribution components (see Table 6.1).

Activities are clustered around the three essentials of the initiative—Market, Cafe, and Community Kitchen. The Market had three distribution components: healthy food retail, mobile distribution of fruits and vegetables, and a Farmers Market. The Cafe also offers a healthy variety of food items. The Community Kitchen has several components including a training area for cooking classes and a facility for local farmers and gardeners to prepare and package foodstuffs.

Outputs

Each project component facilitates training, employment and/or agriculture business development opportunities; supports distribution; increases affordable healthy food options; and provides workshops (see Figure 6.3). **Outcomes** for the project cluster around:

• providing access to affordable healthy food options;
• strengthening local food infrastructure;

Table 6.1 Urban Café and Community Kitchen Logic Model Resources

Collaborator	Project Component					
	Café	Market	Farmers Market	Mobile Market	Community Kitchen	Training & Employment
Neighborhood Residents	Employees, Customers	Employees, Customers	Vendors, Customers	Employees, Customers	Workshop Presenters, Participants, Users	Labor Pool
Burten, Bell, Carr Development, Inc.	Owner, Operator, Manager	Owner, Operator, Manager	Owner, Operator, Manager	Operations, Management	Manager, Programming	Recruitment, Tracking, Monitoring, Training, Jobs
Cuyahoga Metropolitan Housing Authority (CMHA)	Customers	Customers	Sponsors, Customers, Employee Volunteer Opportunities	Sponsors, Employee Volunteer Opportunities	Sponsors, Employee Volunteer Opportunities	
Green City Growers	Suppliers	Suppliers	Vendors	Suppliers	Workshop Presenters, Participants, Users	Training, Jobs
Rid All Green Partnership	Suppliers	Suppliers	Vendors	Suppliers	Workshop Presenters, Participants, Users	Training, Jobs
Ohio State University Extension (OSUE)					Workshop Presenters, Participants, Users	Training, Jobs
Cuyahoga Community College					Workshop Presenters, Participants, Users	Training, Jobs
Local Food Producers	Suppliers	Suppliers	Vendors	Suppliers	Workshop Presenters, Participants, Users	
Cleveland Food Terminal	Suppliers	Suppliers		Suppliers	Sponsors, Employee Volunteer Opportunities	
Local Food Movement	Customers	Customers	Vendors, Customers	Volunteers	Workshop Presenters, Participants	
Vacant Commercial & Vacant Lots	Space	Space	Space	Space	Space	Space for additional Gardens and Farms

Table 6.2 Urban Café and Community Kitchen Logic Model Activities

PROJECT COMPONENT	ACTIVITY
Café	Healthy, Prepared Food Menu
	Use of Locally Provided Commodities (distribution)
	High-level Customer Service
Market	Healthy Food Retail
	Sale of Locally Provided Commodities (distribution)
	High-level Customer Service
Farmers Market	Healthy Food Options
	Sale of Locally Provided Commodities (distribution)
Mobile Market	Healthy, Prepared Food & Produce
	Healthy Snacks
	Marketing & Information Distribution
Community Kitchen	Classes & Workshops
	Local Farmers and Gardeners Prepare and Package Commodities
Training & Employment	Training by Management Consultant
	Cultivation of Additional Community Gardens and Urban Farmers
	Referrals from Child Support Enforcement Agency and TANF Agency
	Marketing and Outreach
	Building of connections to support project
	Documentation of best practices
	Management and reporting

- increasing knowledge;
- improving eating habits;
- providing training, employment, and business development opportunities; and
- improving the neighborhood overall.

More specifically, outcomes resulting from the outputs include:

- Increase access to affordable fresh produce;
- Improve access for low-access areas;
- Make local food more accessible to low-income individuals and families;
- Retain local dollars;
- Increase options/opportunities for affordable healthy food purchases;
- Increase affordable healthy food options for low-income individuals and families;
- Increase consumption of fresh produce and healthy foods;
- Increase number of neighborhood gardeners and farmers;
- Provide a year-round supply of healthy food options;
- Increase community supported agriculture;
- Increase the shift to local food production (farm to table);
- Increase supply chain infrastructure;

- Increase composting;
- Create multi-level community health promotions;
- Increase health literacy;
- Promote health education and health awareness;
- Expand consumption of a variety of healthy foods;
- Increase knowledge of consumption and preparation of flavorful healthy food;
- Improve knowledge of food nutrition and food preparation of youth and adults;
- Improve attitude towards healthy food consumption; Increase demand for fresh produce;
- Increase knowledge of opportunities and experience in the food service industry;
- Increase skills of local residents; and I
- ncrease employment and business development opportunities.

Impact

With the proposed outcomes, the impact is economic development, community building, and a reduction in health disparities (see Figure 6.3).

6.4.2 Urban Farm & Food Entrepreneurs
(ca. June 2012—Awarded $788,673)

The following year I replicated in Youngstown, Ohio, the same efforts utilized for the Bridgeport Market, Café & Community Kitchen—a practical application of the collaboration blueprint (through a design lens).

Food security is a serious issue in Youngstown. Nearly 70% of the census tracts in the city are food deserts, leaving 62% of the population (nearly 42,000 people) food insecure. Youngstown was once an important industrial hub and a center of steel production. The city's failure to diversify meant that the collapse of the steel industry devastated the region, and by the mid-1980s, the city had lost 40,000 jobs, 400 businesses, and $414 million per year in personal income (Calvert, 2016). Opportunities for recovery were continually thwarted, and the industrial monoculture had repressed entrepreneurship. Even with the housing investment and policy decisions that resulted in some reduction of extreme poverty neighborhoods in Youngstown, by the Great Recession most of that progress was erased. In fact, a 2011 Brookings report ranked Youngstown with the highest concentrated poverty rate (49.7%) among primary cities in the largest metropolitan areas (Kneebone, Nadeau, & Berube, 2011). This is critical because, in areas of concentrated poverty, residents are subject to costs and limitations beyond the burden of individual poverty including: limited educational opportunities, poor health outcomes, hindered wealth building, a reduction in private sector investment, and higher prices for goods and services. Further, with more than 22,000 vacant lots, Youngstown has one of the highest per capita vacancy rates in the United States.

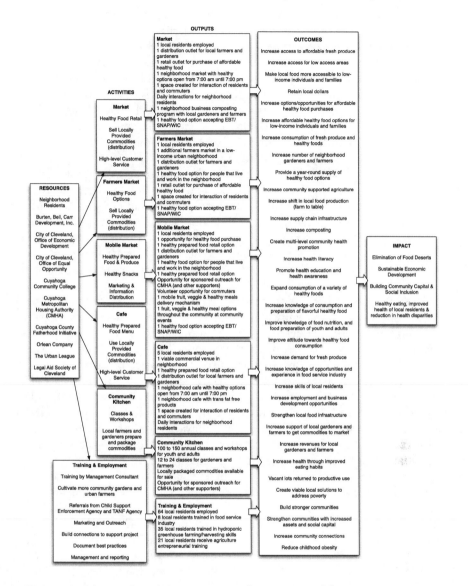

Figure 6.3 Urban Café and Community Kitchen Logic Model

Despite the seemingly insurmountable challenges, Youngstown is working to redefine itself and emerge as a model green city. Youngstown Neighborhood Development Corporation (YNDC), a community development corporation, is on the frontline of this work. In collaboration with the City of Youngstown and Common Wealth, Inc., YNDC proposed a convergence strategy, making use of Youngstown's assets, both physical (i.e., vacant/abandoned land) and human (i.e., unemployed/underemployed poor residents), to develop a placed-based systems approach and scalable transformation strategy to build additional infrastructure for their Iron Roots Urban Farms, as well as create and sustain food entrepreneurs. More specifically, by developing an agricultural entrepreneurship training center with a commercial preparation kitchen to facilitate green jobs education (i.e., building deconstruction and landscaping), community garden education (i.e., building skills of local residents and gardeners to grow, preserve, prepare and consume healthy food and healthy meals), and market gardener training (i.e., classroom and on-farm demonstrations and agricultural training) sustainable economic development can be achieved along with the elimination of food deserts.

The agricultural entrepreneurship training center at Iron Roots Urban Farms is further supported by the Common Wealth, Inc. Lake-to-River Kitchen Incubator. The kitchen incubator provides training to build entrepreneurial acumen, capacity, and marketing skills for increased production and distribution points for healthy food; technical assistance for food businesses; grow-and-freeze training; the necessary infrastructure to support food entrepreneurs (i.e., a cold room, commercial ovens, a commercial kitchen, a thermal processing line, and a vegetable preparation and packaging facility); and distribution points (i.e., local schools, farmers markets, local restaurants, Community Supported Agriculture, corner stores project).

I developed a logic model to describe implementation and illustrate project viability. The logic model articulated the activities necessary for project success.

The **Resources** harnessed to implement the project included the combined experience of the Youngstown Development Corporation (YNDC) and Common Wealth, Inc. (CWI). YNDC has experience in fundraising, fiscal management, and garnering community support and buy-in. YNDC facilitated the complicated land assembly process for market and community gardeners and individuals seeking agriculture business development opportunities. YNDC was the lead agency for recruitment, tracking and monitoring jobs, and business development. CWI also recruited residents and stakeholders to connect to their network of food entrepreneurs. For example, a local school incorporated locally made granola into the school breakfast program. Additional resources included the City of Youngstown for funding and support, Alliance for Congregational Transformation Influencing Our Neighborhoods (ACTION) for networks to thousands of inner city families through their 20 congregations' membership, the Ohio Small Business Development Center for their assistance and no-cost consulting for new food entrepreneurs, and supportive neighborhood residents.

Activities were clustered around marketing, outreach, recruitment, the Iron Roots Urban Farm and Kitchen Incubator, and advanced training. The **Outputs** were realized by the activities. YNDC effectively collaborated with the community and other organizations to actualize the **Outcomes** of the Iron Works Urban Farm and Kitchen Incubator. With the proposed outcomes, the **Impact** of the effort and investment eliminated food deserts and low access areas, and facilitated sustainable economic development, community building, and a reduction in health disparities (see Figure 6.4).

This strategic neighborhood transformation hired, trained, and created entrepreneurship opportunities (42 total) for low-income community residents. This initiative built and expanded a healthy food infrastructure and developed retail outlets, making fresh, affordable, nutritious food available to residents in food deserts. This replicable and sustainable model has served as the catalyst for the green redevelopment of Youngstown, Ohio. A federal grant of $788,673 was awarded to fund this project.

6.4.3 Urban Vineyard and Biocellar
   (ca. November 2012—Opened 10/17/2014)

Neighborhood Solutions is a grassroots nonprofit organization founded and managed by residents in the Hough neighborhood in Cleveland, Ohio. Neighborhood Solutions mobilized neighbors and men from the halfway house in the neighborhood to transform a vacant and abandoned weed-choked lot to a three-quarter acre urban vineyard.[4] Adjacent to the vineyard was vacant land and an abandoned house that was a community eyesore. Neighborhood Solutions secured the house for deconstruction, preserved the basement, and created the nation's first BioCellar.

The creation of a BioCellar adaptively reuses vacant and abandoned properties to extend the growing season. The BioCellar serves as a below-grade growing environment suitable for urban agriculture as well as aquaponics (i.e., fish and crop propagation). Neighborhood Solutions, in collaboration with Upstream Permaculture and the Cleveland Urban Design Collaboration at Kent State University, created this innovative solution for communities suffering from a glut of vacant and abandoned properties. This innovative idea proposes to use urban agriculture as an economic development engine.

The BioCellar increases affordable, local, healthy food access and connects all sectors of a community-based food system (i.e., growing, processing, preparing, eating, retailing, and distribution). Neighborhood residents, individuals returning home from a period of incarceration, at-risk neighborhood youth, and veterans can be trained to grow crops and raise fish. Through food production, the project employs local residents with disadvantaged backgrounds and repurposes vacant homes and idle urban lots to create wealth-building opportunities for residents. With a focus on increasing access, building a community-based food system, creating entrepreneurship and employment opportunities with an eye towards systems level impact, community capacity and economic development is possible. The logic model I developed for the project is presented in Figure 6.4.

6.4.4 Combating Infant Mortality
   (ca January 2014—Awarded $2,000,000)

Infants continue to die at a staggering rate in Cleveland, Ohio. Between 2007 and 2009, Cleveland's infant mortality rate (IMR) was a startling 17.3—more than twice the state rate (7.7) and nearly three times the national rate

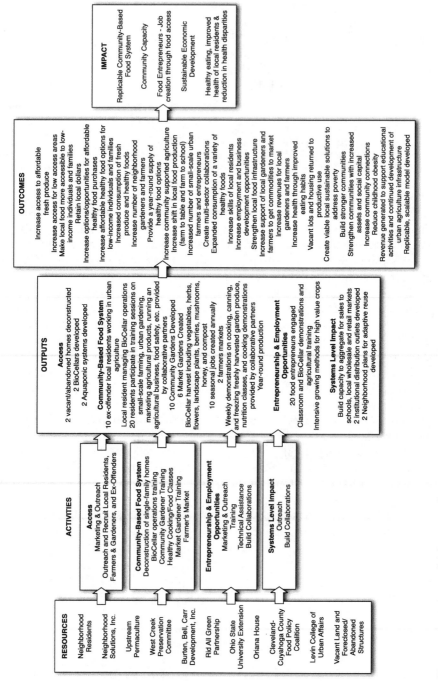

Figure 6.4 Logic Model for BioCellar Community Food Program

(6.1). In fact, early in 2013, the Anne E. Casey Kids Count Program identified Cleveland (tied with Detroit) as having the highest IMR (13.5 as of 2010) of any major American city.

Disparities between white and African American populations are notable and demonstrated an authentic sense of urgency for the Cleveland Department of Public Health. African American babies are nearly 2½ times as likely to die as white infants in the City of Cleveland. For example, in two Cleveland neighborhoods, infant mortality rates are above 27 per 1,000—these rates are higher than those of North Korea, Uzbekistan, Vietnam, and the Gaza Strip. Infant mortality in a third Cleveland neighborhood is slightly above 69 deaths per 1,000 live births. This exceeds the rate in developing countries such as Bangladesh, Haiti, Burma, Cameroon, Sudan, Kenya, Nepal, Pakistan, Rwanda, and Uganda.

The MomsFirst Project (MFP) of the Cleveland Department of Public Health (CDPH) represents the first line of defense in the reduction of disparities in infant mortality and poor birth outcomes experienced by African Americans in the City of Cleveland. The purpose of the proposed MomsFirst Project is to address both the factors that immediately affect a pregnancy (i.e., prenatal care, smoking, obesity, nutrition, substance abuse, perinatal infections, and HIV and other STDs), as well as the social determinants of health in high-risk communities (i.e., poverty, lack of education, violence, and other stressors). This "both/and" strategy reflects evidence-based practices grounded in emerging research and actualizes collective impact.

Recall the five parts of the logic mode—resources/inputs, activities, outputs, outcomes, and impact. For this project, the **INPUTS** were the collaborative partners: Cleveland Department of Public Health (CDPH), MomsFirst Project (MFP), OhioGuidestone, St. Martin de Porres Family Center, May Dugan Multi-Services Center, Friendly Inn Settlement House, Northeast Ohio Neighborhood Health Services, Inc., Cleveland Regional Perinatal Network (CRPN), Planned Parenthood, Southern New Jersey Perinatal Cooperative, Final Draft Communication, and Center on Urban Poverty & Community Development at Case Western Reserve University.

The **ACTIVITIES** were placed into six categories: conduct outreach and engagement, improve women's health, promote quality service, strengthen family resilience, achieve collective impact, and monitor accountability and performance.

Conduct Outreach & Engagement: Provide neighborhood home visits, care coordination and health education functions; Identify medical, home, and personal resources and support systems; Provide community-wide health education and promotion; Provide HealthMobile services.

Improve Women's Health: Outreach and enrollment in health coverage under ACA; Coordination & facilitation of access; Support for prevention and assistance with reproductive life planning.

Promote Quality Services: Service coordination and system integration, Focus on prevention and health promotion, Core competencies for workforce, Standardized curriculum. Strengthen Family Resilience: Address toxic stress, Support mental and behavioral health, Promote father involvement, Improve parenting.

Achieve Collective Impact: Community Action Network, Contribute to collective impact.

Monitor Accountability & Performance: Use quality improvement, Conduct performance monitoring, Conduct evaluation.

Multiple **OUTPUTS** could be realized with multiple collaborative partners and activities: Serve 5700 pregnant women; Conduct 2 Home Visits per month; Provide 5700 screenings for medical homes; Identify 1 to 3 personal resources for participants; Complete 30 community-wide, cross-sector health education promotions; Publish quarterly newsletters; Oversee weekly health promotion and reproductive health care for women, their male partners, and the community at large weekly; Conduct 1 prenatal and 2 postpartum screenings; Provide one-on-one health education, 5700 risk assessments, and 5700 screenings; Use evidence-based and research-based curriculum with all participants adopting standardized curriculum; Conduct every-other-month health education forums; Create 5300 Reproductive Life Plans; Develop agreements for all applicable partners; Identify 50 new participants/partners for CAN; Conduct ongoing identifications of additional services and service providers; Provide developmental screenings for all children with referrals for all at-risk children; Conduct a marketing and social media campaign on safe sleep practices; Develop support groups for breastfeeding; Evaluate performance and provide coaching for all CHWs; Provide testing for all CHWs; Create remediation plans in all needed areas; Train all staff on cultural competency, trauma-informed CM, and validated tools (e.g., ACES, 4Ps Plus); Audit data on all community partners; Integrate Lifecourse theory into all program activities; Deliver trauma-informed care for 5700; Do 5700 intake assessments; Provide education on pregnancy and parenting to all fathers/male partners; Partner with several fatherhood initiatives; Partner with two library systems; Convene ongoing CP; Conduct ongoing quality assurance reviews; Conduct monthly AMG meetings, biannual PSS Surveys, and quarterly data focus groups; Ensure ongoing implementation of best practices for service delivery and achieving better health outcomes; Monitor ongoing reporting of community-level reproductive risk and general reporting to CAN and CPs; Develop CoIIN from regional work.

The outputs facilitate **OUTCOMES** with resulting increases and reductions in key areas: Increase: Outreach, engagement, and awareness; Medical Homes; Healthcare beyond current pregnancy; Personal support systems; Participants with health insurance to 90%; Enrollment of male partners; Well woman visits to 80%; Postpartum visits to 80%; Women, infants, and children who have a medical home to 80%; Services provided to vulnerable populations; Variety of strategies for information delivery; Documented reproductive life plan to 90%; Development agreements; Partners and participants for CAN; Developmental screenings and referrals; Resources for participants with children under age 4; Engagement in safe sleep behaviors to 80%; Awareness by community partners including faith-based community; Abstinence from cigarette smoking to 90%; Well child visits (including immunization) for children between 0–24 months to 90%; Nurse home visits for newborns; Core competencies of all core staff; Increased mentoring for new CHWs; Use of HS Institute TA and federal competencies; Adoption of standardization curriculum project-wide when available; Referrals for 100% of participants to address social determinant challenges outside MFP scope; Information to community; Skills and abilities to address trauma informed case management; Training and tools available to staff; Follow-up services for perinatal depression to 90%; IPV screenings to 100%; Father/partner involvement during pregnancy to 90% and with child 0–24 months to 80%; Reading daily to children 0–24 months to 50%; Fully implemented CAN with 25% participant membership; Leveraging of local, county, and state advocacy; Participation with health initiatives and research contributing to community-wide data collection and measurement targets; Data infrastructure and network to collect, analyze, and report data supporting Collective Impact; Sharing of data and findings; Leadership and excellence in perinatal health leveraging internal capabilities, networks, and placed-based initiatives; Improvements to database and interface; Implement evaluation plans; Reduce: Perinatal depression; Pregnancies conceived within 18 months of previous birth to 30%; Reduce elective delivery before 39 weeks to 10%.

Impact

Eliminate the disparities in infant mortality and poor birth outcomes experienced by African Americans in the City of Cleveland; Address both the factors that immediately affect a pregnancy as well as the social determinants of health in high-risk communities; and Leverage network of cross-sector partners to drive community change, demonstrating leadership and excellence in perinatal health.

The City of Cleveland was awarded $2,000,000 to continue funding the MomsFirst program, which offered innovative solutions to combat infant mortality so that every baby born in Cleveland will celebrate a first birthday.

6.4.5 Social Innovation (ca. April 2014)

In the next example (Figure 6.5), the Raymond John Wean Foundation and three of its largest grantees develop a strategy to target economically disadvantaged communities in Trumbull and Mahoning counties (Ohio) with a programming focus on economic opportunity, youth development and healthy futures. The opportunity for investment in innovation, transformation, and scaling are of critical importance because of the significant challenges to the health and prosperity of the region. Mahoning and Trumbull counties are located in the Rust Belt of Appalachian Ohio. These counties have much higher levels of unemployment and poverty than state and national estimates. Further, the main metropolitan centers of Warren (Trumbull County) and Youngstown (Mahoning County) have staggering levels of unemployment and poverty.

The Wean Foundation invests $4 million annually in nonprofit agencies in Mahoning and Trumbull counties, focusing on community building, building capacity in neighborhood institutions, strengthening ties among residents, and empowering residents to work individually and collectively towards community change.

6.4.6 The Iceberg Project (ca. July 2014—Awarded $741,000)

A community development corporation proposes to create an innovative social enterprise, Beacon Contractors. Beacon Contractors is a construction business committed to developing and supporting low-income entrepreneurs interested in the construction industry and creating sustainable employment or business opportunities. The construction business is not the innovation—it is the adaption of systems thinking to create a viable solution to address the complexities inherent in low-income communities.

In low-income communities, job creation is often only the tip of the iceberg. Beacon Contractors will address the issues above the surface that actualizes self-sufficiency for low-income individuals and their families including jobs, opportunities for career advancement, and entrepreneurship/business creation. In addition, the nonprofit organization, in collaboration with project partners, will address the personal and community barriers below the surface that affect individual success and community development by providing training, supportive services, family support, and community building.

Building upon its development expertise, the community development corporation will secure contracting and subcontracting opportunities to pursue with a highly skilled and well-trained, low income workforce. Beacon Contractors will leverage opportunities such as Section 3 of the HUD Act of 1968 that requires participation goals for low-income residents and the Fannie M. Lewis Resident Employment Law (Chapter 188, City of Cleveland Ordinance Requirements) that requires participation by City of Cleveland residents and low-income Cleveland residents. This systems approach will result in a robust work pipeline to sustain and grow the created jobs and businesses to ensure the Kinsman and Central neighborhoods flourish.

A federal grant for $741,000 was awarded to fund this project. The conceptual model (Figure 6.6) and logic model I developed for the project are presented (Figure 6.7).

RESOURCES

The Raymond John Wean Foundation

Case Western Reserve University

High Impact Nonprofits

Technical Assistance Providers

Capacity Building Consultants

Residents

Civic & Public Leaders

ACTIVITIES

SIF Matched Grants
Economic Opportunity
Youth Development
Healthy Futures

Transformative Innovation
Open & Competitive Subgrantee Selection
Identify Innovative Effective Solutions
Grow Subgrantee Impact

Technical Assistance
Fund Development
Fundraising

Capacity Building
Marketing
Networking
Advocacy
Information Technology
Human Resources
Planning & Programs
Operations & Governance
Performance Measures & Accountability

Evaluation
Subgrantee Assessment
Mixed-Methods Evaluation
Tailored Strategy for Scaling

Evidence-Based & Evidenced Informed Interventions
Examine Management Data
Identify Data Collection Methods, Data Sources & Data Collection Intervals
Track Progress
Develop Performance Measures
Rigorous Evaluation Design
Quasi-Experimental Methodology
Longitudinal Data Collection
Scaling Strategy
Tailored Logic Model & Theory of Change Development
Examine Cross-System Involvement
Track Subgrantee Growth

OUTPUTS

- $5 Million SIF Investment
- $5 Million Matched Investment from the Raymond John Wean Foundation
- $10 million matched SIF pool
- $16 million invested in region over five-years in transformative, evidence-based and informed, scalable solutions
- Social Innovation in three (3) areas for the region: Economic Opportunities, Youth Development & Healthy Futures
- Profile of Subgrantees
- Process for Competitive Selection
- Criteria for Determining Subgrantee Fit with Theory of Change
- Timeline with Stages of selection process
- First Award within 7 months
- Process developed to identify high performance nonprofits that can conduct evaluations
- Clear assessments of readiness and capacity for evaluation
- Interventions achieve moderate and strong evidence of effectiveness.
- Measures of allocating awards so larger amounts go to high impact projects
- Awards from $100,000 to $350,000
- Identification of 25 to 50 promising interventions with a high potential for generating strong impact
- Support all grantees with needed evaluation assistance, technical assistance, and capacity building
- Substantial evaluation of program implementation and program results for all grantees

OUTCOMES

- Increase effective, evidence-informed innovative solutions for the region
- Increase knowledge and utilization of evidence-based and evidence-informed interventions that solve community problems
- Develop transformative approaches that produce strong impact
- Present at least six new solutions or novel adaptions/applications of a solution to a critical regional issue
- Develop evidence-based/informed reciprocal solutions for Trumbull and Mahoning Counties
- Address multiple community challenges concurrently
- Complete Cost/Benefit Analysis of innovative impact and Alternatives
- Increase in evaluation and research on replicable effective interventions
- Increase capacity of high-performing nonprofits in the region
- Reduce 2012 unemployment levels
- Increase employment opportunities in the region
- Reduce poverty levels
- Increase kindergarten readiness levels
- Increase high school graduation rates
- Reduce food insecurity and health disparities
- Expand relationships and cooperation
- Increase leveraging of community assets
- Improve neighborhood operations
- Expand resident participation and leadership
- Expand collaboration and leveraging of assets
  - Improved neighborhoods
  - Empowered Residents
  - Strengthened Organizations
  - Built Networks

IMPACT

Sustained Transformational Change for the Region

Scalable and Innovative Solutions to wicked problems in the Region

Figure 6.5 Program for Social Innovation

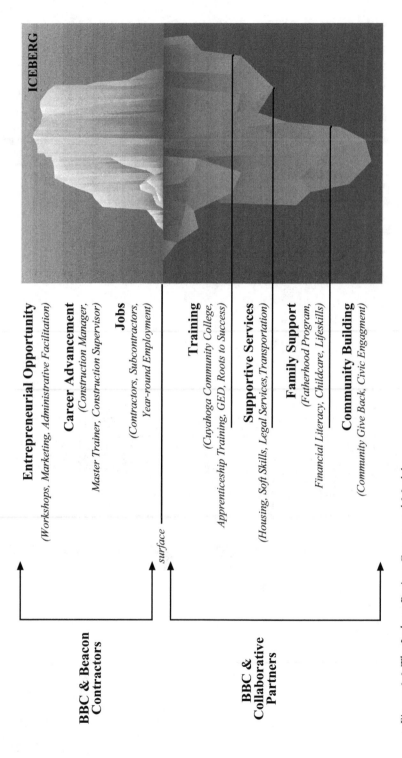

ICEBERG

Entrepreneurial Opportunity
(Workshops, Marketing, Administrative Facilitation)

Career Advancement
*(Construction Manager,
Master Trainer, Construction Supervisor)*

Jobs
*(Contractors, Subcontractors,
Year-round Employment)*

surface

Training
*(Cuyahoga Community College,
Apprenticeship Training, GED, Roots to Success)*

Supportive Services
(Housing, Soft Skills, Legal Services, Transportation)

Family Support
*(Fatherhood Program,
Financial Literacy, Childcare, Lifeskills)*

Community Building
(Community Give Back, Civic Engagment)

**BBC & Beacon
Contractors**

**BBC &
Collaborative
Partners**

Figure 6.6 The Iceberg Project Conceptual Model

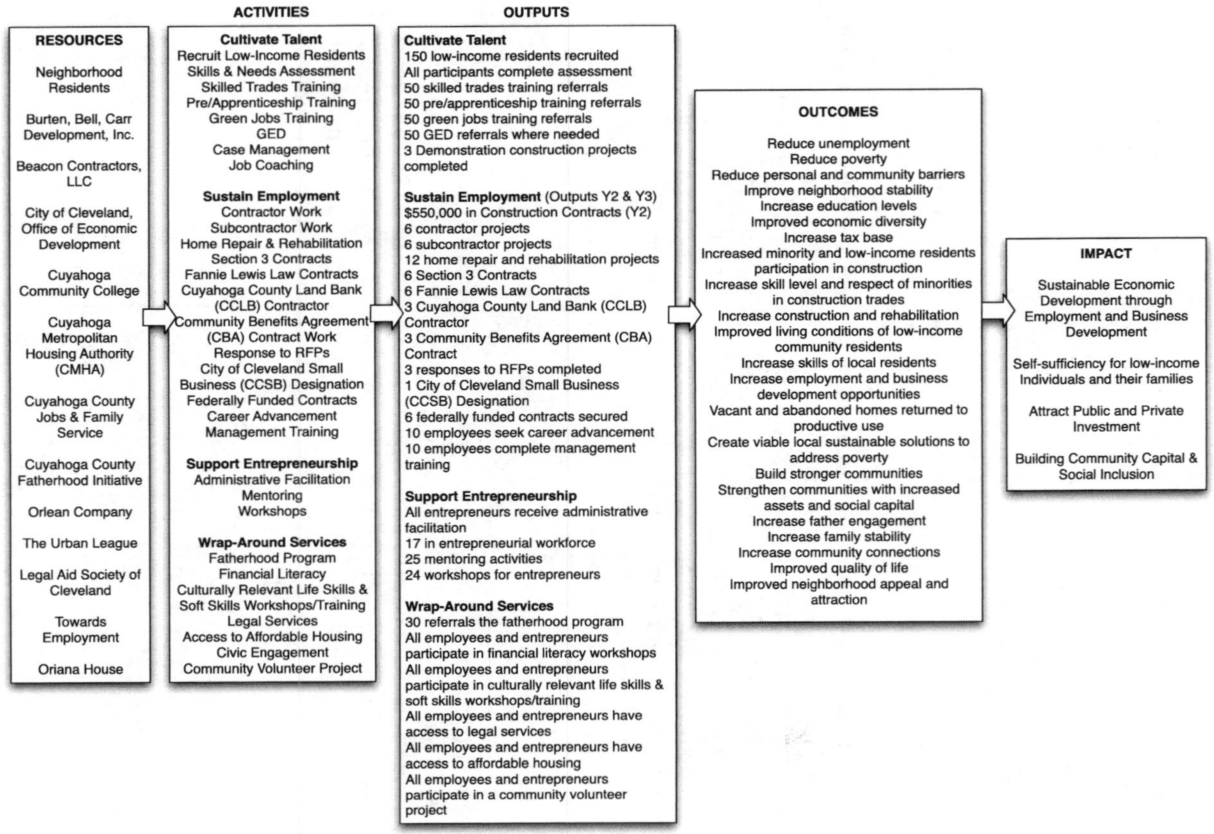

ACTIVITIES

OUTPUTS

IMPACT

RESOURCES

OUTCOMES

RESOURCES

Neighborhood Residents

Burten, Bell, Carr Development, Inc.

Beacon Contractors, LLC

City of Cleveland, Office of Economic Development

Cuyahoga Community College

Cuyahoga Metropolitan Housing Authority (CMHA)

Cuyahoga County Jobs & Family Service

Cuyahoga County Fatherhood Initiative

Orlean Company

The Urban League

Legal Aid Society of Cleveland

Towards Employment

Oriana House

ACTIVITIES

Cultivate Talent
Recruit Low-Income Residents
Skills & Needs Assessment
Skilled Trades Training
Pre/Apprenticeship Training
Green Jobs Training
GED
Case Management
Job Coaching

Sustain Employment
Contractor Work
Subcontractor Work
Home Repair & Rehabilitation
Section 3 Contracts
Fannie Lewis Law Contracts
Cuyahoga County Land Bank (CCLB) Contractor
Community Benefits Agreement (CBA) Contract Work
City of Cleveland Small Business (CCSB) Designation
Federally Funded Contracts
Career Advancement
Management Training

Support Entrepreneurship
Administrative Facilitation
Mentoring
Workshops

Wrap-Around Services
Fatherhood Program
Financial Literacy
Culturally Relevant Life Skills & Soft Skills Workshops/Training
Legal Services
Access to Affordable Housing
Civic Engagement
Community Volunteer Project

OUTPUTS

Cultivate Talent
150 low-income residents recruited
All participants complete assessment
50 skilled trades training referrals
50 pre/apprenticeship training referrals
50 green jobs training referrals
50 GED training referrals
50 GED referrals where needed
3 Demonstration construction projects completed

Sustain Employment (Outputs Y2 & Y3)
$550,000 in Construction Contracts (Y2)
6 contractor projects
6 subcontractor projects
12 home repair and rehabilitation projects
6 Section 3 Contracts
6 Fannie Lewis Law Contracts
3 Cuyahoga County Land Bank (CCLB) Contractor
3 Community Benefits Agreement (CBA) Contract
3 responses to RFPs completed
1 City of Cleveland Small Business (CCSB) Designation
6 federally funded contracts secured
10 employees seek career advancement
10 employees complete management training

Support Entrepreneurship
All entrepreneurs receive administrative facilitation
17 in entrepreneurial workforce
25 mentoring activities
24 workshops for entrepreneurs

Wrap-Around Services
30 referrals the fatherhood program
All employees and entrepreneurs participate in financial literacy workshops
All employees and entrepreneurs participate in culturally relevant life skills & soft skills workshops/training
All employees and entrepreneurs have access to legal services
All employees and entrepreneurs have access to affordable housing
All employees and entrepreneurs participate in a community volunteer project

OUTCOMES

Reduce unemployment
Reduce poverty
Reduce personal and community barriers
Improve neighborhood stability
Increase education levels
Improved economic diversity
Increase tax base
Increased minority and low-income residents participation in construction
Increase skill level and respect of minorities in construction trades
Increase construction and rehabilitation
Improved living conditions of low-income community residents
Increase skills of local residents
Increase employment and business development opportunities
Vacant and abandoned homes returned to productive use
Create viable local sustainable solutions to address poverty
Build stronger communities
Strengthen communities with increased assets and social capital
Increase father engagement
Increase family stability
Increase community connections
Improved quality of life
Improved neighborhood appeal and attraction

IMPACT

Sustainable Economic Development through Employment and Business Development
Self-sufficiency for low-income Individuals and their families
Attract Public and Private Investment
Building Community Capital & Social Inclusion

Figure 6.7 The Iceberg Project Logic Model

6.4.7 Food Hub (ca. July 2014—Awarded $800,000)

Poverty levels for Cleveland are substantial, keeping the city among the 12 poorest in the United States since 2000. In 2014, 34.2% of the population in Cleveland was below the poverty level with 19.2% unemployment. In the area where Hub 55 is located (St. Clair Superior neighborhood), there are census tracts where poverty levels are as much as four times the national average (55.9%) and unemployment is nearly six times the national average (53.5%).

The average cost for a meal in Cuyahoga County is $2.71, but the average monthly SNAP benefit is $1.36 per meal. The resulting gap (-$1.35 per meal) demonstrates the urgency for affordable healthy food options and illustrates why the food insecurity rate for Cuyahoga County is an astonishing 18.7%. For far too many area residents, the ability to eat healthy food is a daily struggle. The current national food system is inefficient and unsustainable: it provides inexpensive food that is often not nutritious and does not benefit local farmers and communities. The current food system also relies on agricultural and transportation subsidies and has contributed to an epidemic rise in obesity, heart disease, diabetes, and other health problems common in the St. Clair Superior neighborhood and other Cleveland neighborhoods. The current food system is also rife with waste: much of what is grown remains unpicked, unsold, dumped in landfills, and otherwise unavailable to hungry, impoverished people.

Despite the challenges, the St. Clair Superior Development Corporation (SCSDC), a community development corporation, is guiding a neighborhood transformation for residents and businesses in its primary service area and the City of Cleveland. SCSDC builds upon existing success; for example, the Cleveland Flea Market with 120 vendors and an excess of 8,000 regular visitors, the Urban Grazing Program managing grassy land in the city with sheep, and the Upcycle St. Clair project to establish a food hub and farmers market and facilitate the development of Hub 55. Hub 55 will improve food security and contribute to community revitalization, creating employment and business development opportunities that did not previously exist for low-income individuals. Hub 55 sparks commercial life, improves Cleveland's east-side neighborhoods, and helps the local economy. The food hub creates a distribution opportunity that will ensure employment for low-income individuals and bring healthy food choices to low-income areas.

The logic model outlines the implementation of the project. Project **RESOURCES** include multiple collaborative partners: Neighborhood Residents; St. Clair Superior Development Corporation; VIP Holdings; Ohio State University Extension; Goodrich-Gannet Neighborhood Center; Community Gardens; St. Martin de Porres High School; Case Investment School; Cuyahoga Metropolitan Housing Authority; Burten, Bell, Carr Development; the City of Cleveland Department of Economic Development; and Producers/Food Entrepreneurs.

ACTIVITIES were clustered around marketing, outreach, recruitment and support; all the components of the Hub 55 (i.e., food hub, farmers market, cafe, brewing company, flex/office space). More specifically: Training, Marketing, Outreach, Recruiting and Support—Marketing; Outreach and Recruit Local Residents, Farmers & Gardeners; Advanced Business & Agricultural Training for Agripreneurs; Business Skills/Entrepreneurial Training; Training by Management Consultant; Cultivate more community gardens and urban farmers; Healthy Food preparation classes and workshops; Referrals from Jobs and Family Services TANF Agency; Marketing and Outreach; Build connections to support project; Youth & School Program; Management and reporting; Collaboration with Choice Neighborhood and HFFI funded project. Food Hub—Healthy local food distribution hub; Regional farm products; Locally-made foods; Develop Direct & Retail Distribution Channels; Regional Food Hub. Farmers Market—Healthy Food Options; Attract supporters across the city; Sell locally produced commodities. Cafe 55—Healthy prepared food; Healthy snacks; Use locally provided commodities. Brewing Company—Support high demand for local craft beer; Regional agriculture sourcing; High-level customer service. Flex and Office Space—Space for food businesses.

The **OUTPUTS** realized by activities include:
Training, Marketing, Outreach, Recruiting and Support:

- Year-round programming for schools and Youth;
- Young Entrepreneur Program with Choice Neighborhood;
- 34 low-income residents employed;
- 30 local residents trained in food service industry;
- 15 local residents receive agriculture entrepreneurial training.

Food Hub:

- 2 local residents employed;
- 1 regional food hub created;
- 1 distribution outlet for local farmers and gardeners;
- 1 retail outlet for purchase of affordable healthy food;
- 1 neighborhood market with healthy options open from 7:00 am until 7:00 pm;
- 1 space created for interaction of residents and commuters;
- Daily interactions for neighborhood residents;
- 1 healthy food option accepting EBT/SNAP/WIC.

Farmers Market:

- 1 new business distribution points for 15 newly created agripreneurs;
- 1 additional farmers market in a low-income urban neighborhood;

- 1 distribution outlet for farmers and gardeners;
- 1 healthy food option for local schools and people that live and work in the neighborhood;
- 1 retail outlet for purchase of affordable healthy food;
- 1 space created for interaction of residents and commuters;
- 1 healthy food option accepting EBT/SNAP/WIC.

Cafe 55

- 12 local residents employed;
- 1 opportunity for healthy food purchase;
- 1 healthy prepared food retail option;
- 1 distribution outlet for farmers and gardeners;
- 1 healthy food option for people that live and work in the neighborhood;
- 1 healthy prepared food retail option;
- Opportunity for sponsored outreach for local schools;
- Volunteer opportunity for commuters;
- 1 healthy food option accepting EBT/SNAP/WIC.

Brewing Company:

- 15 local residents employed;
- 1 viable commercial venue in neighborhood;
- 1 distribution outlet for local farmers and gardeners;
- 1 neighborhood business supporting local craft brewers;
- 1 space created for interaction of residents and commuters;
- High-level customer service.

Flex and Office Space:

- 10 offices available for lease for local businesses;
- 1 opportunity for building businesses;
- 1 example of neighborhood revitalization;
- Opportunity for outreach.

The resulting **OUTCOMES** include:

- Increase access to affordable fresh produce;
- Reduce unemployment and poverty;
- Increase access for low access areas;
- Make local food more accessible to low-income individuals and families; Retain local dollars;
- Increase options/opportunities for affordable healthy food purchases;
- Increase affordable healthy food options for low-income individuals and families;

- Increased consumption of fresh produce and healthy foods; Increase number of urban gardeners and farmers;
- Provide a year-round supply of healthy food options;
- Increase community supported agriculture;
- Increase shift in local food production (farm to table and farm to school); Increase supply chain infrastructure;
- Increased number of agripreneurs;
- Create multi-level community health promotion;
- Increase health literacy;
- Promote health education and health awareness;
- Expanded consumption of a variety of healthy foods;
- Increase demand for fresh produce;
- Increase knowledge of opportunities and experience in food service industry;
- Increase skills of local residents;
- Increase employment and business development opportunities; Strengthen local food infrastructure;
- Increase support of local gardeners and farmers to get commodities to market;
- Increase revenues for local gardeners and farmers;
- Vacant lots returned to productive use;
- Create viable local sustainable solutions to address poverty;
- Build stronger communities;
- Strengthen communities with increased assets and social capital; Increase community connections;
- Reduce childhood obesity;
- Revenue generated to support educational activities and continued development of farm infrastructure;
- Replicable, scalable model developed;
- Increase environmental and business aspects of sustainable market gardening;
- Increased collaborations and partnerships between the local community, businesses and organizations;
- Sound, transparent financial accounting and a sustainable financial plan;
- Increase in creative, appropriate and targeted promotions; Increase in variety of ways to add value to local economies and communities;
- Effective, open-minded and fair management;
- Develop product & brand development for agripreneurs;
- Increase knowledge on small-scale farming, urban gardening, marketing agricultural products, running an agricultural business.

Impact

Inter-organizational collaboration between a nonprofit organization, a for-profit organization and the community actualized the outcomes of Hub 55.

With the proposed outcomes, the impact of this effort and investment includes: Sustainable economic development through the creation of a regional food hub; Building community capital and social inclusion; Agripreneurship—job creation through food access; Business retention and business attraction; Healthy eating, improved health of local residents and reduction in health disparities (see Figure 6.8).

A federal grant for $800,000 was awarded to fund Hub 55.

6.4.8 Public Housing Residents Job Pilot
(ca. April 2015—Awarded $3,000,000)

Jobs Plus is a convergence strategy for a local, place-based, job-driven approach to increased earnings and employment moving public housing residents from surviving to thriving. Jobs Plus represents an evidence-based strategy for advancing employment outcomes and increasing earnings for public housing residents to address acute joblessness and poverty in public housing developments.

For the Jobs Plus Pilot (JPP), CMHA identified two public housing developments (Outhwaite and Carver Park) needing employment services at an on-site job center, changes in rent rules that provided financial incentives to work, and community support for work through neighbor-to-neighbor conversations. In the Central neighborhood, CMHA, in collaboration with the Sisters of Charity Foundation of Cleveland and the Cleveland Municipal School District, is creating conceptualized synergy (the sense that something will be achieved that could not have been attained by any organization acting alone). The addition of the Central JPP to the ongoing efforts of Cleveland Central Promise and Central Choice will result in a convergence strategy where outcomes for public housing residents at Outhwaite and Carver Park include job securement and retention, embracing a culture of work, and necessary support to actualize a positive, long-term financial trajectory and realize family success.

Central JPP staff will embrace the idea of creating strategies while designing and redesigning relevant solutions given available resources and conditions for successful outcomes for public housing residents. Community Weavers will also serve as staff team members for the Central JPP. Weaving will be the principal form of outreach and engagement of public housing residents, as well as the evidence-based strategy for cultivating grassroots leadership. Weaving is an intentional approach for helping people connect to information, opportunity, each other, and most importantly, their own personal power. Public housing residents will be hired and trained to deliberately weave connections and build new connections among public housing residents.

A federal grant for $3,000,000 was awarded to fund the Jobs Plus Pilot. The conceptual drawing I created for the convergence strategy for family success is presented in Figure 6.9.

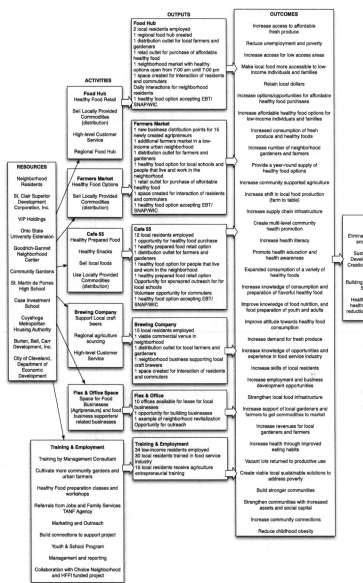

Figure 6.8 Food Hub Logic Model

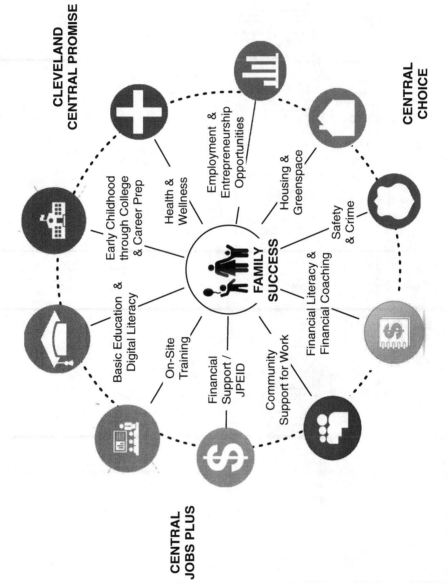

Figure 6.9 Convergence Strategy Conceptual Model

6.4.9 Construction Company (ca. September 2015— Awarded $420,000)

Despite the high unemployment, underemployment, and poverty levels, low educational attainment, and criminal backgrounds, Youngstown Neighborhood Development Corporation (YNDC) has developed a viable business model that both figuratively and literally builds people and neighborhoods in the City of Youngstown. REVITALIZE will create sustainable jobs, improve quality of life, and provide social supports that will enable individuals living on the economic margin to build pathways out of poverty. The REVITALIZE depth (people) and breadth (pipeline) business model has a viable outlook for low-income residents.

For the REVITALIZE depth (people) strategy, YNDC removes both the personal and community barriers that prevent individuals with low income from obtaining and holding jobs and successful careers. For the REVITALIZE breadth (pipeline) strategy, YNDC will build a pipeline of work across a breadth of skills and construction-related activities. Further, YNDC has access to both an abundant housing supply for acquisition and revitalization. In addition to the housing supply, YNDC, through its Community Loan Fund, can provide first-mortgage financing for the purchase of YNDC rehabilitated, owner-occupied housing. The REVITALIZE breadth strategy leverages YNDC's existing relationships, building connections and partnerships for referrals. The depth strategy leverages YNDC access, building connections and partnerships to secure contracts.

The logic model illustrates project implementation. The **RESOURCES** for the project include inter-organizational collaborative partners:

Neighborhood Residents:

- Recruit qualified neighborhood residents;
- Improve civic engagement.

Youngstown Neighborhood Development Corporation (YNDC):

- Supportive services;
- Transportation; Benefits Screening and VITA;
- Financial Literacy; Housing Counseling;
- Loan Pool;
- Affordable Homes for sale and rent.

REVITALIZE Construction Company:

- Rehabilitation of vacant single-family properties owned by YNDC;
- Minor home repair;
- Occupied home repair and rehabilitation;
- Lead abatement;

- Boarding and securing of vacant homes for public and private owners;
- Large-scale grass cutting demolition and clean out of vacant homes, as well as cutting and clearing vacant lots throughout Youngstown;
- Landscaping and snow removal.

City of Youngstown:

- Contracts;
- Section 3 Certification.

Mahoning County Land Bank:

- Contracts.

Youngstown City Schools (ABLE):

- GED Preparation,
- Training, and
- Referrals.

Eastern Gateway Community College:

- Training and Referrals.

Mahoning Columbiana Training Association:

- Training and Referrals.

Mahoning County Jobs and Family Services:

- Low-Income TANF referrals.

Community Corrections Association Community:

- Training, Referrals, and Supportive Services.

Legal Aid:

- Legal services.

Compass:

- Family and Counseling services, financial counseling.

ACTIVITIES possible from resources are clustered around the depth (people) strategy and breadth (pipeline) strategy.

Depth (People) Strategy:

- Low-Income Resident Recruitment,
- Referrals,
- Civic Engagement,
- Skills and Needs Assessment,
- Skilled Trades Training and Referrals,
- Case Management,
- Supportive Services,
- GED Education,
- Financial Literacy,
- Transportation,
- Benefits Screening and VITA,
- Financial Literacy,
- Homeownership Counseling,
- Affordable Rentals,
- Affordable Loan Pools,
- Affordable Housing,
- Job Creation,
- People Rebuilding.

Breadth (Pipeline) Strategy:

- YNDC Real Estate Pipeline,
- Rehabilitation and Construction,
- Vacant Home Rehabilitation,
- Home Repair,
- Lead Abatement,
- Property Management (property maintenance, board-ups, demolition, and clean outs),
- Vacant Land Reutilization (landscaping, cutting, and plowing),
- Neighborhood Revitalizations,
- City of Youngstown Contract Work,
- Federally Funded Contracts,
- Section 3 Contracts,
- Mahoning County Land Bank Contracts,
- Contractor Work,
- Subcontractor Work,
- RFP Responses.

The resulting **OUTPUTS** are also clustered around the depth (people) strategy and breadth (pipeline) strategy.

Depth (People) Strategy:

- 100 low-income residents recruited;
- 23 residents hired;

- All participants complete assessments;
- 50 skilled trades training referrals;
- 20 GED referrals where needed;
- All employees have access to case management assistance;
- All employees have access to supportive services;
- All employees have access to benefits screening and VITA All employees participate in financial literacy workshops;
- All employees have access to housing counseling;
- All employees have access to community loan pool;
- All employees have access to affordable housing.

Breadth (Pipeline) Strategy:

- 25 vacant home rehabilitation projects completed;
- $250,000 in earned income from vacant home rehabilitation;
- 12 occupied home repair and rehabilitation projects completed;
- 100 vacant home clean outs;
- 10,000 annual grass cuts;
- 10 vacant lots repurposed;
- 6 contractor projects;
- 6 subcontractor projects;
- 2 responses to RFPs completed;
- 100 landscaping projects.

The OUTCOMES from the outputs include:

- Reduce unemployment (ensure 23 individuals have sustained employment due to project)
- Reduce poverty (bring at least 16 individuals out of poverty through job creation);
- Reduce personal and community barriers;
- Assist at least 16 individuals with financial counseling, support services, and other.
- Increase education levels (provide at least 23 individuals with access to Lead and Lead Abatement training)
- Increase tax base (sell at least 75 vacant homes to owner-occupants)
- Increase low-income residents' participation in construction (at least 23 individuals employed in LMI neighborhoods)
- Increase construction and rehabilitation (increase amount of construction work by at least 10% annually for each year of 3-year period)
- Improved living conditions of low-income community residents (bring a minimum of 125 low-to-moderate income owner-occupied units into compliance with city code)
- Decrease Housing Vacancy Levels in Strategic Neighborhoods (rehabilitate and return at least 75 vacant homes to occupancy)

- Create viable local sustainable solutions to address poverty (hire at least 16 low-to-moderate income individuals as part of project)
- Build stronger communities (engage at least 500 volunteers annually in blight eradication projects in neighborhoods where homes are being rehabilitated and repaired)
- Strengthen communities with increased assets and social capital (assist at least eight community groups with neighborhood improvement projects)
- Improved quality of life (bring at least 1% of housing units in eight Neighborhood Action Plan areas into compliance through the project and associated collaborative code enforcement efforts);
- Board and secure at least 600 vacant homes;
- Cut grass for at least 2,000 vacant properties across the city.
- Improve neighborhood appeal and attraction (complete at least three neighborhood signage projects);
- Complete at least five projects that improve public facilities in neighborhoods where homes are rehabilitated.
- Improve neighborhood stability.
- Improve economic diversity.
- Increase community connections.
- Increase skills of local residents.

Resulting **IMPACT** includes: Sustainable economic development through employment, Self-sufficiency for low-income individuals and their families, Increased public and private investment; Increased community capital and social inclusion.

A federal grant for $420,000 was awarded to fund this project. The conceptual model I developed for the project is presented in Figure 6.10; the logic model I developed for the project, outlining collaborators, is presented in Figure 6.11.

6.4.10 *Job Readiness for Public Assistance Recipients (ca. May 2016—Awarded $762,539)*

Improving the economic well-being and quality of life for Ohio Works First (OWF) cash recipients is critical work. It necessitates an experienced service provider utilizing innovative, competency-based, and effective job readiness, job placement, and job retention programming, especially given the high levels of poverty and unemployment and the difficult job market in Cuyahoga County. The Centers-El Barrio delivers such programming, transitioning at-risk, disadvantaged, and hard-to-employ Cuyahoga County residents from unemployment and a dependency upon public assistance to employment and economic self-sufficiency through strong corporate partnerships, sector-based career pathways, an established bilingual program, and job retention rates at 72%.

The program embeds drop-in day care service for clients' children at high-quality centers with on-site health and wellness services, along with other

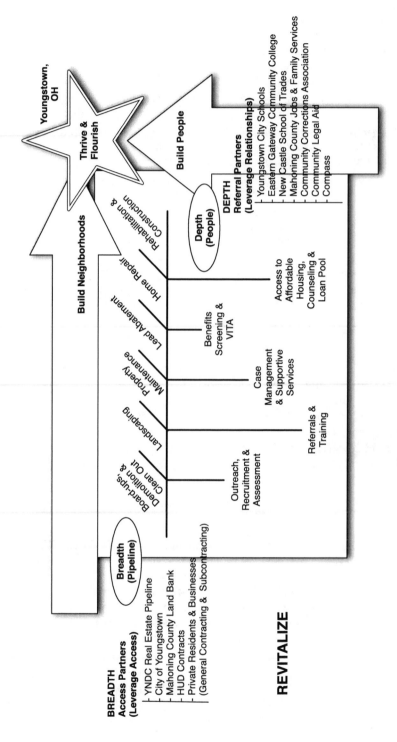

Figure 6.10 Depth (People) and Breadth (Pipeline) Conceptual Model

ACTIVITIES

RESOURCES

- Low-income Youngstown Residents
- Private Residents & Businesses
- Youngstown Neighborhood Development Corporation
- City of Youngstown
- Mahoning County Land Bank
- Youngstown City Schools
- Eastern Gateway Community College
- New Castle School of Trades
- Mahoning Columbiana Training Association
- Mahoning County Jobs & Family Services
- Community Corrections Association
- Community Legal Aid
- Compass

Depth (People) Strategy

- Recruit Low-Income Residents
- Referrals
- Civic Engagement
- Skills & Needs Assessment
- Skilled Trades Training & Referrals
- GED
- Financial Literacy
- Case Management
- Transportation
- Supportive Services
- Access to Affordable Housing
- Homeownership Counseling
- Access to Affordable Rentals
- Access to Affordable Loan Pool
- Benefits Screening & VITA
- Creating Jobs
- Rebuild People

Breadth (Pipeline) Strategy

- City of Youngstown Contract Work
- Federally Funded Contracts
- Section 3 Contracts
- Trumbull County Land Bank Contractor Contractor Work
- Subcontractor Work
- Response to RFPs
- YNDC Real Estate Pipeline Work
- Rehabilitation & Construction
- Vacant Home Rehabilitation
- Home Repair
- Lead Abatement
- Property Management – property maintenance, board ups, demolition, and clean outs
- Vacant Land Reutilization (landscaping, cutting, plowing)
- Revitalization of Neighborhoods

OUTPUTS

Depth (People) Strategy

- 100 low-income residents recruited
- 23 residents hired
- All participants complete assessments
- 50 skilled trades training referrals
- 20 GED referrals where needed
- All employees have access to case management assistance
- All employees have access to supportive services
- All employees have access to benefits screening and VITA All employees participate in financial literacy workshops
- All employees have access to housing counseling
- All employees have access to community loan pool
- All employees have access to affordable housing

Breadth (Pipeline) Strategy

- 25 vacant home rehabilitation projects completed
- $250,000 in earned income from vacant home rehabilitation
- 12 occupied home repair and rehabilitation projects completed
- 100 vacant home clean outs
- 10,000 annual grass cuts
- 10 vacant lots repurposed
- 6 contractor projects
- 6 subcontractor projects
- 2 responses to RFPs completed
- 100 landscaping projects

OUTCOMES

- Reduce unemployment
  - Ensure 23 individuals have sustained employment due to project
- Reduce poverty
  - Bring at least 16 individuals out of poverty through job creation
- Reduce personal and community barriers
  - Assist at least 16 individuals with financial counseling, support services, and other
- Increase education levels
  - Provide at least 23 individuals with access to Lead RRP and EPA Lead Abatement training
- Increase tax base
  - Sell at least 75 vacant homes to owner-occupants
  - Increased low-income residents participation in construction
  - At least 23 individuals employed in LMI neighborhoods
- Increase construction and rehabilitation
  - Increase amount of construction work by at least 10% annually for each year of 3-year period
- Improved living conditions of low-income community residents
  - Bring a minimum of 125 LMI income owner-occupied units into compliance with city code.
- Decrease Housing Vacancy Levels in Strategic Neighborhoods
  - Rehabilitate and return at least 75 vacant homes to occupancy
- Create viable local sustainable solutions to address poverty
  - Hire at least 16 LMI individuals as part of project
- Build stronger communities
  - Engage at least 500 volunteers annually in blight eradication projects in neighborhoods where homes are being rehabilitated and repaired
- Strengthen communities with increased assets and social capital
  - Assist at least 8 community groups with neighborhood improvement projects
- Improved quality of life
  - Bring at least 1% of housing units in 8 Neighborhood Action Plan areas into compliance through the project and associated collaborative code enforcement efforts
  - Board and secure at least 600 vacant homes
  - Cut grass for at least 2,000 vacant properties across the city
- Improved neighborhood appeal and attraction
  - Complete at least 3 neighborhood signage projects
  - Complete at least 5 projects that improve public facilities in neighborhoods where homes are rehabilitated
- Improve neighborhood stability
- Improved economic diversity
- Increase community connections
- Increase skills of local residents

IMPACT

- Sustainable Economic Development through Employment
- Self-sufficiency for low-income Individuals and their families
- Attract Public and Private Investment
- Building Community Capital & Social Inclusion

Figure 6.11 REVITALIZE Logic Model

supports that the agency has to offer. Additionally, all The Centers-El Barrio clients receive on-site health assessment, monitoring, and prevention services for illnesses that affect job readiness and retention and clients have on-site access to counseling, psychiatry, primary care, medication management, and pharmacy services. These are examples of how the work of The Centers is to connect those in need to the right opportunities, relationships, resources, and networks that help build better futures in a comprehensive approach that impacts the entire family.

A county grant for $762,539 was awarded to fund this project. The infographic I developed for the project is presented in Figure 6.12.

6.4.11 Child Advocacy Center (ca. October 2016— Awarded $475,000)

United Way of Greater Cleveland funded an 18-month planning process for the development of a local Child Advocacy Center (CAC). I was hired as a facilitator to coordinate the collaboration of a core Planning Team (12 organizations), and a larger Advisory Team (including additional police departments and social service providers who will work with child abuse victims and serve as a referral sources). The goal of the CAC Planning Process is to build collaborative partnerships, leverage the strengths of Cuyahoga County, and understand other existing CAC models to build an effective model for Cleveland/Cuyahoga County. Key local strengths include the hospital systems, social service providers, and robust government systems, all able to work together on this issue. The CAC planning process has engaged and is supported by the three major hospitals systems—University Hospitals, Cleveland Clinic, and MetroHealth System. University Hospitals has committed to three-half days at the CAC clinic. The hospitals have successfully been doing acute work with victims of child abuse for some time, but they are concerned that non-acute work and ongoing follow-up lacks resources and coordination. Given the strengths of the hospital systems and the social service providers, the significant need and impact targeted for the Cleveland/Cuyahoga County CAC is for ongoing, non-acute work that begins after the first 72 hours of the abuse.

A state grant for $475,00 was awarded as start-up funding for this project where I served as the facilitator (or collaboration maker). The infographic I developed for the project is presented in Figure 6.13.

6.4.12 Health & Wellness Collaborative (ca. October 2016— Awarded $800,000)

The innovative partnership between MidTown Cleveland, Inc., University Hospitals (UH), Sodexo, Hemingway Development, Wholesome Wave, and the Greater Cleveland Food Bank will implement EAT Well, a MidTown Cleveland health and wellness collaborative created to address two key

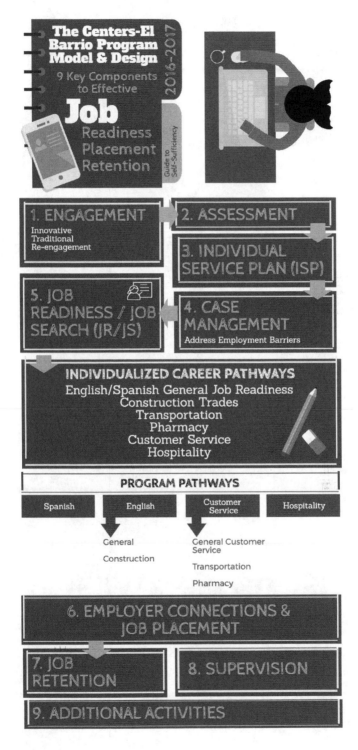

Figure 6.12 Job Readiness Infographic

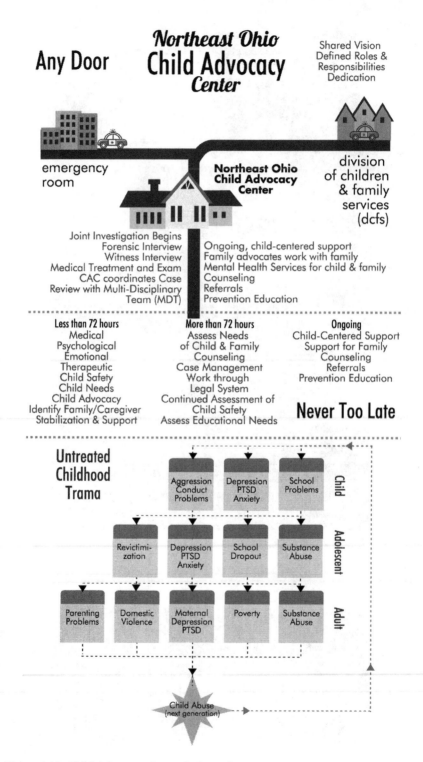

Figure 6.13 Child Advocacy Center Infographic

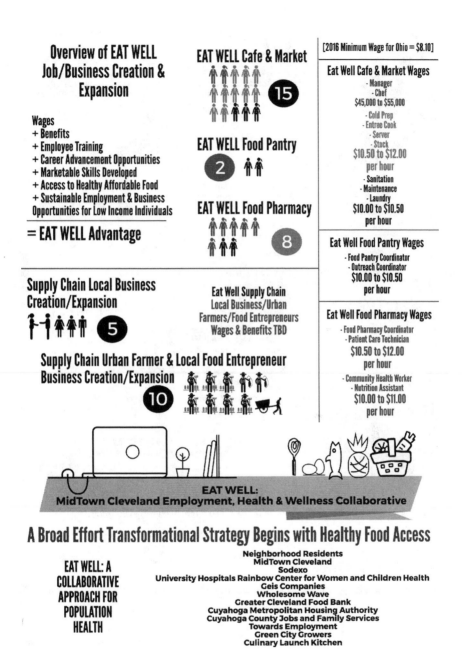

Figure 6.14 Health & Wellness Collaborative Infographics

1 EAT WELL CAFE & MARKET

Great honest food served in a beautifully designed space, accessible and affordable for everyone, everyday. Market will serve the adjacent University Hospitals Rainbow Center for Women and Children Health, as well as other adjacent/local businesses, and community residents. Market will accept EBT/SNAP.

2 EAT WELL FOOD PANTRY & FOOD PHARMACY

Food pantry available for cafe visitors, community residents, as well as children and adults visiting the adjacent University Hospitals Rainbow Center for Women and Children Health who need access to healthy affordable food. The Food Pantry will be operated in partnership with Wholesome Wave and the Greater Cleveland Food Bank to also offer no-cost healthy food options to individuals and families with low income.

- Farmers Market (Support for food entrepreneurs, complement Eat Well Cafe, Market, and Food Pantry; build community linkages)

- Double Value Produce Perks ("Two for One" nutrition incentive doubling SNAP purchasing power of fruits and vegetables)

- Community Distribution & Redemption of Double Value Produce Perks and Produce Prescriptions (Redeemable at Farmer's Markets, Mobile Markets, and Corner Stores)

- Produce Prescriptions (Distributed by Medical Providers, Nutritionists, Community Health Workers, and eligible for redemption at the Eat Well Market, Eat Well Food Pantry, other Healthy Food Financing Initiative sites, and community sites)

- Kid's Pantry (Designed for kids to build healthy eating habits and reduce risk of hunger)

- On-site Nutrition Education in the Nutrition Learning Kitchen (Cooking Classes/Workshops, Shopping Classes, Group Care Workshops, and Group Education Classes/Workshops)

EAT WELL POPULATION HEALTH MANAGEMENT PROGRAMS 3

- Food as Medicine Program (Virtual Counseling and Public Daily Educational Programs)

- Stop Hunger Servathon (Every April, partners join forces to fight hunger locally)

- Feeding Our Future® (a summer meal program leveraging the Sodexo supply chain to provide enjoyable, nutritious meals to children)

- Stop Hunger Food Drive (Annual Fall food drive where non-perishable food items are donated to the Food Pantry)

- Food Donations (Sodexo donates surplus perishable and non-perishable food to the Food Pantry)

- Ohio Benefit Bank (Innovative online services for public benefits, tax credits, and work supports screening)

Figure 6.14 (Continued)

social determinants of health: access to healthy affordable food and employment. MidTown Cleveland and UH have collaborated with local cooperatives employing hundreds of local residents and offering health care benefits and equity. EAT Well creates critically needed access to healthy, fresh, sustainable food at little or no cost to community residents, hospital visitors, and individuals and families with low-income.

Fifty percent of people living in Cleveland live in a food desert and a "food swamp" (overabundance of fast food and unhealthy food options compared to healthy food options)—a recipe for disease. It's time to EAT Well. The goal is self-sufficiency, a sustained commitment to healthy eating, and a strengthening of the local food system. Via jobs and helping individuals, parents and children will be able to make healthier food choices and change the course of their lives. EAT Well creates 32 employment and business opportunities; (2) brings healthy, affordable food choices to high need communities; and (3) leverages cross-sector institutional partnerships to implement population health management programs modeling a scalable transformational strategy.

A federal grant for $800,000 was awarded to fund the health and wellness collaborative. The infographics I developed for this inter-organizational collaboration are presented in Figure 6.14.

Notes

1. www.carthage.edu/continuing-studies/graduate-studies/bdi/
2. To build connections to practice, I created a social media Twitter hashtag (#buildbettercollaborations) to categorize messages and stimulate ongoing conversations about successful collaboration.
3. www.bbcdevelopment.org
4. http://chateauhough.org

References

Argyris, C., & Schon, D. (1978). *Organizational learning: A theory of action approach.* Reading, MA: Addision-Wesley.

Bossert, S. T. (1988). Cooperative activities in the classroom. *Review of Research in Education, 15*(1988–1989), 225–250.

Boyatzis, R. E., & McKee, A. (2005). *Resonant leadership: Renewing yourself and connecting with others through mindfulness, hope, and compassion.* Boston, MA: Harvard Business School Press.

Boyatzis, R. E., Rochford, K., & Taylor, S. N. (2015). The role of the positive emotional attractor in vision and shared vision: Toward effective leadership, relationships, and engagement. *The Impact of Shared Vision on Leadership, Engagement, and Organizational Citizenship, 6*, 6–18.

Brown, T. (2009). *Change by design: How design thinking transforms organizations and inspires innovation.* New York, NY: HarperCollins.

Brown, T., & Wyatt, J. (2010). Design thinking for social innovation. *Stanford Social Innovation Review, 8*(1), 31–35.

Calvert, K. (2016). the rebirth of a city. *Economic Development Journal, 15*(2), 24.

Dillenbourg, P. (1999). What do you mean by "collaborative learning?" In P. Dillenbourg (Ed.), *Collaborative-learning: Cognitive and computational approaches* (pp. 1–19). Oxford, England: Elsevier.

Fall, R., Webb, N., & Chudowsky, N. (2000). Group discussion and large-scale language arts assessment: Effects on students' comprehension. *American Educational Research Journal, 37*(4), 911–941.

Gray, B. (1989). *Collaborating: Finding common ground for multiparty problems.* San Francisco, CA: Jossey-Bass.

Jack, A. I., Boyatzis, R. E., Khawaja, M. S., Passarelli, A. M., & Leckie, R. L. (2013). Visioning in the brain: An fMRI study of inspirational coaching and mentoring. *Social Neuroscience, 8*(4), 369–384.

Jiang, L. (2008). The nonprofit sector: Examining the paths and pathways to leadership development. In *Wharton Research Scholars Journal*. Philadelphia, PA: University of Pennsylvania, 51–86.

Kneebone, E., Nadeau, C. & Berube, A. (2011). *The re-emergence of concentrated poverty: Metropolitan trends in the 2000s.* Metropolitan Opportunity Series, November. Washington, D.C.: Metropolitan Policy Program at Brookings. Retrieved from http://www.brookings.edu/~/media/Files/rc/papers/2011/1103_poverty_kneebone_ nadeau_berube/1103_poverty_kneebone_nadeau_berube.pdf

Lai, E. R. (2011). *Collaboration: A literature review.* Pearson Research Report, New York, NY: Pearson. Retrieved from http://images.pearsonassessments.com/images/ tmrs/Collaboration-Review.pdf

Levitt, B., & March, J. G. (1988). Organizational learning. *Annual Review of Sociology, 5*, 319–340.

McLaughlin, J., & Jordan, G. (2004). Using logic models. *Handbook of Practical Program Evaluation, 2*, 7–32.

Mercer, N. (1996). The quality of talk in children's collaborative activity in the classroom. *Learning & Instruction, 6*(4), 359–377.

Mottner, S., & Wymer, W. (2011). Nonprofit education: Course offerings and perceptions in accredited U.S. business schools. *Journal of Nonprofit & Public Sector Marketing, 23*(1), 1–19.

Murdock, A., Tekula, R., & Parra, C. (2013). Responding to challenge: Comparing nonprofit programmes and pedagogy at universities in the United Kingdom, Spain and the United States. NISPAcee *Journal of Public Administration & Policy, 6*(2), 69–95.

National Center for Charitable Statistics (NCCS). (2013). *The nonprofit almanac 2012.* Retrieved from http://nccs.urban.org/statistics/quickfacts.cfm

Salamon, L. M., & Sokolowski, S. W. (2005). Nonprofit organizations: New insights from Quarterly Census of Employment and Wages (QCEW) data. *Monthly Labor Review, 128*, 19–26.

Salamon, L. M., Sokolowski, S. W., Haddock, M. A., & Tice, H. S. (2013). *The state of global civil society and volunteering: Latest findings from the implementation of the UN Nonprofit Handbook*, Working Paper, No. 49. Baltimore, MD: Center for Civil Society Studies.

Tierney, T. J. (2006). The nonprofit sector's leadership deficit, Stanford Social Innovation Review. Retrieved from http://www.ssireview.org/articles/entry/the_leadership_ deficit

Webb, N. M. (1995). Group collaboration in assessment: Multiple objectives, processes, and outcomes. *Educational Evaluation & Policy Analysis, 17*(2), 239–261.

Wood, D., & Gray, B. (1991). Toward a comprehensive theory of collaboration. *Journal of Applied Behavioral Science, 27*(1), 139–162.

Appendix A
Interview Protocol for Study I

1. Tell me about yourself, your experience in housing development, and about your organization

   a. Personal history and previous experiences working in private/ nonprofit/government sector

2. Tell me about the _____ project.

   a. Probe for project impetus

      i. How was it started?
      ii. Who was involved?
      iii. How did the team come together? When did participants (including respondent) get involved?
      iv. What was the strategy for the project?
      v. How and when was project strategy developed?
      vi. Why was this strategy adopted? What was it about this project (or the team) that suggested this was the best approach?

   b. Probe for timeline

      i. Describe the evolution of the project.

   c. Probe for perspectives on roles and responsibilities

      i. Who did what?
      ii. Who was in charge? How was leadership exercised? To what extent was leadership shared? How did others respond to leader? Did leadership change over time?

   d. Probe for organization structure and process

      i. How were decisions made?
      ii. Concrete example (Can you think of a key project decision that stands out in your mind? Tell me about it. What was the decision? Who was involved? Who did/said what? How did others react? How was the decision received? With what consequences?)
      iii. How did the work get done?

      iv. How were problems solved?

      v. Concrete example (Can you think of a specific problem or challenge that occurred and had to be resolved in order for the project to move forward? Tell me about it. What was the problem/challenge? Who was involved? Who did what? How did the solution emerge? How was it decided? How was it executed?

      vi. What "changed" during the project?

      vii. Concrete example. What caused the change? Who initiated it? Who was involved? What were the results/consequences?

3. Thinking back over the course of the project, can you recall a specific time when you felt things were going exceptionally well? Tell me in as much detail as you can about an event or instance that stands out in your mind when you felt very positive about how the project was developing.

    a. What was going on then? Who was involved? What were they doing? What made it "feel" right?

4. Reflecting back over the course of the project, can you think of a specific time when things were not going so well? Tell me in as much detail as you can about a particular event or instance that transpired during that time.

    a. What was happening? Who was involved? What did they do/say? When? How? Why? What happened next? What did you do? How/why?

5. Thinking back about your experience in multisector collaborations, can you compare this project with another you have participated in?

    a. For respondents describing an effective project: Can you recall a different project in which you were involved in the recent past that was not as effective as this one? Tell me about it. (Tease out contrasts, e.g., differences in structure, process, and leadership)

    b. For respondents describing a less effective project: Can you recall a different project in which you were involved in the recent past that was more effective than this one? Tell me about it. (Tease out contrasts, e.g., differences in structure, process, and leadership)

Appendix B

Table of Constructs for Study II

Construct	Reference	Scale Item (D=deleted item)
Autonomy 6 items, 5-point Alpha = 0.86 Alpha for this study based on 3 items = 0.777	Items adapted from Hughes & Morgan (2007)	1. Our team members are permitted to act and think without interference. 2. Our team members perform jobs that allow them to make and instigate changes in the way they perform their work tasks. 3. Our team members are given freedom and independence to decide on their own how to go about doing their work. 4. Our team members are given freedom to communicate without interference. (D) 5. Our team members are given authority and responsibility to act alone if they think it to be in the best interests of the project. (D) 6. Our team members have access to all vital information. (D)
Shared Vision 6 items, 5-point Alpha = 0.85 (Chen) Alpha = 0.78 (Rickards) Alpha for this study based on 6 items = 0.899	Items 1, 2 & 3 adapted from Chen et al. (2008) Items 4, 5, & 6 adapted from Rickards et al. (2001)	1. We have a clear view of team direction. 2. We have a shared vision of team future achievements. 3. We have a shared vision of team goals. 4. We have a shared vision of team purpose. 5. We have strong loyalty to team purpose. 6. We have no confusions over team purpose.

(Continued)

(*Continued*)

Construct	Reference	Scale Item (D=deleted item)
Boundary Spanning 4 items, 5-point Alpha = 0.81 Alpha for this study based on 4 items = 0.803	Items adapted from Faraj & Yan (2009)	1. The team encourage its members to solicit information and/or resources from beyond the organization. 2. The team encourage its members to try to influence important stakeholders on behalf of the team and its work. 3. The work of the team depends upon information and/or resources actively solicited by team members. 4. The team values team members for making use of their relationships with others on behalf of the team.
Performance 5 items, 5-point Alpha = 0.92 Alpha for this study based on 6 items = 0.874	Items adapted from Lui & Ngo (2004) (building from Saxton, 1997)	1. Overall, we are satisfied with the performance of this team. 2. The team has realized the goals we set out to achieve. 3. This team has added to the long-term success of relevant stakeholders. 4. This team has completed a project to high standards. 5. I am proud of this team.
Design Attitude 6 items, 5-point Alpha for this study based on 4 items = 0.818	Developed from Gaskin & Berente (2011); Boland & Collopy, 2004	1. We embrace an entrepreneurial spirit (finding new problems and solutions). 2. We think outside the box (beyond past decisions and known solutions). 3. We develop new solutions to old problems/decisions. 4. We discover stakeholder/customer needs and requirements. (D) 5. We try new concepts given available resources. 6. We iterate through trial and error driven by the belief that things can get better if we try more. (D)

Collaboration Checklist Tool
12 items, 5-point *Score*
Interpretation:
0–20: collaboration experiencing a number of challenges.
21–40: collaboration demonstrating some strengths and progress, however some problem areas.
41–60: collaboration has strong components and poised for growth.

Items adapted from Borden & Perkins (1999)

1. Was started because of existing problem(s) and/or the issue being addressed required a collaborative response
2. Has clear goals that are shared and understood by the members
3. Members have a history of working cooperatively and solving problems
4. Understands the person to be served, including their culture and values
5. Leadership facilitates and supports team building, and capitalizes upon diversity and individual, group and organizational strengths
6. Members have clear roles and responsibilities that are well understood and fulfilled by the members
7. Has open and clear communication. There is an established process for communication between meetings
8. Members are connected and have established informal and formal networks/interactions at all levels
9. Has access to needed resources. Resources refer to four types of capital: environmental, in-kind, financial, and human
10. Has a plan for sustaining membership and resources
11. Identifies needed skills or knowledge and seeks to recruit new members (i.e., partner organizations - lay and religious) to acquire the skills or knowledge
12. Collects data to measure need and the achievement of goals over time

Appendix C
Table of Constructs for Study III

Construct	Reference	Scale Item (D=deleted item)
Performance 5 items, 5-point Alpha = 0.92 Alpha for this study based on 4 items = 0.846	Items adapted from Lui Ngo (2004; building from Saxton, 1997)	1. Overall, we are satisfied with the performance of this team. 2. The team has realized the goals we set out to achieve. 3. This team has added to the long-term success of relevant stakeholders. 4. This team has completed a project to high standards. 5. I am proud of this team. (D)
Innovativeness 3 items, 5-point Alpha = 0.81 Alpha for this study based on 3 items = 0.832	Items adapted from Hughes & Morgan (2007)	1. We actively introduce improvements and innovations in our business 2. Our business is creative in its methods of operation. 3. Our business seeks out new ways to do things.
Shared Vision 6 items, 5-point Alpha = 0.85 (Chen) Alpha = 0.78 (Rickards) Alpha for this study based on 6 items = 0.899	Items 1, 2 & 3 adapted from Chen et al. (2008) Items 4, 5, & 6 adapted from Rickards et al. (2001)	1. We have a clear view of team direction. 2. We have a shared vision of team future achievements. 3. We have a shared vision of team goals. 4. We have a shared vision of team purpose. 5. We have strong loyalty to team purpose. 6. We have no confusions over team purpose.

Construct	Source	Items
Design Attitude 6 items, 5-point Alpha for this study based on 4 items = 0.818	Developed from Gaskin & Berente (2011); Boland & Collopy, 2004	1. We embrace an entrepreneurial spirit (finding new problems and solutions). 2. We think outside the box (beyond past decisions and known solutions). 3. We develop new solutions to old problems/decisions. 4. We discover stakeholder/customer needs and requirements. (D) 5. We try new concepts given available resources. 6. We iterate through trial and error driven by the belief that things can get better if we try more. (D)
Autonomy 6 items, 5-point Alpha = 0.86 Alpha for this study based on 3 items = 0.777	Items adapted from Hughes & Morgan (2007).	1. Our team members are permitted to act and think without interference. 2. Our team members perform jobs that allow them to make and instigate changes in the way they perform their work tasks. 3. Our team members are given freedom and independence to decide on their own how to go about doing their work. 4. Our team members are given freedom to communicate without interference. (D) 5. Our team members are given authority and responsibility to act alone if they think it to be in the best interests of the project. (D) 6. Our team members have access to all vital information. (D)
Boundary Spanning 4 items, 5-point Alpha = 0.81 Alpha for this study based on 4 items = 0.803	Items adapted from Faraj & Yan (2009)	1. The team encourage its members to solicit information and/or resources from beyond the organization. 2. The team encourage its members to try to influence important stakeholders on behalf of the team and its work. 3. The work of the team depends upon information and/or resources actively solicited by team members. 4. The team values team members for making use of their relationships with others on behalf of the team.
Team Interaction (Active listening) 3 items, 5-point Alpha for this study based on 6 items = 0.786	Lingham (2004)	1. Members listen carefully to each other. 2. Members consider all sides of an issue before acting on it. 3. Members take their time to listen before talking.

Index